THE LOOK OF THE PAST

How can we use visual and material culture to shed light on the past? Ludmilla Jordanova offers a fascinating and thoughtful introduction to the role of images, objects and buildings in the study of past times. Through a combination of thematic chapters and essays on specific artefacts – a building, a piece of sculpture, a photographic exhibition and a painted portrait – she shows how to analyse the agency and visual intelligence of artists, makers and craftsmen and make sense of changes in visual experience over time. Generously illustrated and drawing on numerous examples of images and objects from 1600 to the present, this is an essential guide to the skills that students need in order to describe, analyse and contextualise visual evidence. *The Look of the Past* will encourage readers to think afresh about how they, like people in the past, see and interpret the world around them.

Ludmilla Jordanova is Professor of Modern History at King's College London. Her publications include *History in Practice*, (third edition 2013).

THE LOOK OF THE PAST

Visual and Material Evidence in Historical Practice

LUDMILLA JORDANOVA

CAMBRIDGE
UNIVERSITY PRESS

CAMBRIDGE
UNIVERSITY PRESS

University Printing House, Cambridge CB2 8BS, United Kingdom

Cambridge University Press is part of the University of Cambridge.

It furthers the University's mission by disseminating knowledge in the pursuit of education, learning and research at the highest international levels of excellence.

www.cambridge.org
Information on this title: www.cambridge.org/9780521709064

© Ludmilla Jordanova 2012

First published 2012
4th printing 2016

Printed in the United Kingdom by Clays, St Ives plc

A catalogue record for this publication is available from the British Library

Library of Congress Cataloguing in Publication data
Jordanova, L. J., author.
   The look of the past : visual and material evidence in historical practice /
   Ludmilla Jordanova.
      pages cm
   Includes bibliographical references and index.
   ISBN 978-0-521-88242-2 (hardback) – ISBN 978-0-521-70906-4 (paperback)
   1. Historiography – Methodology.   2. History – Study and
   teaching.   3. Visual literacy.   4. Material culture.   5. Art and
   history.   6. Architecture and history.   7. Historiography and
   photography.   I. Title.
   D16.J744   2012
   907.2–dc23   2012019021

ISBN 978-0-521-88242-2 Hardback
ISBN 978-0-521-70906-4 Paperback

For my granddaughter, Elsa Kay,
born 20 September 2009

and

In memory of my uncle, Richard,
died 5 May 2009

CONTENTS

COLOUR PLATES
(between pages 26 and 27, and 170 and 171)

BLACK AND WHITE ILLUSTRATIONS

PREFACE AND ACKNOWLEDGEMENTS

The Look of the Past examines the ways in which historians can use images and objects in their arguments; it seeks to evaluate such uses, and to see how they might be extended. Put in its broadest terms, it considers how thinking with the eyes about the past actually works, and probes the claims that result. This is a huge field, and I have had to impose limits in terms of time, place and medium on the scope of the volume to make it manageable. I focus on examples from the seventeenth century onwards, take most of my examples from Europe and North America, and exclude, with regret, the important fields of film studies and media studies, but pay attention to the insights art history can bring to history.

I am building here on the approach I took in *History in Practice* in seeking to bring to the surface assumptions, attitudes and modes of address so that they can be held up for critical inspection. One distinctive feature of *The Look of the Past* is the four short essays on specific objects. The subject of each one has been chosen with a number of criteria in mind. Naturally I wanted items that I felt enthusiastic about. The idea was also to include diverse genres, media, geographical areas and periods – I chose architecture (late seventeenth-century England), sculpture (mid-seventeenth-century Italy), photography (twentieth-century United States) and painting (early twentieth-century France). I could just as well have chosen metalware, porcelain, costume, furniture, industrial tools, tapestries, stained glass, scientific instruments or medals, and other times and places. The essays are designed to illustrate a range of historiographical issues and to ground points that are made at a more general level in the chapters with which they alternate.

I hope that undergraduate and postgraduate students, as well as their teachers and general readers, will find the book helpful. It cannot, however, provide background or basic information on the many topics it mentions. A brief note on how to use the book may be found on pages xviii–xix. It is not feasible to illustrate every object I refer to – apart from anything else, the costs would be prohibitive. It should be remembered that any reproduction is a poor substitute for seeing the real thing. If this book encourages more historians to treat museums and art galleries, churches and houses, public art and the built environment as an integral part of their professional experience and as potentially rich evidence for their thinking, teaching and writing, I would be delighted. I am deeply indebted to the many who already do so.

The Look of the Past touches on the ethics of using items of visual and material culture in historical work. We are thoroughly familiar with ideas about footnotes and plagiarism, which are about the moral obligations incurred by anyone doing academic work. A concern with fairness, accuracy and acknowledging the roles of those who made things in the past are present throughout the book. My comments are as relevant to publishers as they are to authors. Those who write and publish history are only one part of a bigger picture that includes owners and sellers of reproduction rights, internet providers, professional picture researchers, and the makers. Because it is now so easy to steal, change, distort, chop up and trivialise images in digital form, this is a good time to think about the distinctive responsibilities that scholars at all stages of their careers incur when using them.

In reflecting upon these broad issues I have incurred innumerable debts, many of which are indicated by the works cited. In addition, it is a pleasure to acknowledge some special kindnesses. I thank Richard Fisher and his colleagues at Cambridge University Press; the Master and Fellows of Downing College, Cambridge; Martha Macintyre; and my colleagues and students in the Department of History at King's College, London, and at the University of East Anglia in the School of World Art Studies and Museology. I have had the privilege of supervising a number of doctorates that have helped to shape my ideas in this area and I trust their authors know how much I learned from them. The experience of being a Trustee of the National Portrait Gallery in London between 2001 and 2009 has been crucial for this book; in particular, contact with artists and with those who commission and display portraits helped me think about the processes and relationships through which objects are made and used. Members of staff at the Portrait Gallery have been marvellously helpful, patient, supportive and inspiring.

I have drawn upon the resources of a number of institutions: Cambridge University Library, the National Library of Scotland, the Heinz Archive at the National Portrait Gallery, London, the Sainsbury Centre for Visual Arts, Norwich, the Scottish National Portrait Gallery, the Churchill Archives, Cambridge, the Bodleian Library, Oxford, and the Courtauld Gallery, London – I thank the staff of those institutions most warmly. I am indebted to all the providers of images, some of whom were extraordinarily generous in their help. At Cambridge University Press, Raihanah Begum was tireless in sorting out the rights for images, in tracking pictures down and in making suggestions. Her input has been indispensable.

It is customary to thank 'friends and relations', and I am delighted to do so, although it is not possible to mention everyone by name. I have greatly valued the feedback from the seminars and conferences where some of these ideas have been presented. Conversations with many people have helped me clarify my thoughts and given me useful suggestions – my warm appreciation goes to them all. A number of people read drafts of all or part of the book: Raihanah Begum, Lizzy Cowling, Nathan Crilly, Simon Ditchfield, Florence Grant, Lauren Kassell, Paul Kerry, Lucy Kostyanovsky, Howard Nelson, Steve Smith, Stephen Taylor, Michael Watson, Koji Yamamoto and anonymous readers. I deeply appreciate their assistance. The first essay benefited from the kindness and the scholarship of David McKitterick of Trinity College, Cambridge. Viccy Coltman helped and encouraged me with the second essay. I am also particularly grateful to Karen Amies, Stephen Brogan, Michael Bury, Melissa Calaresu, Caroline Campbell, Becky Conekin, Lars Fischer, Francesco Filangeri, Ralph Hawtrey, Phillip Kelleway, Vanessa Lacey, Angela McShane, Alison Morrison-Low, Vita Peacock, Marcia Pointon, Andrew Riley, Michael Rowe, Alison Rowlands, Sara Selwood, Michal Sofer, Tatyana Stoicheva, John Styles, Martha Vandrei, Rachel Worth and many others, for their assistance in the preparation of this volume. Howard Nelson helped with photography and provided invaluable support during the final stages of completing the book. Heartfelt thanks goes, as always, to close friends and family.

Thomas Puttfarken died, totally unexpectedly, just as I was beginning to write *The Look of the Past*. I think of him as my principal art-historical mentor: when I took an MA in his department at Essex in the 1980s, I benefited hugely not only from his kindness and his scholarship, but from his incisive questions, his rigorous approach to looking, and his concern with art-historical reasoning. I am unsure what he would have made of my arguments, only certain I would have been immeasurably enhanced by the opportunity to discuss them with him – he is deeply missed.

Ludmilla Jordanova

Cambridge, 10 October 2011

HOW TO USE THIS BOOK

Like every author, I hope my book will be read cover to cover! If so, three points should be borne in mind. First, it contains two types of chapter and these are signalled clearly to the reader. Five numbered chapters address large themes and big issues. The interspersed essays examine specific items and suggest some of the ways in which historians might engage with pieces of visual and material culture. By design they address four distinct media and historical contexts. The thematic chapters also contain examples, if briefer ones, in the form of words and images. Second, endnotes following chapters and essays provide details of quotations and essential supporting material. Third, there is a discussion of 'Further Reading' following the endnotes. The Index should help readers track down where a particular work, author or maker is mentioned. The captions are also indexed.

Readers should be aware, however, that *The Look of the Past* is not a guide to existing historical work that uses visual and material evidence. Furthermore, it only cites materials in English unless an essential work is only available in another language. It gives examples, samples what has been done already, and suggests possibilities, but makes no further claims than that. Secondary materials from a number of contexts and periods are deliberately used to convey the range of approaches and subject matter that are relevant to the book. A brief bibliography of reference works at the end should help readers to pursue matters further. Every major collection and visitor attraction now has a website, and although these vary greatly in the quality of the images and supporting information provided, they are worth using. Because they are so easy to locate using search engines, they have not been listed.

However, it is possible to use *The Look of the Past* somewhat differently, for example, by taking the essays as self-contained mini case studies. Although there are a number of threads that run through the entire volume, I hope the thematic chapters, too, can be read as distinct and accessible arguments on issues that are, it seems to me, of importance for the practice of many kinds of history.

The illustrations are designed to be integral to the arguments in the book, and the captions can be used to think about what historians need to tell their readers when including images in their writings. Basic information on each item depicted, such as size and medium, date and current location, is, if possible and relevant, given there. In addition to providing such data when available, most captions also discuss the works in question, if briefly. Being as precise as possible on such matters helps historians deploy visual and material evidence effectively, and hence the captions should be seen as central to the book's purpose. Black and white pictures and cues to them may be found in the text, numbered in bold thus **1, 2** and so on. Coloured plates are inserted in two places, and are indicated by roman numerals **I, II** and so on. Lists at the front of the book give brief details for both series. Photography credits, which acknowledge the providers of illustrations as opposed to indicating their content, are given at the end. Readers will notice images of the cantilever railway bridge over the Firth of Forth in Scotland in the book. Inspired by Michael Baxandall's brilliant essay on it in *Patterns of Intention*, published in 1985, and by my own love of Scotland, they act as visual cues for bridging passages.

Assembling illustrations for publication is expensive and time-consuming, hence their selection has necessarily been shaped by practical considerations, such as cost, availability and the length of time it is necessary to wait for images to be delivered. Such constraints are a major consideration for scholars working with images and objects. The author and publishers would be delighted to be informed of any corrections required, and express once again their appreciation of the many people and institutions that enabled these illustrations to be included in *The Look of the Past*.

A HANDBAG?

The Archive at Churchill College, Cambridge houses important collections of twentieth-century political and scientific papers, including those of Margaret Thatcher, the only female British Prime Minister to date. Photographs, objects that she was given or owned, press clippings, letters, papers generated during her career and much more may be found there. Gift exchange is central to political life. For instance, it is possible to trace her increasing closeness with Ronald Reagan through the ever more affectionate inscriptions upon photographs he gave her. I There are medallions and medals, Christmas cards, her clothes diary, coins, certificates and plaques, keys, pens and postcards. All are deposits of political ideas, aspirations, events and relationships.

The Archive also contains one of her handbags. Housed in a special box, it is popular with visitors. We might consider it a relic. Yet when it was first offered to them, the then archivist was quoted as vehemently refusing it: 'This is a storm in a handbag. It is ridicule and reticule. We haven't got any handbags, and as far as I know, we are not going to get any handbags. We are in the business of conserving documents.'[1] When he made this declaration in the early 1990s, the archive already contained items that were not conventional 'documents' – in fact, most archives are rich in visual and material culture. His words are an implicit challenge to historians to articulate the precise nature of their interest in handbags and the like. *The Look of the Past* seeks to meet that challenge.

What can be learned from this very dark navy, crocodile-skin bag, which still smells of its owner's perfume, the role of handbags in Thatcher's life and reactions to them? **1** Handbags are mainly women's wear, and assumptions are made, for example about their contents, that reveal gendered stereotypes. Discussing Thatcher's feminine aspects was part of the attempt, arguably unsuccessful, to come to terms with the exceptional coalition of femininity and power that she manifested. The new verb 'to handbag' derives from her time in office and it expresses precisely that troubling combination of femininity and power – the sense that this domineering politician was profoundly problematic. Some were strongly drawn to her; nonetheless, they had to manage the unusual situation that had brought a woman, intensely aware of herself as such, to great political heights.

Thatcher's speeches were on a size of paper designed to fit into her handbag. She herself saw it as a special item: 'anything I want to keep quiet is normally in my handbag so it is not left lying around. Things do not leak from my handbag.'[2] That others saw it similarly is revealed by Julian Critchley's remark, 'she cannot see an institution without hitting it with her handbag', and by George Schultz's 1992 quip, 'you are the only person so far to whom has been awarded the Order of the Handbag'.[3] Photographs and cartoons showed her with handbag in hand. So when she was described as 'a rather bossy, hand-baggy sort of lady', a phrasing with no male equivalent, further reflection is warranted.[4]

The difficulties faced by women with exceptional and seemingly unprecedented amounts of public power, and by those who work with them, merit consideration. Historians are familiar with this situation from, for example, the reign of Elizabeth I, whose artful control of her own image reveals the centrality of visual and material culture, a point monarchs and political leaders eagerly grasp. Remarks about Thatcher's manner, appearance and accoutrements helped manage a situation for which many were psychologically unprepared. To focus this onto a quintessentially feminine object brought relief, sometimes comic relief. Her handbag became convenient shorthand, a gender-saturated tag, a condensed symbol, like Churchill's cigar or Wilson's pipe. **II** Note how neatly cigars and pipes fit with masculine imagery. Commentators struggled with Thatcher's forceful policies, practices and personality, partly because she was also capable of exercising erotic allure. Her handbag – for her a genuine symbol of womanliness – was turned into a weapon when it suited her. Equally, it was used by those who resisted her forcefulness and deployed the idea of a handbag to put her down. An apparently trivial aspect of the look of the past offers rich insights into responses to Britain's first female Prime Minister.

1 Margaret Thatcher's handbag, dark blue leather and other materials, 29.3 cm wide × 21.5 cm high × 13.3 cm deep, Churchill Archives Centre, Cambridge. It is evident from photographs that Thatcher owned a number of handbags and we may reasonably assume that her selection of these was as careful as her choice of clothes. The style of these bags, worn hanging from the forearm or held by the handles, is identifiable as traditional, and characteristic of upper-class British women of the period, including the royal family.

NOTES

1 I am quoting from a newspaper clipping in the Churchill Archive.
2 Iain Dale, ed., 'As I said to Denis...': the Margaret Thatcher Book of Quotations (London, 1997), p. 27.
3 Ibid., pp. 99 and 180.
4 Ibid., p. 124.

FURTHER READING

Oscar Wilde's play The Importance of Being Earnest (1899), available in many editions, is a good starting point for thinking about handbags and their resonances. Wilde was unusually perceptive about the roles images and objects played in people's lives; see also his short novel The Picture of Dorian Grey (1891). Literary sources provide a rich fund for historians interested in the imaginative worlds that images and objects generate. See, for example, Bill Brown, A Sense of Things: the Object Matter of American Literature (Chicago, 2003).

Thatcher herself has been much written about: the abridged version of John Campbell's two-volume biography is useful, Margaret Thatcher: Grocer's Daughter to Iron Lady (London, 2009). For very different approaches, see Heather Nunn, Thatcher, Politics and Fantasy: the Political Culture of Gender and Nation (London, 2002); Richard Vinen, Thatcher's Britain: the Politics and Social Upheaval of the Thatcher Era (London, 2009); and Wendy Webster, Not a Man to Match Her: the Marketing of a Prime Minister (London, 1990). Webster is highly critical of Thatcher; she is perceptive on many points and discusses her hats.

On political imagery, classic works include Roy Strong, The Cult of Elizabeth: Elizabethan Portraiture and Pageantry (London, 1999; first published 1977), and Gloriana: the Portraits of Queen Elizabeth I (London, 2003; first published 1987); and Peter Burke, The Fabrication of Louis XIV (New Haven, 1992).

Elizabeth Roberts, ed., Margaret Thatcher: a Life in Pictures (Lewes, 2009), contains a wealth of images, including plenty with handbags. On handbags more generally, see Caroline Cox, Bags: an Illustrated History (London, 2007), which discusses Thatcher, but as if she always used the same bag, which was not the case. See also Judith Miller, Handbags (New York, 2006), which is aimed at collectors and has little text, but many fine illustrations.

The website of the National Portrait Gallery in London can be used to explore images of Churchill and his cigar, Wilson and his pipe, depictions of Thatcher in a range of media and portraits of other British political leaders.

Introduction

Starting points

As in the present, so in the past, the sense of sight shapes experience. The material world is a visual world, which impacts upon human beings through their eyes, and is intimately bound up with touch. Historians can only benefit from approaching the past with a vivid appreciation of these points, with a willingness to consider what people looked at, how they looked and the roles of objects designed to be looked at. Sight has long been accorded privileged status: that the expression 'I see' means 'I understand' neatly reveals the point. The diversity and complexity of what was seen, and made to be seen, demands our attention. Texts, one element within the visual life of earlier times, play a dominant role in historical practice. In this book I explore how artefacts, which are seen, touched, made, displayed, bought and sold, and through these processes yoked to texts, can be turned to good account by historians.

In doing such work historians recognise that definitions and experiences change in fundamental ways, as do materials, skills and values. Thus ways of seeing themselves have altered, as have assumptions about how visual effects are achieved, and the agency of supernatural forces in images and objects. My focus is on that part of the material world that has been created by human beings in order to invite visual reactions. It comprises many, but by no means all, made things. I generally refer to them as artefacts, which could include items whose origins once posed a puzzle, such as fossils, and found objects, such as shells, placed in specially designed settings. **2** Artefacts mediate past ideas and experiences, making them ripe for historical analysis.

2 Scallop shell of a pilgrim from Santiago de Compostela, thirteenth century, Musée archéologique de Grenoble. The scallop shell has long been a sign of pilgrimage, having initially been associated with those who returned from Santiago, the principal shrine to St James the Great in an area where scallops are plentiful. The holes in this example suggest it was attached to clothing. Such signs were widely recognised and metaphorically rich. Sir Walter Raleigh, in a poem written the day before his death in 1618, evoked the idea of a 'scallop-shell of quiet'.

I use the phrase 'the look of the past' to suggest that the appearances of things themselves constitute rich historical evidence, which merits careful evaluation. The veritable explosion of interest among historians in recent times in thinking visually indicates that such evaluation is well underway. In this book I set out some of the arguments to consider when we examine the look of items made and used in the past. Many of these – playing cards, inn signs, church interiors, coins and advertisements, for example, were probably seen by large swathes of the population. **3** At every social level, visually significant artefacts were ubiquitous. Not only did they help to mould ways of life, but many also expressed and commented upon contemporary issues in their own ways. Made items bear the imprint of both makers and of their originating contexts, and it is reasonable to assume that many people noticed and responded to their visual properties. Artefacts, then, may be treated as providing historical testimony and of diverse kinds. When historians deploy such testimony, it helps to be as clear as possible about the claims that are being made. My principal purpose is to work towards such clarity.

Many objects and images were produced by specialists, such as artists, engravers, sculptors, designers, potters, furniture-makers and so on. These are diverse occupations, and those who practised them were producers with differing commitments to, and investments in, visual effects. But they all used their honed visual intelligence and skills, such as manual dexterity, to produce items they wanted to be looked at and appreciated. Whatever their social status, they were masters of looking, who paid careful and conscious attention to the visual properties of their products. Considerable problem-solving was often involved: choosing the right materials, selecting an appropriate design, developing visual idioms to suit particular markets and so on. These specialists contributed directly to the look of past and while going about their business, they inevitably engaged with artefacts from previous eras. The look of their pasts was often present, in a mediated form, in what they made. Workshop traditions, and an awareness of the achievements of earlier generations, along with a sense of clients' requirements, shaped their endeavours. While it is important to recognise that some makers were more concerned with visual effects than others, useful, everyday objects – the appearance of which was shaped by practical considerations, such as the cost of materials and labour – benefit from the careful attention given to more obviously 'aesthetic' items. Thus it is always worth asking about the visual properties of made items and exploring their potential for generating historical insights, while recognising that those possessing greater complexity and fashioned with higher levels of awareness may yield historical insights more readily.

People in the past had their own ways of observing and interpreting what they saw. Sometimes there is direct evidence of this, in writings that told people how to read facial expressions or hand gestures, for example. Cf. **42** Any records of past modes of looking can be used to study the ways in which visual experience was understood and has altered. These issues arose in many places, such as theories of the visual arts, conduct books, discussions of performances, manuals on how to preach, as well as in literary works, including plays, poetry and novels and unpublished sources, letters and diaries, for instance. Written materials help reveal ways in which looking was important in past societies and attended to by many constituencies. Probing the look of the past involves paying close attention to words as well as to images and objects, and to the relationships between what historians see and what was seen in the past. We acknowledge, then, that vision has a history, and that objects necessarily played a central role within it.

3 Coin, of the denomination known as an angel, 1606–7, gold, 4.48 grammes, British Museum. The ubiquity, diversity and visual properties of coins make them of general interest to historians. When portraits are included they provide the most common representations of human heads. This example is from the reign of James I of England and is pierced for use in the ceremony of touching for the King's Evil. French and English monarchs were thought to be able to cure scrofula by touching sufferers. In such an artefact, the special powers of rulers are doubly affirmed, by the coin being issued in their name and by the modification connected with a ritual that manifested their divine attributes.

Assumptions

All historical works rest on assumptions, some of which their authors recognise and avow, while others are so deeply embedded that they are difficult to bring up for critical inspection. I outline my own briefly here to enable readers to take account of them in the following pages. The use of images and objects as historical evidence turns out to be a topic that elicits strong feelings. Perhaps this is connected with anxieties about their reliability, especially given the allure some images and objects are known to exercise. I argue that such forms of seduction can be turned to good effect and need not deter historians from engagement with sources that are numerous, diverse and eloquent, and neither more nor less 'reliable' than other forms of evidence. My own responses guided the choice of example for the four short essays and acted as a spur to curiosity. This approach is perfectly compatible with a systematic examination of the objects in question, which demands the deliberate management of personal responses. I further assume that, when possible, such examination should begin with first-hand knowledge of the item in question. The internet is useful as a reminder, but not as a substitute for direct looking, which allows viewers to appreciate texture, dimensions and scale – features that prompt visual analysis.

One fundamental assumption of *The Look of the Past* is that a historical account containing diverse evidence is a worthy goal for the discipline. My ideal is an integrative form of history – the past itself was hardly divided up in the ways contemporary historical practices imply. Developing an integrative approach is not about quantity – more rather than fewer sources – but about bringing a range of types and genres of evidence together meaningfully. If any given theme – fear of degeneration, celebration of motherhood, critique of luxury, for example – is present not just in institutions, but also in literature, memoirs, treatises and newspapers, it is worth pursing that range of evidence, tracking the commonalities and differences. A fuller and more convincing historical account should result from this range, as it does from considering prints, medals and buildings, paintings, textiles and pottery as integral to our understanding of past phenomena. When working in this way historians track imaginative processes in the past, using their own in a disciplined manner in order to do so.

I further assume that when historians use visual and material evidence, it is worth being explicit about how and why, so that their workings are available for critical inspection. I therefore seek to spell out the kinds of reasoning involved. This approach risks stating the obvious, but that is preferable to being vague about how a visual source contributes to an argument or why an image is placed where it is in a publication. I endeavour to discuss the issues that arise when historians use objects and images in language that is as plain as possible. There are many introductions to visual culture, art history and material culture that set out a range of theoretical approaches and debates and outline the principal methods deployed. I take another tack, and use either specific objects or themes and concepts as my focus. By the end of the volume, readers will have been exposed to the basic issues that, in my view, the use of visual and material evidence raises for historians.

The significance of visual and material culture in people's lives and the existence of both major shifts and continuities in attitudes to objects are hardly in doubt. I am assuming that a broad case can be made for their value and relevance; hence the task of historians is to mobilise such evidence as effectively as possible, making clear their assumptions and moves. The items that fall into the categories 'visual and material culture' are strikingly diverse; as a result it is not always possible to generalise about how they are best used. Accordingly, conceptualising their precise historical pertinence in each case is a worthwhile exercise and this is what the short essays are designed to do. So, this volume aims to offer helpful suggestions and examples, both by laying out the bigger issues and by discussing specific instances. Yet there are general observations to be made, and they may be found throughout the book and underpinning them are some key beliefs. For example, I find the notion of mediation indispensable. Objects act as mediators; they cannot be simple reflections of an independent state of affairs, a point that applies as much to photography, for example, as to painting. Every made item results from human attention and skill; when ideas pass through consciousness and social practices – these are entwined – they are transformed in the process. This is as true of a child's drawing or a homemade garment as it is of artisanal products or acclaimed works of art. It follows that historians will find languages that stress active change, such as translation and transformation, more helpful than those evoking passivity, of which 'reflection' is the prime example.

The precise significance with which objects are endowed varies markedly with time and place, and within a given society. Yet the assumption that some artefacts are capable of embodying people and attributes is remarkably widespread, making the notion of embodiment analytically useful. Portraits, for example, are taken to stand for and evoke the person depicted. They can substitute for them after death or during their absence: both literally and metaphorically a portrait can embody a person. Similar phenomena are at work in relics and icons, in objects used during a Christian Mass and a coronation service. **III** The relationships between human beings and certain potent objects, which embodiment expresses, constitute major historical phenomena, ones that have been picked up in literature when writers, such as Nathaniel Hawthorne and Oscar Wilde, have explored the magical powers with which some objects and images have been endowed. People invest things with elaborate meanings, which, as we know from the case of souvenirs, do not depend upon them being expensive or made from precious materials: working out how this happens is of central importance for the field of history.

Through production processes, as well as through subsequent transactions and forms of display and use, meanings are added to materials. Some substances may already be resonant, as gold, alabaster and gemstones were. Historians who use artefacts engage with the people who made, handled, traded and used them. It is through such agents that images and objects have active lives, acquire power and are esteemed. It seems that myths around making are as old as human societies, which suggests something of the significance of this activity, especially when the results are highly valued, rare, symbolically dense or endowed with extraordinary powers. The story of the sculptor Pygmalion, told in Ovid's *Metamorphoses*, is a case in point. He made a statue of a woman so beautiful that he fell in love with her, and Venus, the goddess of love, granted his wish that the woman come to life.

Historians are generally eclectic creatures, and I am no exception. There are numerous tools and approaches that we can use, and it is incumbent on us to select them thoughtfully and in an informed manner. For instance, I have found art history to be a rich source of ideas, approaches and conceptual frameworks. It is itself a diverse discipline, encompassing a range of practices and theories, and one that can be generative for historians. In addition, I draw on other perspectives and fields as and when I find them useful. There can be no single method or approach for doing the sorts of work I explore here. They begin with careful looking and move on to description, analysis, contextualisation and comparison. Such operations are effective because artefacts arise out of social relationships, acting as mediators, not as mirrors, and can become dense with meanings, habits and conventions. Given the heterogeneity of the material worlds, these features are present in different ways and to diverse degrees, as it is our job to discover.

Decisions

The secondary literature that pertains to the themes of this book, like the primary sources that are potentially relevant to the look of the past, is simply vast. Difficult decisions had to be made to keep its scope manageable. Accordingly I excluded film, partly because an extensive literature exists about its role in historical practice. I only touch on media studies briefly when discussing audiences. While I use the idea of visual culture, visual culture *studies* with its focus on the present and most recent past, is not my primary concern here, although I am indebted to much recent work in the field, which is cited as appropriate. I draw most of my examples from 1600 onwards, because those who work on earlier periods, and have fewer sources at their disposal, have been inspiring pioneers when it comes to blending visual and material evidence into historical accounts and have long practised integrative forms of history. It seems that as sources proliferate the closer we get to the present, the harder it is to achieve such thorough integration. For practical reasons, most of my examples are drawn from Europe and North America, the geographical areas upon which I have previously worked. Furthermore, there are many types of artefact that are not mentioned here, such as arms and armour, vehicles, games and toys. The forms of argument mooted here can, however, be applied to any made item. A book such as this is inevitably the result of pragmatic decisions and authorial preferences.

Key themes

A number of themes that run through *The Look of the Past* are mentioned here so that readers can look out for them and reflect upon them.

They raise broad questions about historical practice and the relationships between scholars and sources. The first is agency, and in particular the ways historians can use productively the fact that the form and function of every artefact have passed through the minds and bodies of people who exercised choice in the past. Acts of patronage, exchange and display entail agency too. Like consumers, makers of objects and images manifest forms of visual intelligence, preferences and skills, which entitle them to be understood as historical actors, as witnesses to past states of affairs. Many different kinds of agency are involved, offering correspondingly rich historical opportunities. A significant proportion of made things was designed to elicit visual reactions. My second theme, then, is spectators' responses, which, although they may be difficult to document, are of major historical importance. How do we understand and conceptualise such reactions, and find evidence of audiences? How are potential audiences imagined by makers when they are working?

Third, I consider the skills that are needed for working closely with images and objects, which is an interdisciplinary and comparative enterprise. In keeping with the whole tenor of the book, I seek to be as explicit as possible about the range of skills involved, including the ability to describe, and then analyse and contextualise, visual evidence. In the process, historians generate verbal accounts. Everything, analytically speaking, is carried in the words used to describe, explain and interpret the evidence that artefacts present. So, the fourth theme could be summed up as 'word and image'. Translations, indeed all the intricate dynamics between these modes, are central to current forms of historical practice that involve thinking with the eyes, as they have been to people in the past.

The fifth theme concerns what I think of as the problem of levels. It is a characteristic of the discipline of history that it ranges between and connects phenomena that are concrete and abstract, local, national and international, individual and collective. Clear and convincing articulations between these levels are required. Nowhere is this more pressing than in the case of artefacts, which, if they are to be integrated into historical accounts, need to be linked to more abstract phenomena and also to explanatory frameworks. The role of theory in historical practice, a related matter, is the sixth theme snaking through the book. The fields that specialise in studying visual and material culture give more prominence to theory than most historians do, for whom it is frequently no more than a part of the philosophy of history that has little to do with their business as usual. Those who are interested in historical theory have shown surprisingly little concern for probing the conceptual challenges of working with visual and material culture, for analysing their place within the discipline of history or for learning from theoretical reflection in adjacent fields.

The final theme is the ethical dimensions of using non-written evidence. When historians work with artefacts, they incur the same obligations as when deploying written and spoken evidence, which are managed through acknowledgements, footnotes, bibliographies and permissions. Adaptations of these devices help to cultivate a careful, engaged visual attention that is the opposite of the unthinking use of illustrations, which, regrettably, remains common. It is always worth analysing how images are used in publications, as this reveals the attitudes of authors and publishers to visual and material evidence.

Terminology

Finding the most generative vocabularies and apt analytical terms is vital for historians who use visual and material evidence. Given the heterogeneity of images and objects, I often use the terms 'visual culture' and 'material culture' as catchalls. But they carry distinctive connotations, largely because disciplines are now organised around them and they stand in implied contrast to other terms, such as art and archaeology. For example, 'visual culture' implies a study that is more inclusive than art history, since 'art' suggests aesthetic entry requirements. Sometimes, 'visual culture' indicates an interest in contemporary phenomena, such as film, television and advertising and debates concerning their interpretation. In this sense it overlaps with media studies and film studies, which are rightly concerned to give popular culture its due. 'Visual culture' includes design, fashion and photography as well as art: not only is it inclusive, but it is also open to theoretical perspectives from the social sciences, post-modernism and critical theory. It is possible to use the phrase 'visual culture', which generally signals an interest in working across media, in a more explicitly historical manner, to suggest the array of items at a given place and time that possess visual interest. **IV**

'Material culture' is even more generously inclusive in implying any made item, especially those in three dimensions. Material culture *studies*, with its close relationships with archaeology and anthropology, has been informed by the social sciences, and also by traditions that study artefacts in everyday life. It recognises the dynamism of objects as they change location and hands. Aesthetic criteria are relatively unimportant. The most ordinary objects come under the category 'material culture', items that are as important for the way they feel and are used as for how they are looked at. Geographers, with their preoccupation with the social organisation of space, have been drawn to the study of material culture, while social theorists are interested in 'stuff' in general. I use 'material culture' inclusively, especially when I want to suggest the diversity of objects that historians can consider, while my priority remains the possibilities for analysing their appearance.

Although they possess distinct resonances, there are important points of overlap between 'visual culture' and 'material culture'. For example, apart from dreams and visions, most images are 'material'; a picture is generally also an object. I use 'image', a more complex notion than is immediately apparent, to refer to many forms of representation, and vary the terms in a quest to avoid tiresome repetition. When I speak of objects, things, items, artefacts or pieces, I am excluding neither most images nor buildings. **V** Although buildings are in many respects unlike objects made by an individual or a small number of people, I hope that my approach works with architecture, as the first essay aims to show. Architectural history tends to operate as a distinct specialised field, but there is no reason why it should be not further integrated into mainstream history.

Even seemingly innocent terms such as 'craft' and 'design' are freighted with assumptions about social status, with the 'fine' arts generally accorded more cultural prestige than the 'decorative' ones. Similar issues of hierarchy apply to 'artist' and 'artisan', and where possible and appropriate I opt for a more neutral word, such as 'maker' or 'producer'. Beyond rough categories such as 'art' and 'craft', more detailed languages of description and further forms of classification are needed. It is possible to turn to materials and medium, genre and date, beginning an account with such basic information. Technical precision is also required, so that the print method, for example, needs to be given its proper name. Then it is necessary to speak of colours, shapes, composition and so on, and we necessarily have recourse to metaphor. Even seemingly straightforward tasks, such as the use of style terms, 'baroque' and 'neo-classical' for instance, to classify objects, turn out to be fraught with complexities. Historians are wordsmiths by trade, and we need to be especially attentive, meticulous and imaginative in our use of language, especially when drawing upon a range of disciplines. Accordingly, *The Look of the Past* is about the ways historians talk and write about things, as well as about how the past was experienced visually and is transmitted to us through the sense of sight.

Interpretation

There are innumerable ways of talking and writing about visual experiences and the phenomena that generate them, which are shaped by authors'

S. Munition gehört nur dem Tommy hinter den Tanks!

NUR DIE RUHE KANN ES MACHEN

Durchgefahrene Tanks erledigt die Artillerie!

4 'Nur die Ruhe kann es machen' ('Gently does it'), acquired 1919, 90 cm wide × 47.8 cm high, Cambridge University Library. This intriguing poster is printed on the back of a map of Belgium. The slogan may also be translated as 'take it easy' and was a common expression of the time, including in popular songs. The text on the left-hand side reads: 'Save small-arms fire for the Tommies behind the tanks'; and on the right: 'The artillery will deal with any tanks that get through'. Thus the poster was presumably aimed at German soldiers in training.

commitments and preferences and the contexts in which they operate. I do not advocate a particular method or approach here, except insofar as paying careful, focused attention to items of visual and material culture is the indispensable foundation for taking them seriously. Historians will interpret them in a range of ways, as they do texts, periods and places. These processes are commonly evoked through the idea of 'reading'. While notions of interpretation may be widely applied, we might well avoid using terms that simply assume the similarities between, say, books and images, as they can distract attention from the distinctive ways in which visual media work. 'Reading' is sometimes taken to imply that there are 'messages' to be decoded, which downplays the ambiguity and complexities of both artefacts and texts. Images designed to persuade, as in propaganda and advertising, may have been intended to convey 'messages', yet even they frequently work at a number of levels. **4** The model of reading messages is too reductive to do justice to many visual and material sources.

The point about 'messages' is especially important because of the dramatic recent growth in public history. The major role of museums, galleries, parks and other visitor attractions in communicating aspects of the past depends upon the display of artefacts and the inculcation of a sense of the past through visual experience. Simplified 'messages' abound. It is essential that historians are able to critique such installations from an informed position. Thus I hope *The Look of the Past* will make a contribution to the critical evaluation of public history and the interpretations offered there.

Disciplines

The idea of interdisciplinary history is now well established, with a dedicated journal that has been in existence since 1970. When historians use visual and material evidence, it would be odd not to engage with the range of relevant specialised fields, some of which are recent developments and manifest a strong commitment to interdisciplinarity. Museology, or museum studies, is a good example of a relatively new and growing field that is interdisciplinary and eclectic. Although a great deal of attention is paid to current public policy in relation to museums, considerable work has also been done on collections, collecting, institutions, and forms of display in the past, making the boundaries between museum studies and history quite fuzzy. As issues around the preservation of valued remnants of the past loom ever larger in public life, the relationships between history and other areas with an interest in 'heritage', such as geography, are likely to become closer. As we have noted, visual culture studies, which is avowedly interdisciplinary, is willing to embrace contemporary theoretical debates that themselves transcend conventional boundaries. By contrast, another relevant field, conservation studies, is highly technical, deploying cutting-edge scientific methods capable of yielding results that can change historical interpretation. Then there are also what can be called meta-disciplines, such as philosophy and psychoanalysis, both of which have had considerable impact upon visual studies, and as a result touch our concerns here. Historians interested in using visual and material culture can thus expect to interact with many other disciplines and to do so in a variety of ways from learning about the nuts and bolts of materials and production processes to engaging with conceptual frameworks.

Structure

Five thematic chapters, with four interspersed case studies, follow this introduction in a structure designed to prompt reflection upon a range of analytical levels. Chapter 1 considers matters that come up immediately when historians use artefacts: description and evidence. It explores the nature of historians' descriptions, their capacity to lead into analysis and the ways in which things can be made into evidence. Having considered how images and objects become historical evidence, I provide next a short essay to examine how this can be done, using a building from the late seventeenth century. Since buildings, even when associated with a single architect, are produced by many hands, this essay introduces the key theme of agency. Chapter 2 suggests the ways in which understanding the making of objects, through the study of materials and production processes, can assist historical analysis. The essay that follows takes a renowned and controversial work by a polymath – a chapel and its central piece of sculpture – through which we consider design, collaboration and style.

Periodisation, the subject of Chapter 3, is of central importance for historians of visual and material culture. Period specificity, often invoked using style terms, is a complex phenomenon. Historians can usefully reflect upon the exact ways in which artefacts express and reveal historical moments. Then the third essay discusses a mid-twentieth-century photography exhibition, paying particular attention to one specific item within it, which has been taken to epitomise the time at which it was made. It touches upon questions concerning audiences and the nature of visual display, which are developed in the following chapter. Chapter 4 considers the complexity and elusiveness of audiences, both implied and actual, alongside the settings and contexts that are crucial for the interpretation of displayed artefacts. An early twentieth-century painted portrait depicting a man appreciatively handling a statuette forms the subject of the last essay. Finally, Chapter 5 examines a way of thinking – comparative analysis – of fundamental importance for historical work with images and objects.

The Look of the Past is addressed to those who practise and are fascinated by that broad field we call 'history', who wish to reflect on its procedures, and who are curious about an aspect of it that is of growing significance. It deals with a subject where open and collaborative relationships with other fields are essential. Thus *The Look of the Past* is an interdisciplinary enterprise, which nonetheless maintains a focus on the manner in which historians use visual and material evidence, drawing upon centuries of curiosity about just what old stuff reveals about past times.

FURTHER READING

The relationships between history and visual culture have been explored by, among others, Francis Haskell, *History and its Images* (New Haven and London, 1993); Peter Burke, *Eyewitnessing: the Uses of Images as Historical Evidence* (London, 2001); and Robert I. Rotberg and Theodore K. Rabb, eds., *Art and History: Images and their Meanings* (Cambridge, 1988). Many recent books provide introductions to visual culture. Examples include Matthew Rampley, ed., *Exploring Visual Culture: Definitions, Concepts, Contexts* (Edinburgh, 2005); Elizabeth Edwards and Kaushik Bhaumik, eds., *Visual Sense* (Oxford, 2008); Gillian Rose, *Visual Methodologies: an Introduction to Researching with Visual Materials*, 3rd edn (London, 2012); and Malcolm Barnard, *Approaches to Understanding Visual*

Culture (Basingstoke, 2001). *Visual Culture*, ed. Charles Jenks (London, 1995), is a classic example. Two relatively new journals are worth noting, *Journal of Visual Culture* (2002 onwards) and *Visual Culture in Britain* (2000 onwards), and the older *Visual Studies* (1986 onwards). See also Jane Kromm and Susan Bakewell, eds., *A History of Visual Culture: Western Civilization from the 18th to the 21st Century* (Oxford, 2010).

Useful works on material culture include Steven Lubar and W. David Kingery, eds., *History from Things: Essays on Material Culture* (Washington DC, 1993); Chris Tilley *et al.*, eds., *Handbook of Material Culture* (London, 2006); Karen Harvey, ed., *History and Material Culture: a Student's Guide to Approaching Alternative Sources* (London, 2009); and Ian Woodward, *Understanding Material Culture* (Los Angeles, 2007). Carl Knappert, *Thinking Through Material Culture: an Interdisciplinary Perspective* (Philadelphia, 2005), is a stimulating attempt by an archaeologist to 'explore the basic theoretical issues – the status of objects and of the humans producing and using them – by looking at developments in a range of fields that confront such questions in relation to objects in the contemporary world' (p. vii). He considers art history but not history, nonetheless historians can learn much from his analysis. The *Journal of Material Culture*, first published in 1996, indicates the scope of the field. Daniel Miller, *Stuff* (Cambridge, 2010), is an example of a book about the importance of studying 'material things', which manifests little interest in their appearance. See also the special issue of *Critical Inquiry* on 'Things', 28/1 (2001); Sherry Turkle, ed., *Evocative Objects: Things We Think With* (Cambridge, MA, and London, 2007) and Judy Attfield, *Wild Things: the Material Culture of Everyday Life* (Oxford and New York, 2000).

A sense of art history as a field may be gained from Marcia Pointon's *History of Art: a Student Handbook*, 4th edn (London, 1997), and Michael Hatt and Charlotte Klonk, *Art History: a Critical Introduction to its Methods* (Manchester, 2006). Eric Fernie, ed., *Art History and its Methods: a Critical Anthology* (London, 1995), provides a selection of texts about the interpretation of art from the sixteenth century to the early 1990s. A more demanding but comparable collection, which includes texts from the mid-eighteenth century onwards, is Donald Preziosi, ed., *The Art of Art History: a Critical Anthology* (Oxford, 1998). It forms part of the excellent Oxford History of Art series designed to provide authoritative introductions to major art-historical subjects. An example of my art-historical mentor's work is Thomas Puttfarken, *The Discovery of Pictorial Composition: Theories of Visual Order in Painting, 1400–1800* (New Haven and London, 2000). A valuable work is Robert S. Nelson and Richard Shiff, *Critical Terms for Art History*, 2nd edn (Chicago, 2003), which provides a sort of keywords for art history and includes terms such as mediation, meaning/interpretation, style, gender and identity. See also Jonathan Harris, *Art History: the Key Concepts* (London, 2006); Raymond Williams, *Keywords: a Vocabulary of Culture and Society*, 2nd edn (London, 1988); and Tony Bennett *et al.*, eds., *New Keywords: a Revised Vocabulary of Culture and Society* (Malden, MA, 2005).

William Whyte's article 'How do Buildings Mean? Some Issues of Interpretation in the History of Architecture', *History and Theory*, 45 (2006), pp. 153–77, is extremely useful. *History and Theory* has published relatively little on visual and material culture broadly defined, but see their special issue on *Photography and Historical Interpretation*, 48/4 (2009). Anthropologists have reflected upon the roles of 'art' and artefacts in their field, for example: Alfred Gell, *Art and Agency: an Anthropological Theory* (Oxford, 1998); Amiria Henare *et al.*, eds., *Thinking Through Things: Theorising Artefacts Ethnographically* (London, 2007); and Cristina Grasseni, ed., *Skilled Visions: Between Apprenticeship and Standards* (New York and Oxford, 2007).

Other works relevant to issues raised in the Introduction are, in alphabetical order by author: James Aulich, *War Posters: Weapons of Mass Communication* (London, 2007), esp. ch. 2; John Barnicoat, *A Concise History of Posters* (London, 1972); Marc Bloch, *Royal Touch: Sacred Monarchy and Scrofula in England and France* (London, 1973; first published 1924); Stephen Brogan, 'The Royal Touch', *History Today*, 61/2 (2011), pp. 46–52; Kenneth Gross, *The Dream of the Moving Statue* (University Park, PA, 2006; first published 1992); Martin Kemp, *Christ to Coke: How Image Becomes Icon* (New York and London, 2011); David Large, *Berlin* (London, 2001); Teofana Matakieva-Lilkova, *Icons in Bulgaria* (Sofia, 2000; first published 1994); Edwin Mullins, *The Pilgrimage to Santiago* (Oxford, 2001; first published 1974); Martin Jessop Price, *Coins: an Illustrated Survey 650BC to the Present Day* (London, 1980), chs. 12–15; Ovid, *Metamorphoses*, completed in AD 8 and available in many editions; Alexandra Richie, *Faust's Metropolis: a History of Berlin* (London, 1998); Robert Rosenstone, *Visions of the Past: the Challenge of Film to our Idea of History* (Cambridge, MA, 1995); and John Styles, *Threads of Feeling: the London Foundling Hospitals Textile Tokens, 1740–1770* (London, 2010).

Stuart Clark's *Vanities of the Eye: Vision in Early Modern European Culture* (Oxford, 2007), takes a wide-ranging look at the ways in which sight was understood and debated in one particular historical era. The American writer Nathaniel Hawthorne wrote extensively about art, vision, appearances and artefacts supercharged with significance – see, for example, *The Marble Faun* (first published 1860).

My own historiographical positions are developed in *History in Practice*, 2nd edn (London, 2006; 3rd edn 2013), see, for example, the chapter on Public History; 'Image Matters', *Historical Journal*, 51 (2008), pp. 777–91; 'Visualising Identity', in *Identity*, ed. Giselle Walker and Elisabeth Leedham-Green (Cambridge, 2010), pp.127–56; and 'Approaching Visual Materials', in *Research Methods for History*, ed. Simon Gunn and Lucy Faire (Edinburgh, 2012), pp. 30–47.

1   Description and evidence

A description

To write this chapter I am sitting at a cheap, oval, gate-legged table bought at IKEA in the early 1990s; the wood is yellowish, and I have worked at it intermittently in the intervening years. I could describe where the IKEA store is, the journey there and back, the person I was with, where the table has been positioned in places I have lived, its dimensions, and what is currently on its surface. One item stands out. **VI** It is a female figure about six inches high and two inches wide, made of a grey, stone-like substance. She has long hair, flowing robes, a simple, stylised feminine face and is holding a jar. A gift from someone I worked with long ago, she is, I find, beautiful and evocative. I assume my little statue is a modern replica of an early Christian figure, although I am not expert enough to date its template without research. Presumably the figure it represents is Mary Magdalene, whose attribute is a jar, to suggest the ointment she carried to Christ's empty tomb on Easter morning.[1] We can compare her with other three-dimensional depictions of this widely depicted woman, such as Donatello's standing wooden figure and Canova's statue of the repentant Magdalene. **5** and **6** Mine is different: small, serene and mass produced – there are obvious marks from the mould on the sides, suggesting that the material was originally liquid in form. Mary Magdalene shares my table with a simple elegant modern lamp, purchased at a major department store, which takes a tiny halogen bulb, as well as books and papers, items such as paperclips, a stapler that must be at least forty years old, Tipp-Ex, assorted pens and pencils, cards, envelopes, files, sticky labels and much more.

5 *St Mary Magdalen*, by Donatello, ?1453–5, wood, 188 cm high, Museo dell'Opera del Duomo, Florence. This work is both mysterious and arresting. Its original purpose, like the date it was made, is unknown. Its expressive qualities are not, however, in doubt. Donatello has depicted Mary, a symbol of penitence and reform, in her extended period of solitary repentance, her long hair covering her body. Although her limbs are shown as being strong, the face looks ravaged, marked by suffering.

Description and history

The themes of this book have been hinted at in a single paragraph. I called my brief account a description: as we shall see, 'description' covers a multitude of literary forms, including captions, criticism, inventories, novels, stage directions and sales catalogues. Those who consider items of visual and material culture in their historical work are interested in how they have been described in the past. My main concern in this chapter, however, is with the role played by description in historical practice and its contribution to the processes of turning artefacts into evidence.

The description of my table and items on it could have continued, more or less indefinitely, ramifying into autobiography, accounts of manufacturing and retailing, materials, design, and the accoutrements of academic and personal life. The paragraph operated at a number of levels: I gave some physical details, used evaluative terms, such as 'beautiful', 'elegant' and 'evocative', to suggest emotional and aesthetic responses, and alluded to the significance one item in particular held for me, mentioning how it was made as well as its association with a specific period of my life. Such levels, together with the conceptualisation of links between them, contribute to a sense both of the past and of the kinds of history it is possible to write; they hint at the complexities of using things in academic accounts.

The ways in which images and objects can play an active part in historians' accounts is the subject of this book. With the fullness of the term 'history' in mind, I can assert that the opening paragraph of this chapter was indeed *historical*, in alluding to a Christian figure and the history of materials, for instance. My aged stapler is made of painted grey metal, most new ones are coloured plastic. All the objects mentioned, like their constituent parts, could be historically located; it is possible to specify roughly when the item in question was made, where the idea for it came from, how it was marketed and used. Then there is the biographical history through which possessions are given significance, by association with people, times and places. Through such connections, as well as by virtue of their physical properties, artefacts prompt analytical, aesthetic and emotional responses.

It is probably impossible to describe fully any given object – a simple diagram or sketch may communicate its appearance more efficiently. But

6 *Penitent Magdalene*, by
Antonio Canova, 1794–6,
marble and gilded bronze,
90 cms high, Palazzo Bianco,
Genoa. In Canova's version, the
posture of the figure, kneeling
and gazing down meditatively,
together with the skull, conveys
a strong sense of penitence. So
too does the cross she holds.
It not only reminds viewers of
her closeness to Christ – she
was the first to see him after
the Resurrection – but also of
her capacity to meditate upon
his suffering during her years
of isolation in the wilderness.
Mary's famous long hair is
present, but does not dominate
the figure as in Donatello's
statue. Note the smoothness
and sensuality of the marble
in contrast to Donatello's
corrugated wood. Canova
made relatively few statues of
religious figures. This one was
exhibited, to acclaim, in the
Paris Salon of 1808, a strikingly
secular setting, and it is not
immediately apparent how it
would work in a sacred space.

the creation of descriptions is an unavoidable element of scholarship on
the visual and material worlds. While there are limits to verbal description, it is the task of some fields – poetry, drama, fiction, for example – to
keep finding new ways of approaching it. Perhaps this is also a task for
the discipline of history, and if so, it is helpful if its practitioners develop
skills for describing what they see and mobilising the results as evidence.
Both generating descriptions and endowing items with the status of historical evidence are active processes involving the self-aware honing of
a range of skills.

7 Pages 28 and 29 from *Universal: a Catalogue of Appliances*, London, 1929, each page 21.7 cm wide × 28.2 cm high, Cambridge University Library. This catalogue was produced 'for the trade only', by L. G. Hawkins and Co., of Drury Lane, London. It illustrates and describes a range of electrical goods from curling irons and hot plates to meat choppers and vibrators. It provides an excellent example of verbal descriptions and visual representations for a highly specific purpose – persuading shopkeepers to sell their goods. The images of washing machines are designed to show their appearance, key features of them and something of their workings. From such publications, we can make informed inferences about their audiences, including about their anticipated visual skills.

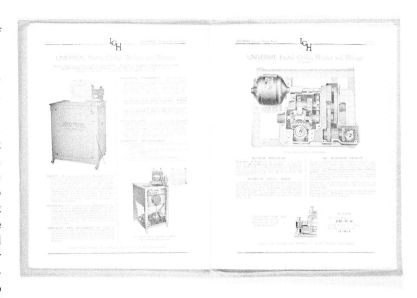

What is description?

'Description' here refers to an account, in words, of a person, an event, an object, indeed any phenomenon worthy of attention. The contexts in which descriptions are offered are, however, strikingly varied: instruction manuals for household appliances, exhibition catalogues, guidebooks, newspapers, encyclopaedias, advice books, programmes to accompany performances and many more. **7** The numerous, distinct purposes of description suggest equally distinct forms of writing. There is no one way of describing something, although in historiographical contexts, the basic features of an artefact, such as size and medium, certainly need to be included.

One form of description, referred to by the Greek term *ekphrasis*, deserves mention here. This is a rhetorical device in which a work of art is evoked, often graphically and dramatically, in another medium – a painting in a poem, for instance. *Ode on a Grecian Urn*, written by the English poet John Keats in 1819 is a well-known example, even if it is hardly a 'description' in our sense. *Ekphrasis* is used to mean an account in words of the visual experience prompted by a striking piece of art. Such descriptions are designed to provoke vivid emotions in the reader, perhaps to deepen their understanding of objects, characters, plots, themes, and of themselves. Ekphrastic writing not only provides direct historical insights into the visual worlds in which they were composed, but suggests ways in which it is possible to craft an account of what one sees. Examples of *ekphrasis* help historians to understand and deploy their own and their readers' responses in writings on visual and material culture.

In order to appreciate the role that description can play in historical practice, it is worth listing the functions it is capable of performing. Some of these, conveying instructions, for example, are less central to our concerns here, but others, such as engaging an audience, definitely are. Five related functions of description are pertinent in this context. First, producing an account enables the historian to identify the features that interest them, and that render the object in question of scholarly value. Next, descriptions help to evoke their object of study in readers' minds, engaging their audience in a lively manner. An effective description achieves a third end by conveying the materiality of the artefact in question, using words to establish its physical features. Fourth, description draws attention to the salient features that will be integral to the historical argument. It makes them explicit and available for analysis. Finally, description is a form of sharing, of building up a common understanding, not only of specific images and objects, but of ways of talking about, conceptualising and explaining them. Description and interpretation are intimately connected.

The links between description and evidence, the other key term of this chapter, are now emerging. Evidence is a relative term, a source is evidence *for* a hunch, a hypothesis, an argument or a claim. Descriptions act as bridges between sources and interpretations of them. Detailed accounts have the potential to provide evidence for historians, not just because they contain information and (sometimes) plain records of relevant phenomena, but because the language in which they are expressed is already processing authors' responses and ideas. There is no clear dividing line between description and analysis. In undertaking analysis, historians' minds are already full of questions, some of which are designed to assess the kinds of evidence they have in front of them. Returning to and refining further a description are integral parts of assessing and deploying visual and material evidence and of clarifying historical questions.

Let me be more explicit about what a description ideally contains. I say 'ideally' because inevitably states of preservation, the ability to handle a work, and the availability of related information, such as provenance, are limiting factors. Descriptions start with physical properties: size, shape, colours, materials, subject matter, genre, date, maker and so on. These sound straightforward, but present their own challenges. While size can be conveyed, albeit imperfectly, through numbers, any discussion of composition, shape and colour has to convert the visual experience of the writer into words. The literary talents of the describer, as well as the variety of ways in which descriptors, such as crimson, peacock blue (which, for many people, is green) and cream, are interpreted, shape a process best described as translation. Furthermore, numbers convey size imperfectly because they are abstract without a measuring device and comparisons to hand: size is most readily apprehended through the human body and its surrounding space – taller than the average person, as wide as the beholder can spread their arms, from here to the door and so on. Indeed viewers might be positively encouraged to think about scale in such a way, and writers to provide descriptions that bring scale to life. Including the historical location and hang of works when these are known, extends the capacity of a description to contextualise objects.

Descriptions then progress to the life history of an artefact: who made it and why, how much it cost, where, how and by whom was it given and received, bought and sold, used and displayed, how it has been seen and interpreted. The consideration of provenance – the record of the ownership of a work – reveals how it is possible to move from the attributes of an object to broader issues, such as the role of gifts, forms of association between people and possessions, and markets. Provenance is rarely visible; although information attached to an item is sometimes relevant, more often it depends on ancillary documentation. These questions apply as much to the settings of objects – frames and display cases, for example – as they do to objects themselves. For historians, the nature of any collaborations during production processes are likely to be of special interest; information about who, exactly, made or modified an artefact is especially precious evidence of social relationships. Such evidence can sometimes be derived from extremely close scrutiny, for example, of the kind undertaken by conservation specialists, who produce their own kinds of description, demanding technical understanding.

Attention and time

There are many forms of description, and the skills required to produce an effective one are an important part of historical expertise. There is a concept that unites different types of description and makes the necessary skills explicit: attention. In this context 'attention' is a combination of sustained careful looking, mental focus, concentrated reflection and consideration, and thoughtful, self-aware writing. Descriptions are produced by writers paying close attention to the object in question and they elicit the reader's attention in turn. Paying attention is a capacity that has to be cultivated. Certain types of discipline are required for it to function fully, such as, when viewing a painting or piece of sculpture, systematic and meticulous looking, measuring and then recording the results. Descriptions have to be actively generated so the more self-awareness and experience involved the better. When is it appropriate to produce an austere, plain description that eschews overt terms of evaluation and when one that revels in adjectival richness? Careful description facilitates comparisons between objects, by means of which differences and similarities that are fundamental for interpretation are identified. Such comparative analysis lies at the heart of all work with images and objects.

There are further reasons for placing special emphasis on attention. Attention is a feature of making as well as of viewing artefacts. Indeed one of the main purposes in analysing them is gaining an understanding of the kinds of attention that have been paid during processes of design and production, working out how this can be used as evidence and assessing how it corresponds to responses of users and audiences. Attention is a facet of visual intelligence. Many makers expect it of their audiences, and put specific features in their work to be noticed and appreciated by those who pay careful attention. The term 'connoisseurship' describes close, discriminating forms of visual attention; it has been applied especially to the inspection and evaluation of valued works of art by privileged elites. This quality of visual attention is generative in numerous contexts. The processes that take place when we pay attention are of three broad kinds: somatic, mental and emotional. In practice these overlap, but noting the existence of these types helps us to recognise what a complex phenomenon 'attention' is. Scale, for example, is often registered first by the body, as are colour and texture, whilst assessing subject matter and genre primarily involves mental operations. Somatic, like emotional, awareness may begin more or less intuitively, but can then be brought up to a more conscious level of full attention quite deliberately. It is for these reasons that our capacity for paying attention needs to be trained.

Attention implies time spent looking, and, if possible, repeated visual engagement with objects of study. It is possible to see features on second or third inspection that were simply not noticed initially. Each session of looking takes time. The spectator is likely to move around, especially when viewing three-dimensional objects. The challenges of generating a verbal description are especially great when there is no single vantage point. Furthermore, objects and images change with time, both in how they appear and physically. One obvious way in which they do so is as a result of light. A piece of marble sculpture, for example, when in a setting that admits natural light, changes many times in the course of a day because of shadows and the quality of sunlight that falls upon it.[2] Objects and images also age, and this too needs to be taken account of, especially when making observations about painted colours. Paying careful attention to such effects helps to generate a satisfying description.

Time also affects description through habituation. Items deployed repeatedly, that are perhaps over-exposed, as happens when they are

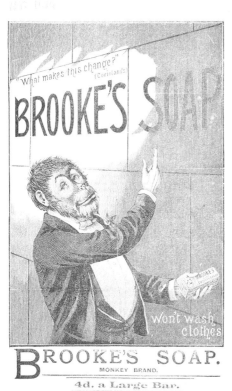

8 Advertisement for Brooke's soap, 1892, 14 cm wide × 22.5 cm high, Cambridge University Library. The monkey dressed up in formal attire is particularly striking to modern viewers, especially in the light of the extensive satirical imagery that followed the publication of Charles Darwin's *On the Origin of Species*, in 1859. Such images revealed deep anxieties about the boundaries between human beings and animals, and between racial and ethnic groups. The reference to a play by Shakespeare is also noteworthy. The wording is persuasive and exuberant. This advertisement, so different from ones using Millais's painting, begins to alert us to the range of visual idioms that co-existed.

part of big advertising campaigns, cannot subsequently be seen in the same way. Two forces are at work here. First, they become associated with something to which they have no intrinsic connection. The use of a painting of a little boy by the British artist John Everett Millais in advertisements for soap is a prime example. Painted in 1885–6, it depicts his grandson Willie James in a 'costume reminiscent of those worn by boys in portraits by Gainsborough and Thomas Lawrence' painted in the late eighteenth and early nineteenth centuries. The bubbles he is blowing remind viewers of the transience of life. It was bought first by the *Illustrated London News* and then by T. J. Barratt of Pears soap: it served, to the artist's disapproval, to advertise this product, and was retitled 'Bubbles'. Owned by Unilever, which took over Pears, it is currently on long loan to the Lady Lever Art Gallery, National Museums of Liverpool.[3] **8**

When the second force operates, the image itself becomes over-familiar, stale, even hackneyed, so that it is difficult, perhaps impossible, to look at it and describe it dispassionately. An excellent example of this phenomenon is Leonardo da Vinci's *Mona Lisa*. She too is used commercially, to promote the Louvre Museum in Paris, and on items for sale. She is also a brand in her own right, not something with which a separate product has been linked in order to promote it. Many well-known artists are brands, with the result that a limited number of works are indeed over-exposed. Huge numbers of people see them many times, becoming habituated to them. There are currently millions of bags, mats, paper napkins, ties and t-shirts with reproductions of Impressionist paintings on them, especially by Claude Monet. An interesting and noteworthy phenomenon in its own right, fully worthy of historians' attention, it sheds light on taste, museum financing and patterns of consumption. Inevitably it also becomes it harder to treat such works as historical evidence of the times in which they were made, and renders the need for adequate description all the more urgent.

Classification and hierarchy

Even before historians move to deliberately describe a thing, they have already made assumptions and performed a mental operation that will, whether they like it or not, shape their responses to it. That mental operation is the categorisation, deploying several criteria, of the object in question. During a first glance, an artefact is being placed in rough categories, such as the possible period in which it was made, its purpose, interest and quality. Genre and medium can also be fairly quickly appraised. The precise date and place of making may be more difficult to ascertain immediately. Categorisation and assumptions about value are deeply entwined, whether the value is economic, aesthetic, personal or linked with materials. Already several types of classification have been mentioned; in judging any single item, they are integrated, largely unconsciously, when forming an initial overall impression.

Classification is the most widespread way of imposing order and meaning upon the world and its constituent objects. This is obvious enough in science, especially in botany and zoology, which simply could not function without workable taxonomies. As the anthropologist Mary Douglas showed, all aspects of human life are constituted by overlapping forms of classification, which are charged with emotional, religious, personal and moral meanings. Historians working with visual and material culture are taking account of a number of taxonomies, those imposed by markets, by art worlds, by institutions and so on. In the discipline of history we are constantly classifying both sources and types of historical writing, for example, by genre (monograph, journal article, textbook), by content or approach (legal, social, political, feminist) and by method (econometrics, psychohistory, oral history).

One of the challenges in working with visual and material culture is the existence of pervasive systems of classification, which we bring to our work, without necessarily being fully aware of doing so. The common division between work done with the head and with the hand, with the former being accorded higher status, is particularly problematic, not least because in practice the production of artefacts requires both kinds. Within the so-called 'fine' arts, the academic hierarchy of genres, so prominent in the seventeenth and eighteenth centuries, has left its mark. History painting, which depicted great deeds and stories from the past, was at the top, and was considered more intellectually demanding on artists. Lower down were portraits, still life and scenes of everyday life. There lingers a corresponding tendency to see the history of quotidian existence as less intellectually challenging than, say, political history, and newer genres and media, such as television and graffiti, as less worthy of analysis. For example, some historians argue, and others readily agree, that paintings produced in a royal or noble court shed light on that court; they are capable of doing so because courts were centres of power. The same people, however, might find a fire screen, a table or a walking stick less historically eloquent. The explanations for their value judgements are certainly complex, but they hinge, at least in part, on a long-standing assumption that the so-called decorative arts are lower in commonly deployed hierarchies than, say, oil painting on canvas, and especially than paintings by 'great masters', such as Titian, Velasquez, Rubens and van Dyck, all of whom can be described as court painters. Here 'lower' implies less skilful and demanding, cheaper and altogether more routine.

Such forms of classification are inseparable from *social* hierarchies. Portraits of rulers by major artists seem obviously historically 'significant', while a chair or table, whose maker is, if known at all, less likely to be famous, does not. In the former case, ancillary documents have better survival chances, and the agency of sitter, patrons and artists is easier to imagine. Such responses concern class, status, power and authority; large paintings of monarchs by fêted artists exercise an allure that differs markedly from that of furniture made and used by regular folk. The former pertain to matters easily deemed significant, whereas furniture can seem trivial. There are historically specific social hierarchies of occupations and of the institutions with which they were associated. Both are linked with the nature of markets. While such hierarchies of people, organisations and objects vary, versions of them are reinforced in myriad ways, but above all by institutions, such as museums and art galleries, the international businesses that buy and sell objects, and schools and universities, which study, marginalise or ignore them. All these phenomena are relevant to acts of describing.

The existence of domesticated, taken-for-granted classification systems is one of the main reasons why it is productive for historians to look at images and objects afresh. The goal is to provide, at least initially, as 'neutral' descriptions of them as is feasible, and to put aside, insofar as possible, preconceptions about their worth, whether historical, aesthetic or monetary. Description can be used knowingly to bracket off hierarchies, because the focus is on paying attention and giving intellectual value to a thing irrespective of its alleged aesthetic, economic or social status. It encourages us to think in open-minded ways with artefacts.

Captions and titles

In order to illustrate and extend the points already made about description and evidence, I turn to some specific examples, beginning with captions, which in many publications offer the most basic accounts readers come across. I then move from captions to entries in reference books and guidebooks, and on to criticism, a genre that helps us to consider what the distinctive features of academic writing about images and objects may be.

Captions are one of the most fundamental and accessible types of description. I have chosen examples from a highly diverse exhibition with an accompanying publication. Entitled *Choice: 21 Years of Collecting for Scotland*, and organised by the National Galleries of Scotland, the exhibition included more than 350 objects, in diverse media, from numerous countries and spanning many centuries. The book contained 204 of them, organised by date of production not of acquisition. Number 1 was a Roman Bust, while the last entry was a piece of sculpture dated 1999. Here is the caption for the latter: '204 Mona Hatoum b. 1952 *Slicer*, 1999 / Varnished steel and thermoformed plastic. 104 × 117.5 × 93 cm / Purchased with assistance from the National Art Collections Fund 2005 [GMA 4782]'.[4] Above it is a colour photograph (24 cm wide × 19 cm high) of an object familiar to many as a kitchen utensil. A great deal of information is given here in a compact way, although it does not reveal anything about the colour of the object – the plastic is white. Nor does it *interpret* the object in any way. Every item is photographed in colour, thus readers are invited to enjoy the beauty of the acquisitions themselves. The book displays works of art – paintings, drawings and prints, furniture, medals, photographs, and sculpture – defined broadly enough to include a landform commissioned in 2003 for the grounds of the Scottish Gallery of Modern Art in Edinburgh. This publication, and others like it, are full of openings for historical work, especially around processes of collecting, the taste associated with an institution and its leaders, and the diverse manner in which works are acquired: purchase, bequest, gift, funded by charitable bodies, accepted in lieu of inheritance tax, and commission. Thus institutional histories may be embedded in, if not made fully explicit by, a basic description. The objects in *Choice* can be made into evidence of processes of collecting, of taste, of Scottish public culture, and much more.

There are, however, some striking omissions. The caption does not reveal the price paid, nor, for items purchased, their source, whether a dealer, an auction house, an organisation or individual. While it is understandable that there are sensitivities about such matters, it is worth reflecting upon the lack of public discourse about money and its impli- cations for historical understanding. For example, captions for items displayed in publications and galleries could include their cost when known, with the current equivalent, and source. Furthermore, *Choice* omits provenance, which would allow readers to extend their under- standing of objects' life histories. Since it does not 'interpret', it does not overtly evaluate either, except insofar as membership of the collections confers implicit aesthetic value. Another category of information is often given when works of art are described – a list of references to scholarly

9 *Camden Town Murder*, by Walter Sickert, *c*.1909, pencil heightened with white chalk on paper, 24.8 cm high × 20 cm wide, Private Collection. The woman's naked body is open and curvaceous, while the man, who is slighter and fully clothed, is standing behind her and seems to be touching her shoulders gently. The bed in the foreground perhaps suggests an erotic encounter, while the curtain in the background provides visual interest.

discussions of them. In my experience these are rarely complete, but they provide a useful starting point.

Two further features of descriptions in exhibitions and their catalogues invite comment. First, they chime with modernist styles of displaying art, which involve spacing works out on white, or at least plain, walls, and treating them as separate units, accompanied by brief labels. When works are grouped together, they are usually categorised by country and period of origin, but this mode of presentation does not diminish the sense of each work as autonomous – we might call this approach 'atomistic'. Second, works are given titles, but it is rare to find these explained or explored in any way. Sometimes they have been provided by the makers themselves, at others by dealers, owners, curators or writers. Since titles metaphorically frame the object in question, they shape the way viewers categorise what they see. Hence it matters whose titles they are, when and in what context they were formulated. They may appear to be the most innocent of descriptions, but that is not the case. If the pencil and chalk drawing by Walter Sickert, from around 1909, which shows a clothed man standing behind a naked woman, his hands on her shoulders, were entitled 'Intimacy' or 'The Massage', both plausible titles given the content of the sketch, the image would be seen as benign. **9** In fact, it has been called 'Camden Town Murder', allowing one curator to see it as 'convey[ing] a sense of threat and sexual danger', although I see no *visual* evidence in the image itself to sustain that view.[5] Both these features – styles of hanging and titles – reinforce the need for forms of contextualisation to supplement and supplant an atomistic approach. Scholars can supply these, eschewing the idea that objects are autonomous, self-evident and transparent. Description is a first step in the process.

Choice included furniture. Note how this caption differs from the one quoted above: '66 Italian (Rome or Turin) c. 1720 / One of a pair of carved giltwood sofas / Purchased 1991', with its marked lack of specificity with respect to the maker, the place of origin, the date of production and dimensions.[6] Some of this information may not be known, and the result is an impoverished sense of agency, which easily fits into a stereotype – 'art' is made by named individuals; by contrast, 'furniture', which belongs to the decorative arts, arises, unspecifically, from unnameable workers.

The exhibition and catalogue also contained a sculpture: '169 Ernst Barlach 1870–1938 / Das schlimme Jahr 1937 / [The Terrible Year 1937], 1936 / Wood (oak). 142 × 31 × 28.5 cm / Purchased with assistance from the National Art Collections Fund (William Leng Bequest) 1987 / [GMA 3036].'[7] **10** It is a simple, stylised and veiled female figure, in a long gown, standing on a plinth, no hands are visible, only the feet, in a reddish, lightly burnished wood. 'Wonderfully soulful' is how one guidebook describes it.[8] Who was Barlach, how might *he* be described? Biographies, of whatever length, are a particular type of description, sometimes associated with portraiture. 'Portrait' is commonly used in the titles of books offering detailed accounts of a person or phenomenon. A recent dictionary of art and artists gives Barlach about a column, a bit less than the painter Max Beckmann ('German painter'), born fourteen years later, about the same as Canova ('Italian sculptor') and very much less than Donatello ('Florentine sculptor'). Dates of birth and death are provided, and a tag – in Barlach's case, 'German sculptor' – followed by amplification, such as training, type of work undertaken, significant life events, achievements, works and so on. For example: 'Following a visit to Russia, moved by the earthy simplicity and piety of the Russian peasant, he devoted his art to making images of figures visualized in a semi-medieval style, expressing alienation from the modern world and mankind's need of God.'[9] This sentence mentions a specific event, seeks to convey Barlach's responses to an experience, gives a brief account of his art, and classifies it using style and period terms. Words that might easily go unremarked, such as 'earthy' and 'devoted', are evocative. 'Devoted' reinforces 'piety'. The entry also *interprets* Barlach by associating him with big themes such as 'alienation'. Later on we learn, 'In 1937 many of his public works were removed or destroyed and 381 Barlachs were taken from public collections; some of them toured as "Degenerate Art".' **53** This sentence is more descriptive and less evaluative, it provides a bare account of events with which many readers are likely to have some familiarity, bringing their own emotions and prejudices to that particular phase of Barlach's life. This biographical account, however brief, does begin to situate him in the political and artistic contexts of his time. It thereby opens the way for an understanding of the connections between the content of his art, his life and the situation in which he lived.

10 *Das schlimme Jahr 1937* (*The Terrible Year 1937*), by Ernst Barlach, wood (oak), 142 cm high × 31 cm wide × 28.5 cm deep, Scottish National Gallery of Modern Art, Edinburgh. This work was actually made in 1936; it was given its title the following year because of the Degenerate Art Exhibition, which opened in Munich and then toured to thirteen other cities in Germany and Austria. It included works by Barlach among 650 items from thirty-two public museums. In total this free show was seen by more than 3 million people. Many works by Barlach were destroyed by the Nazis. See also **53**.

From the catalogue and the dictionary, we begin to gain a sense of how *Das schlimme Jahr 1937* could be mobilised as historical evidence. Taking such an insight further requires fuller accounts of the connections between art, life and context. Connections of this type are compellingly explored by Thomas Crow in *Emulation*, which concerns art in the equally politically charged situation of the French Revolution.[10] In principle such accounts offer fresh insights and historical depth. But a biographical entry in a dictionary, designed to provide a brief handle on an artist, does not enable readers to envisage what Barlach's art looked like. Few if any verbal accounts achieve this. In order for an image or object to be *activated* as historical evidence, it is highly desirable to see it in the flesh, and then generate a description of it that acts as a bridge into the analysis, and to provide an adequate image in publications. Representing in words works meant to be viewed from more than one angle, or those in materials, such as white marble, that do not photograph well, is particularly challenging. We may usefully distinguish between historical work on 'degenerate art' as a broad phenomenon, which is concerned with numerous items in that particular category, and analyses driven by direct engagement with specific artefacts. The latter demands an exploration of forms of visual intelligence in the period, and requires closer attention to individual objects, their makers and their immediate contexts. Careful, accurate and detailed description of the things themselves is then essential, whilst it is optional, if highly desirable, when writing about 'degenerate art' in general. The project of understanding the label and its deployment operates at an analytical level that is distinct from the study of one maker and his works.

Any self-respecting description must include the principal physical features of an object, but, as we have seen, description is much more than this. It is hard to avoid evaluative and emotive terms, and the result is necessarily shaped by writers' prior experience and the values that shape their contexts – the immediate reason for looking at an object or image informs any description that results. Furthermore, since description is actually a cluster of genres of writing, it can be constructed in a variety of ways and for a variety of purposes. Readers are invited to analyse the four essays and the captions in this book as examples of description. Guidebooks, a distinct genre, provide further instructive examples of description.

Guides and buildings

Consider the following sentences from the *Rough Guide to Scotland*: 'The religious wars of the Covenant (1639–44) and invasion of Cromwell

(1650) initially discouraged contemporary building in the **seventeenth century**. However, it did see the final development of the **Early Scottish Renaissance**, marked by regular, symmetrical plans, the use of pediments and other decorative details of Classical origin, and an ordered dignified façade'.[11] In fact, despite references to specific events, this passage is quite abstract. Notions such as 'Renaissance' and 'Classical' have a range of meanings, referring to complex phenomena for which they are merely convenient shorthand. Such terms, which allude to both style and period, play a major role in description. There is a double danger here. On the one hand, they are handy labels. Readers are likely to have some familiarity with them, but little sense of what, exactly, they refer to. On the other hand, they are far from neutral: the idea of an early Scottish Renaissance sounds impressive, and perhaps elevates Scottish architecture by association with Renaissance works elsewhere. Thus there is an *implicit* interpretation of architecture in Scotland and its periodisation, and a claim about the impact of historical events upon building patterns. In addition, terms such as 'pediment' and 'façade' are deployed, which are, in a sense, technical. Specialised vocabularies play a central part in description.

The importance of technical language is immediately apparent if we turn to the famous *Buildings of England* series, first compiled under the leadership of Nikolaus Pevsner between 1951 and 1974. Each volume contains an extensive glossary, which defines terms such as 'weepers' and 'acanthus', and eight pages of drawings, which illustrate architectural forms from different periods, such as medieval buttresses, roofs and spires, and types of construction.[12] The drawings are more economical and efficient than verbal accounts. Such apparatus allows the entries on each building to be as precise and compact as possible. One complete entry for a building, Norwich railway station, gives a flavour of the work: 'THORPE STATION. The first station was built in 1844 to receive the line from Yarmouth. It was in an Italianate style with a bell-tower but was replaced in 1886 with the present structure in a "freely Renaissance" manner, as *The Builder* expressed it. Classical and symmetrical but with a French pavilion roof. The material is red brick with Bath stone dressings; the dome has zinc scales and the architects were the Great Eastern Railway Architect *W. N. Ashbee* in conjunction with *John Wilson*, the company's engineer. After damage in World War II the concourse was rebuilt and the original decorative ironwork (by *Barnard, Bishop and Barnard*) replaced with the present steel members. There was refurbishment of the passenger facilities in 1974–5.'[13] **VII** This description provides four main types of information: the life history of the building, the styles adopted, the materials used, and the main people involved in its construction. Although accessible, the entry is precise in its use of terminology. Architectural history has a large specialised vocabulary.

Such technical languages generally operate in three related registers. First, there are descriptions of the materials and visual properties of the artefact; second, these produce distinctive visual effects, which need to be articulated accurately, and then there are ways of describing that are important for specialists, and especially for buyers and sellers, as they affect desirability and price. As with architectural terms, it is efficient and economical to be able to speak of such things in a way that is accurate and precise. These are the building blocks upon which other types of discourse are erected.

This brief discussion alerts us to the audiences who are implied by each description. Historians, and practitioners of other disciplines, form particular audiences, which are quite distinct from collectors and dealers and those for whom artefacts primarily generate visual pleasure. The complexity and diversity of audiences, whether past or present, are worth bearing in mind. They help to shape forms of display and are present in the consciousness of those commissioning and making artefacts. All descriptions are written with an awareness of potential audiences; in the case of labels in museums and galleries, they are often composed in consultation with those seeking to widen participation, and avoid the use of long or technical words that would be off-putting to first-time visitors.

Criticism

Nikolaus Pevsner was, among other things, an architectural critic; he only selected those buildings deemed worthy for inclusion in his books. The commentaries of critics differ in some significant respects from labels, captions and reference books – yet all grapple with the challenges of description. Although criticism is not a unified, homogeneous genre and has changed markedly over time, it does have some defining features: the personal voice and authority of the critic, the critic as mediator between makers and audiences, the drive to make sense of what is seen, and to evaluate it. In the case of criticism most readers are *unlikely* to see the objects being discussed for themselves, which endows critics' descriptions with particular interest. They need to evoke some sense of the works and their manner of display in readers' minds. Thus critics seek to bring to life what they have seen for readers, whose thoughts, preferences and purchases may be shaped in the process.

Here is an example, from a review of a photographic exhibition I did *not* see, written in 2008: 'In *Aspens*, a few pale glimmering trees approach

gingerly out of darkness. You look: they appear to look back at you. In *Redwoods*, the tree columns rise instead like ancient architecture holding up the sky. People and cathedrals: each metaphor is achieved through extreme variations of depth of field and contrast.' **11** The works in question are by the American photographer Ansel Adams. Laura Cumming suggests that these two 'contrasting photographs … express his emotional experiences of nature'. The description contains and expresses the critic's responses. It is impossible to recognise the photographs in question from these words alone, but they communicate a strong sense of the aesthetic status with which she endows his work. They contain both claims about Adams and his emotional experiences, and assumptions about the nature of art. The trees are explicitly likened to people and cathedrals, and the photographs treated as if they were (almost) animate.[14]

At first sight it might seem as if such writing occupies a territory distant from that of historical prose, partly because the latter relies on research and scholarly apparatus, criticism on personal authority. In addition, critical language is relatively unfettered: yet the permit critics

11 *Aspens, Dawn, Autumn, Dolores Canyon, Colorado, 1937*, by Ansel Adams, 1937. Adams is best known for his photographs of the American West, and especially of Yosemite National Park. He was devoted to the outdoors and to the preservation of the environment. His photographs are widely reproduced, for example on postcards and calendars. A modest man, he was also part of the movement to establish the serious artistic credentials of photography. This image, with its exquisite precision, may be interpreted as a celebration of natural forms.

have to express their reactions, feelings and opinions is worth considering further. In description lie the seeds of analysis; composing descriptions is an acquired skill that needs to be disciplined and honed. The viewer's feelings and experience can never be purged from the process. Whereas critics may give free rein to them, historians are more likely to feel restrained. Nonetheless, we can and should use the full range of our reactions to probe the ways in which a given object produces specific effects. Such responses can be used to enhance understanding. Further, historians' accounts need to be evocative for readers and conveying reactions in writing constitutes an important element within any argument. It is naïve to suppose that description can be value free. Hence it is best to be aware, insofar as this can be achieved, not only of one's own preconceptions, but of the reactions, which are sometimes extremely powerful, that looking at objects and images brings. There are thus a number of ways in which reading and reflecting upon criticism from a range of periods can be helpful to historians.

Criticism, which flourished in recognisably modern form for the first time in the eighteenth century, constitutes significant historical evidence in its own right. Contemporary responses to works of art are telling and frequently surprising; they are especially rich for eras before photography was widespread. Thus the history of criticism – who wrote commentaries, in what terms, in which publications, and their impact – is an important subject. The roles of critics – from major figures such as Denis Diderot, whose comments circulated in manuscript form, to popular and controversial critics in our own time – are of considerable historical interest. The study of criticism helps shed light on audiences, institutions, patrons, the status of individuals, media and genres, on taste, and, most important for our present purposes, it reveals languages of description at particular historical moments.

Conclusions

Providing descriptions of sources is a vital task for historians. Descriptions activate our materials, especially visual ones, which, contrary to what is sometimes assumed, never speak for themselves. Rather, images and objects need intellectual energy to be applied to them in order to acquire the status of historical evidence. In the process of providing a description, ideas that lead to analysis and interpretation begin to surface, and ways of tying artefacts to other sources, both verbal and visual, emerge. There is a strong sense that objects can 'speak', a sense that is nurtured by literary accounts of the impact of works of art, especially portraits and figurative statues, and by common forms of speech.

Such assumptions deny the agency of the scholar-viewer; it is as if all they have to do is 'listen'. Rather, the use of items of visual and material culture within historical argument requires a disciplined approach that actively turns them into evidence and then mobilises them within an argument.

There are many reasons why things cannot 'speak', and should not be treated as if they were autonomous, transparent and self-evident. It is philosophically untenable for scholars to project human qualities onto objects, to treat them as if they were animate beings, however tempting, poetic and common it may be. Objects require contextualisation so that the settings in which they were made and used are brought to the fore – if there is agency it lies, less in things themselves than in the people who produce, commission, use and display them. Artefacts may, of course, be endowed with agency – the phenomenon is common enough in both past and present – but in an academic context we painstakingly unravel the processes whereby this occurs, rather than using language that perpetuates misleading assumptions about their status.

Historians frequently encounter artefacts in a radically decontextualised state; in the case of flat art that tends to mean on a plain wall, in a frame, with a brief caption and a title that may have been added later. In this state they are divorced from the physical settings and relationships in which they were born and then used. Description alone cannot remedy such decontextualisation, but the series of questions it implies – where, what, how, by whom and so on – lead directly into contexts. A further reason why things do not automatically 'speak' to us is that we have lost many of the references, skills and appetites that viewers, patrons and makers in the past took for granted. Scholarship aims to restore them, with description as one vital stage of the restoration process.

Description may be conceptualised as a kind of translation. It renders visual and tactile experiences into words that are accessible to readers and that form the groundwork of interpretation. During this process it is best to take as little as possible for granted, to make what is seen as explicit as possible. It requires the mastery of certain skills and vocabularies, together with attentiveness to the precise use of language and the ways in which complex visual experiences can be expressed in many kinds of prose. There is indeed a checklist of matters that any basic description should include, where these are knowable, such as names of makers, medium, size, palette and provenance. The terms 'visual culture' and 'material culture' are all-encompassing – they cover many things where much basic information is not available. This situation does not lessen the value of such a list, but suggests it needs to be used flexibly. Categorisation is an inescapable part of description. Historians are inevitably affected by existing systems of classification, which carry social baggage. There are hierarchies of objects, of people who made them, and of those who care for and study them now, although these are complex, even within a single society. Historical research picks up the assumptions of the places and times being studied and ideally distinguishes them from those of succeeding generations and of historians' own situations. The process of generating a description, if undertaken with self-awareness, lays the groundwork for explanation; and explanation presupposes the prior existence of historical questions and problems upon which artefacts can shed light. In this way, images and objects become evidence, with 'description' as the activity that brings evidence into analytical focus. During these processes earlier descriptions become valuable sources.

NOTES

1 James Hall, *Subjects and Symbols in Art*, rev. edn (London, 1979), p. 202.
2 This occurs in the Cornaro Chapel, which is the subject of the second short essay.
3 Jason Rosenfeld and Alison Smith, *Millais* (London, 2007), p. 184, which also reproduces the advertisement.
4 *Choice: 21 Years of Collecting for Scotland* (Edinburgh, 2005), p. 255. I have used / to indicate the end of each line.
5 Barnaby Wright, ed., *Walter Sickert: the Camden Town Nudes* (London, 2007), p. 24. See also David Peters Corbett, *Walter Sickert* (London, 2001), p. 37, which discusses titles in connection with the Camden Town series of works: 'Sickert retitled his works with abandon'.
6 *Choice*, pp. 104–5.
7 *Ibid.*, p. 215.
8 *The Rough Guide to Scotland*, 6th edn (London, 2004), p. 114.
9 N. Lynton and E. Langmuir, *The Yale Dictionary of Art and Artists* (New Haven and London, 2000), p. 46. Compare this with the biography in Stephanie Barron, ed., *Degenerate Art: the Fate of the Avant-Garde in Nazi Germany* (Los Angeles and New York, 1991), pp. 196–8.
10 Thomas Crow, *Emulation: Making Artists for Revolutionary France* (New Haven and London, 1995).
11 *The Rough Guide to Scotland*, 5th edn (London, 2002), p. 786 (bold in original).
12 Nikolaus Pevsner and Bill Wilson, *Norfolk 1: Norwich and North-East*, 2nd edn (New Haven and London, 2002; first published 1997), pp. 739–64; the drawings are on pp. 748–55.
13 *Ibid.*, p. 334 and plate 104.
14 Laura Cumming, 'King of the Wild Frontier', *The Observer* (6 April 2008), p. 19 of the review section.

FURTHER READING

On Mary Magdalene, who has been extensively portrayed in a range of media, see Susan Haskins, *Mary Magdalen: Myth and Metaphor* (London, 1993). On Donatello, there is John Pope-Hennessy, *Donatello: Sculptor* (New York, 1993), and on Canova, Fred Licht, with photographs by David Finn, *Canova* (New York, 1983).

On description and visual culture, see Svetlana Alpers, *The Art of Describing: Dutch Art in the Seventeenth Century* (Chicago, 1983). Specifically on *ekphrasis*, there is Stephen Cheeke, *Writing for Art: the Aesthetics of Ekphrasis* (Manchester, 2008). He discusses Keats and provides a useful bibliography on pp. 190–9. The field of rhetoric more broadly is also relevant. Introductions to rhetoric are: Robert Cockcroft and Susan M. Cockcroft, *Persuading People: an Introduction to Rhetoric* (Basingstoke, 1992), and James A Herrick, *The History and Theory of Rhetoric*, 4th edn (Boston, 2009), which includes a brief discussion of the rhetoric of display (pp. 270–1) and a useful bibliography and glossary.

Paying visual attention is a theme of much art-historical writing. Arguably no one was more lucid on the matter than Michael Baxandall, for example, in *Patterns of Intention: On the Historical Explanation of Pictures* (New Haven, 1985). Lorraine Daston, 'Attention and the Values of Nature in the Enlightenment', in *The Moral Authority of Nature*, ed. Lorraine Daston and Fernando Vidal (Chicago and London, 2004), is insightful on forms of attention in the eighteenth century and their broad significance. Tim Barringer's *Men at Work: Art and Labour in Victorian Britain* (New Haven and London, 2005) is just one example of a book containing some impressive descriptions.

A lively, if idiosyncratic, approach to the Mona Lisa as an icon and to the status of art is Darian Leader, *Stealing the Mona Lisa: What Art Stops us from Seeing* (London, 2002). Cf. Martin Kemp, *Christ to Coke: How Image Becomes Icon* (Oxford and New York, 2011), who also discusses the Mona Lisa. Victoria Alexander, *Museums and Money: the Impact of Funding on Exhibitions, Scholarship, and Management* (Bloomington, 1996), raises important questions.

The anthropologist Mary Douglas wrote many accessible works outlining her ideas, for example, *Purity and Danger: an Analysis of the Concepts of Pollution and Taboo* (London, 1966) and her edited volume *Rules and Meanings: the Anthropology of Everyday Knowledge: Selected Readings* (London, 1973). Classification is a classic anthropological theme and a major topic in the history of science; see, for example, Chrissie Iles and Russell Roberts, eds., *In Visible Light: Photography and Classification in Art, Science and the Everyday* (Oxford, 1997); Nigel Rapport and Joanna Overing, *Social and Cultural Anthropology: the Key Concepts*, 2nd edn (London, 2007); and Peter Dear, *The Intelligibility of Nature: How Science Makes Sense of the World* (Chicago and London, 2006).

On artistic hierarchies, Gill Perry and Colin Cunningham, eds., *Academies, Museums and Canons of Art* (New Haven and London, 1990), esp. part 2, is useful; works on 'craft' cited in ch. 2 are also relevant.

The literature on individual artists who played a central role in early modern courts is vast. On court culture more widely, John Adamson, ed., *The Princely Courts of Europe: Ritual, Politics and Culture under the Ancien Régime, 1500–1750* (London, 1999), is a good place to start. See also Clarissa Campbell Orr, ed., *Queenship in Britain, 1660–1837: Royal Patronage, Court Culture and Dynastic Politics* (Manchester, 2002).

The literature in English on Ernst Barlach, who was a writer as well as an artist, is sparse, but the historian Peter Paret has examined the conflicts between the sculptor and the Third Reich in *An Artist Against the Third Reich: Ernst Barlach 1933–1938* (Cambridge, 2003). On the Degenerate Art Exhibition of 1937, see Stephanie Barron, ed., *Degenerate Art: the Fate of the Avant-Garde in Nazi Germany* (Los Angeles and New York, 1991), which includes a room-by-room reconstruction of the exhibition. The idea of degenerate art was not new in the 1930s; see, for example, George Bernard Shaw, *The Sanity of Art: an Exposure of the Current Nonsense about Artists Being Degenerate* (London, 1908), which was a critique of Max Nordau's *Degeneration* (first published in 1892). See also Max Nordau, *On Art and Artists* (London, 1907).

On Pevsner, who died in 1983, see Simon Bradley and Bridget Cherry, eds., *The Buildings of England: a Celebration Compiled to Mark Fifty Years of the Pevsner Architectural Guides* (Beccles, 2001).

Ansel Adams was a major figure in twentieth-century photography, hence there is an extensive literature on him; for example, Jonathan Spaulding, *Ansel Adams and the American Landscape: a Biography* (Berkeley and London, 1995). A good introduction to his work is *Ansel Adams: Four Hundred Photographs* (Boston and London, 2007).

On criticism, see Richard Wrigley, *The Origins of French Art Criticism: From the Ancien Régime to the Restoration* (Oxford, 1993). Some of Diderot's salon criticism is included in *Selected Writings on Art and Architecture*, trans. and ed. Geoffrey Bremner (London, 1994). See also Michael Fried, *Absorption and Theatricality: Painting and Beholder in the Age of Diderot* (Berkeley and London, 1980). Fried himself is also a critic, see his *Art and Objecthood: Essays and Reviews* (Chicago and London, 1998). Also see James Ackerman, *Origins, Imitation, Conventions: Representation in the Visual Arts* (Cambridge, MA, 2002), ch. 1: 'On the Origins of Art History and Criticism'; Donald B. Kuspit, *Clement Greenberg: Art Critic* (Madison, WI, and London, 1979); Chris Murray, ed., *Key Writers on Art: From Antiquity to the Nineteenth Century* (London and New York, 2003) and *Key Writers on Art: the Twentieth Century* (London, 2003); Paul Smith and Carolyn Wilde, eds., *A Companion to Art Theory* (Oxford, 2002); and the three anthologies on *Art in Theory*, which together cover the period 1648–2000 and were edited by Charles Harrison and Paul Wood (Oxford, 1998,

2000 and 2003 (2nd edn)). They contain many kinds of writing on art including evaluative commentaries, i.e. 'criticism'.

Many of the issues discussed in this chapter, especially those concerning description and terminology can be pursued through reference books, see pp. 234–5. Exhibition catalogues are particularly valuable because they take the task of description extremely seriously. They are cited throughout this book.

On the idea of things speaking, see, for example, Lorraine Daston, ed., *Things that Talk: Object Lessons from Art and Science* (New York and London, 2004), which includes a discussion of Millais's *Bubbles*, and my review in the *British Journal for the History of Science*, 39 (2006), pp. 436–7.

For diverse discussions of 'evidence', see Andrew Bell *et al.*, eds., *Evidence* (Cambridge and New York, 2008).

Bridge

The brief essay that follows seeks to demonstrate how these points about description and evidence operate in practice. I chose a building – the Wren Library at Trinity College, Cambridge – of exceptional beauty and resonance, which bears on many historical themes. I offer a description of it, mention the existing evidence, and indicate some of the themes and questions it prompts us to consider. The nature of description varies with the item being described, and buildings offer special challenges. For example, they are rarely static. Buildings are composites and invite careful descriptions of both inside and outside. Many, like the Wren Library, are settings for works of art and a vast array of other kinds of objects, such as furniture, books and manuscripts. It is vital to pay attention to the location and architectural contexts in which artefacts are found. There is an established relationship between history and architectural history, which is currently being strengthened. While it may seem to strain the meaning of 'artefact' to apply it to a building, which is a constellation of made things, the approaches outlined in this book are fully applicable to architecture.

ESSAY

A 'sumptuous structure': the Wren Library at Trinity College, Cambridge

A special building

The phrase, 'that sumptuous structure', comes from a letter dated 12 August 1689 sent by John Evelyn to Samuel Pepys.[1] **VIII** It was written before the library, which bears the name of its famous designer, was completed in 1695. Evelyn's praise for the building joins the many words that have been written over more than three centuries to express admiration for a building that is indeed exquisitely beautiful. It is also exceptionally well documented with Wren's original drawings, a long letter from him about his ideas, information from the college's archives, and the library itself surviving. Quickly recognised as both an important piece of work by Sir Christopher Wren and a significant example of the category 'library', this building has received considerable attention from scholars. There is, for example, a 'biography' of its first 150 years, and it is usually mentioned in writings about Wren himself.[2] It is, then, a jewel in the crowns of the architect and of the college. This library is renowned, not just for its appearance but also for its contents – carvings and busts, for example, as well as books and manuscripts. Yet such an account gives little sense of why historians in particular might pay close attention to it. In this essay I approach the Wren Library in such a way as to suggest some of the general issues that historians face when using buildings as evidence, as well as some of the historical questions upon which they can be brought to bear.

The 'biography', published in 1995, marked the 200th anniversary of the library's completion by placing the available documentation, especially Wren's drawings, in the public domain. The essays it contains touch on many important historical questions, but their purpose was necessarily different from mine. They provide a strong base of evidence for the history of the library, interpreting this evidence in order to give as complete and authoritative an account as possible of the first century-and-a-half of its existence. I have the privilege of taking this excellent book as a starting point. In discussing a structure that I too find enchanting, I mention themes discussed elsewhere in *The Look of the Past*, from description to comparative analysis.

Before describing the building itself, however, some cautionary remarks are in order. When I say 'the Wren Library', my referent is perfectly clear. It is possible to stand and look at 'it'. Yet it is not really an 'it' at all, since we are dealing with a complex composite, made up of the architectural structure, permanent fittings, such as book cases, decorative schemes, both inside and out, and contents – books, manuscripts and all the other accoutrements of a library. Historians discussing these elements might think of them as distinct registers. In addition, 'the Wren Library' conjures up sets of ideas, associations and images that transcend any particular constituent element. For example, to Robert Smith, Master of Trinity College between 1742 and 1768, it was a temple to the college's great men, and hence the embodiment of his idea of its identity.[3] Furthermore, the building is, and always has been, in a state of evolution, even if the shell has changed little since completion. By 'evolution', I do not mean to imply 'improvement', rather that Wren's plans and ideas and the final structure that exists today, match well but not perfectly. The interior of the building especially changed for many reasons, some of which we will encounter over the next few pages. So did its setting alter. The historian's goal is to consider buildings holistically without losing a sense of the processes through which they came, and are still coming, into being. Users and viewers are integral to such an approach. The Wren Library has been a tourist attraction ever since it was in the process of being built: it is both a famous building and a working library. Thus guidebooks to Cambridge can also shed light on how the building was understood.

A partial description

The building in question is made of warm yellow stone, and sits behind grassy banks not far from the river. The internal dimensions give some sense of its scale: 191 feet long, 40 feet wide and 38 feet high. In shape, it is an oblong box, with one side facing the river, the other looking into the college, and across to the hall. **12** It formed the fourth side of, and thereby completed, Nevile's Court; existing buildings were extended on the north and south sides to meet up with it. The elevations of these two wings were remodelled in the 1750s, and in this respect we do not see what those in 1695 did, although the view from the river is unaltered. In fact, the Wren Library is a raised building supported by several rows of columns, which form a cloister walk. The elevation is different on the two sides; in both cases, Wren 'tricks' the viewer about the location of the floor, which is considerably lower than external appearances suggest. The large windows are

12 The Wren Library, seen from Nevile's Court, with the college hall behind the photographer, by Howard Nelson, 2011.

high above floor level inside the library, yet they appear to extend to the floor when the building is viewed from the outside. Four statues on the roof – of Divinity, Law, Physic and Mathematics – and a relief over the central arch adorn the inner side of the exterior, which could be called 'classical'.

The inside – with its high windows, black and white marble floor, busts, statues, woodcarvings and furniture – is dramatic. **IX** High bookcases jut into the huge room, on top of which are busts, of ancients on one side, and of moderns on the other. There are further busts lower down, placed on pedestals. The end of each bookcase is adorned with exuberant limewood carvings, most of which are by the renowned sculptor Grinling Gibbons. The 1829 statue by Bertel Thorwaldsen of the poet Lord Byron, who had studied at the college, stands at the far end, placed there in 1845 after failing to find a home in Westminster Abbey and being deemed unsuitable for Trinity's chapel. There is another statue inside the library of the politician and courtier, the Duke of Somerset, Chancellor of the University from 1689 until his death, and a patron both of the library and of Grinling Gibbons, who made the statue too, probably in the early 1690s. It stands in one of a pair of niches (these were not in Wren's original design), on the south wall; the other has remained empty. In that same wall is a remarkable stained-glass window, added in the eighteenth century, which includes the figures of George III, Sir Isaac Newton, Francis Bacon and Britannia. Other windows are of clear glass, flooding the library with light. A few large portraits are hung on the walls, while four smaller ones are attached to the panelling at either end of the room – all recognise important patrons and donors. From even this brief account, the complicated nature of the interior, which changed markedly over the century-and-a-half after its completion, is apparent.

We can register change in two further ways, having already noted that the stained-glass window arrived nearly eighty years after the building was completed, and that niches were built to accommodate Somerset's marble statue. First, the original ceiling was not as Wren designed it. The flat ceiling was altered in the nineteenth century to something very much closer to his original wishes. Second, the arrangement of busts and of some of the furniture has changed since 1695. Wren's original idea was for full-length figures to be mounted on top of the bookcases: 'The statues will be a noble ornament they are supposed of plaister, there are Flemish artists that doe them cheap'.[4] The current busts of ancients and moderns, mostly of plaster, are of a kind that was fairly standard in the eighteenth century; they were installed after the building was completed. By this point, busts were a recognised part of library decoration. But the current arrangement of the lower busts was not completed until the nineteenth century. **40** Some of these are visible in an engraving of the library after 1832 but before 1845 when Byron's statue was installed, since this is not shown in the print. Furthermore, these lower-level busts are quite different in character from the upper ones in being of marble and depicting college luminaries; they were custom-made by leading eighteenth-century sculptors such as Roubiliac and Scheemakers, and the names of sitter, artist and patron may be found on each one.

Subjects included Francis Bacon, Isaac Newton, Isaac Barrow and Robert Smith. In addition to being an inspirational figure for those, like the early Fellows of the Royal Society, who were interested in natural philosophy, Bacon, who studied at Trinity in the 1570s, was powerful as Lord Chancellor under James I. Isaac Newton also studied at the college, and was a Fellow there when his *Principia Mathematica* was published

13 Photograph of wooden furniture, designed by Wren, date of design not documented, in the Wren Library, Trinity College, Cambridge. An undated sketch for a reading-desk, stand and stool exists, which is probably by Wren.

in 1687. His reputation as a genius was extraordinary, and made visible in many ways in the college. Isaac Barrow, himself a student at Trinity in the 1640s, had initiated the whole library project, although he did not live to see it completed. Robert Smith, who first joined the college in 1708, was a generous benefactor.

It was not only 'decorative' elements, such as busts, that changed; the furniture did too. Wren himself designed the tables and stools in the bays, which remain in use to this day. **13** But for much of its early life the library was a museum as well as a repository of books and manuscripts. Extra bookcases were added in the centre of the library in the mid-nineteenth century and a mixture of objects was displayed on top of them. There are still a few display cases in the library, although they are of an unobtrusive design. They contain treasures from the collections, mostly famous, beautiful and rare books and manuscripts. A relic – a lock of Sir Isaac Newton's hair – is also on display.

The account of the building given so far is hardly exhaustive; for instance, it has not detailed the shape of the windows, or the nature of the columns and frieze. Nor has it described the range of responses to the library and depictions of it, which are certainly central to a rounded engagement with it. But it has begun to sketch in links between the Wren Library, the college and a range of individuals, especially those whose linked intellectual activities chimed so harmoniously with Trinity's sense of itself, which persists to this day, as intellectually pre-eminent, especially in what came to be called the natural sciences. We shall return shortly to Wren himself, who was distinguished in natural knowledge as in architecture, and to his networks, after considering some of the ways in which the building has been written about in an architectural context.

Architectural historians consider the library

So far, my emphasis has been on giving an accessible account of the Wren Library that suggests its interest for historians while eschewing technicalities. The only specialised term used has been 'elevation', which refers to the external façade of a building.[5] Many aspects of the library's construction, however, are of technical interest, as we shall see in a brief discussion of the way architectural historians have approached the matter.

Dear Margaret – As you can see, I agree with every word you are saying. I always do. Warmest Friendship. Sincerely Ron

I   Photograph given to Margaret Thatcher by Ronald Reagan, White House official press image, taken 2 June 1988, 25.4 cm wide × 20.3 cm high, Churchill Archives Centre, Cambridge. The occasion was a dinner for Reagan in the Pillared Room on the first floor of 10 Downing Street, also attended by George P. Shultz, who is seated next to Thatcher. In addition to the interest of the photograph and inscription, there is Thatcher's presentation of self – the immaculately coiffed hair, expensive suit and prominent jewellery – which is reminiscent of contemporary royal style. The setting too invites careful scrutiny: the damask-covered walls, fireplace, portraits, vases and candelabra, all of which possess historical resonance.

Harold Wilson by Ruskin Spear, oil on canvas, exhibited 1974, 51.1 cm high × 31.8 cm wide, National Portrait Gallery, London.

II

Spear has made the pipe central to his depiction of Wilson, rather than a mere accoutrement. The puffs of smoke are witty and visually bold; they even cover one of the sitter's eyes. Executed in strong, broad and perfectly discernible brushstrokes, this portrait is evocative of the sitter, even if it is strikingly untraditional. Yet it is in no way disrespectful, and manages to suggest intense concentration, perhaps even the steamed-up atmosphere that characterises many high-level political meetings. Wilson was a Labour Party politician, who entered the House of Commons when he was twenty-nine, and became Prime Minister at forty-eight. Depictions of him frequently included his pipe, which may be understood as his trademark, handy in identifying him, for example, in cartoons. Wilson sat for Spear in his official London residence, 10 Downing Street.

III

The Virgin Hodegetria,
eighteenth century, tempera on
wood, 28 cm high × 21 cm wide,
National History Museum,
Sofia, Bulgaria. 'Hodegetria'
means 'she who shows the way'
and is used of icons where the
Virgin Mary holds Christ on
her left arm, and gestures to
him as the way to salvation. This
example, indebted to the style
of Mount Athos painters, shows
how enduring medieval modes
of representation were. It may be
by Monk Zachery from Mount
Athos, who painted several
icons in the Rila Monastery,
south of Sofia. Icons play an
active role in worship.

Image from 'Threads of Feeling' online exhibition, depicting the textile token and written entry for Foundling number 2584, a girl, admitted 27 October 1756, The Foundling Hospital, London. This expensive silk fabric and fringe from about 1750 are part of a collection of around 5,000 pieces of material in the institution, which was founded in 1739 to care for children whose parents were unable to keep them. Each baby was meticulously documented, for instance, by keeping scraps of fabric that would identify them. The result is an extraordinary archive of everyday textiles which, taken together, provide insights into the visual and material culture of the period.

Postcard of the Brandenburg Gate, Berlin, photographer and date not known, probably 1960s, 14.8 cm wide × 10.5 cm high, Cambridge University Library. The gate was designed by Carl Gotthard Langhans, and constructed 1788–91. This postcard depicts an iconic object, one of Europe's best-known landmarks, which stands at the end of Unter den Linden, the famous avenue of linden trees. The gate's design blends triumphal arch and city gate. City gates were important structures both economically and socially since they regulated people and assisted in the collection of taxes, while also possessing clear symbolic significance. The gate has recently been restored. Prints show Napoleon entering Berlin on 26 October 1806 through the Gate, and its resonances have accrued further in recent times.

VI

Top of a table used for work.
Photograph taken by the author, 2011.
Note the distinctive design and colours
of the paperclips, the tatty old metal
stapler, the lamp and the statue – a
combination of everyday objects of
different ages and a treasured personal
possession laden with associations.

VII Norwich railway station, photographed by the author, 2011.

VIII

A view of the Wren Library, Trinity College, Cambridge, taken on the river side, by Howard Nelson, 2011. The outside of the stained-glass window, discussed in the essay, is visible on the upper right.

IX

Photograph of the interior of the Wren Library, Trinity College, Cambridge.

 *Giuseppe Cappellani*, by Guiseppe Cappellani and Francesco Filangeri, 2007, digital photograph. The Sicilian photographer Francesco Filangeri is interested in artisans and their representation, and thinks of himself as an artisan. This portrait depicts the person who taught him photography, that is to say the master to whom, metaphorically speaking, he was apprenticed. Cappellani, who took the picture using a remote control, is offering the viewer a chance to participate in the activity of which he was himself a skilled exponent. Filangeri set up the lighting, and 'framed' the shot. The beauty of the camera, the tool of the photographic art or craft, is a central element of this image.

XI Dragonfly table lamp, designed by Clara Driscoll and made by Tiffany Studios, c.1900–1906, leaded glass and bronze, 71.1 cm high × 55.9 cm diameter, New York Historical Society. Louis Comfort Tiffany was a highly successful American artist and designer, whose work in stained glass is particularly well known and easy to recognise. He produced, however, on an industrial scale, as is evident from the range of designs known to exist. Tiffany was an employer of artisans and artists, whose names were usually suppressed; he worked on stained-glass windows for churches, and interior decoration, as well as producing paintings, jewellery, pottery and art glass. Originally trained as a painter, Tiffany's career illustrates both the multiple roles those who produce material and visual culture may occupy, including entrepreneur, and the way in which a name can become associated with artefacts. In 1906 this lamp cost $175, when the average wage per hour was seventeen-and-a-half cents.

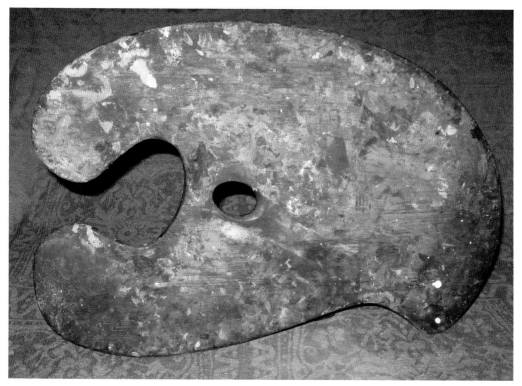

XII Palette belonging to George Frederick Watts, wood and oil paint, 54 cm high × 36 cm wide × 0.7 cm deep, Watts Gallery, Compton, Surrey. Palettes are often used as the occupational accoutrement of painters, for example in portraits and self-portraits. They are also memorabilia, displayed to the public in the case of prominent artists, and may be understood as a type of relic. This one has been used on both sides.

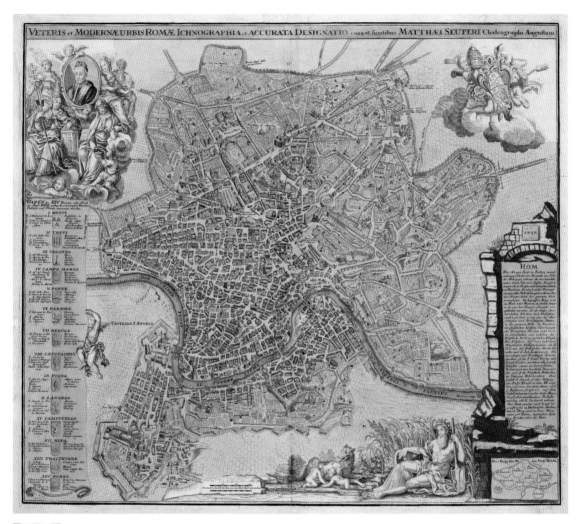

XIII

Veteris et Modernae Urbis Romae Ichnographia et Accurata Designatio, cura et sumtibus Matthaei Seuteri Chalcographi Augustani (Plan and Accurate Map of the Ancient and Modern City of Rome, by Matthew Seuter, Imperial Engraver), no date, 60 cm wide × 52.2 cm high, Cambridge University Library. Matthaeus Seutter the elder, who was based in Augsburg and worked as an engraver, globe-maker and map publisher, died in 1757. Presumably this work dates from earlier in the eighteenth century, but after 1731 when he was appointed Imperial Geographer to Karl IV. In addition to representing the position and shape of buildings' footprints, it also shows elevations and roofs. This map, orientated with east at the top, includes a history of Rome, a sketch of its seven hills and a list of churches in the various parts of the city. Santa Maria della Vittoria is the first church shown on the right of the Strada di Porta Pia, which enters the city on the top left-hand side of the map.

Teresa of Avila's Vision of the Dove by Peter Paul Rubens, c.1614, oil on panel, 97 cm high × 63 cm wide, Fitzwilliam Museum, Cambridge. Rubens painted Teresa a number of times. Here he depicts a vision the saint experienced on the eve of Pentecost in 1569, when the Holy Spirit appeared to her in the form of a Dove: 'very different from those we see on earth, for it had not feathers like theirs but its wings were made of little shells which emitted a great brilliance…' These words come from chapter XXXVIII of her *Life of the Holy Mother Teresa of Jesus*.

XV

Photograph of the Cornaro
Chapel in Santa Maria della
Vittoria, Rome, by Francesco
Filangeri, 2011. Here we get an
impression of the ensemble and
the two spectators provide a
sense of scale. Note especially the
relationship between the man on
the left, and the central sculpture.
Both sets of busts are visible in
the photograph.

XVI   Photograph on the museum's website of the Victorian Street, York Castle Museum, UK. This is a particularly interesting example of reconstruction, where a lot of ancillary information is provided. The website proclaims: 'the fabulous street of Kirkgate has been magically brought to life as part of a massive revamp'. 'Magically' suggests the powerful illusion, created through visual and material culture, of actually being in a Victorian street, rather than a critical approach to understanding the Victorian period. Such reconstructions are necessarily sanitised; they fit with common assumptions about what the 'Victorian' look is.

XVII *Time and Death*, by Caterina de Julianis, before 1727, coloured and moulded wax relief, frame is 83 cm high × 108 cm wide, Victoria and Albert Museum, London. This Italian *memento mori* (reminder of death) was probably made in Naples, by a nun who specialised in such work, and was inspired by the work of the famous wax modeller Gaetano Zumbo. With a host of gruesome details, it conjures up the ghastliness of death and decay so that onlookers contemplated their own mortality. Its first home was probably a church.

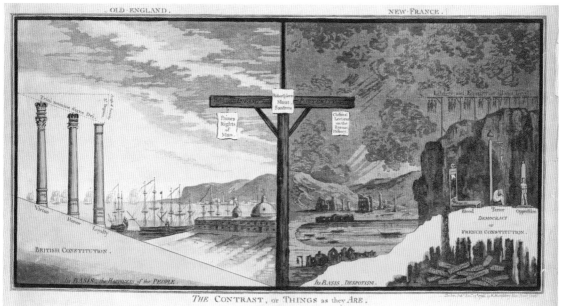

The Contrast, or things as they are, by James Gillray, 1796, hand-coloured etching, 35 cm high × 63.5 cm wide, British Museum. The device of contrasting England and France on single print as a way of attacking the latter was deployed by Gillray on several occasions. Here the guillotine acts as one piece of visual shorthand for the terror and oppression he deplored. The print is supercharged with details all contributing to the same idea, conveyed through the elaborate intertwining of word and image, that 'Old-England' is superior to 'New France'. Note Gillray's use of emotive keywords, such as 'virtue' and 'blood', and their close connection with visual motifs.

XIX

Button, by Josiah Wedgwood and Sons, 1780–1800, cut steel set with a jasparware plaque, diameter 4.4 cm, Victoria and Albert Museum, London. The button, which shows signs of the Zodiac, includes the shade of blue that is still associated with Wedgwood. Josiah Wedgwood's business partner Matthew Boulton pioneered the combination of sparkling cut steel with jasparware, a material Wedgwood developed.

Here I consider a number of approaches to Wren's work, beginning with one designed for wide audiences.

In the *Oxford Dictionary of National Biography* (*ODNB*), the building is discussed in the entry for Wren by Kerry Downes, an architectural historian, who, quite naturally, emphasises its role within Wren's oeuvre and life, calling it 'his most elegant building':

> The library of Trinity College, Cambridge, was entirely in Wren's hands although directed from London. It is … the grandest library in Cambridge. His drawings and an accompanying letter … illuminate his design in exceptional detail. It is a traditional European collegiate library – a long upper room above a cloister walk – but it is much more … A new site was available: the open river end of Nevile's Court, whose sides comprised ranges of lodgings with ground-level arcades … Decoration is sparing and scrupulously classical … Trinity Library consists of disparate exterior and interior linked by an unseen common structure … With a logic worthy of twentieth-century frame building, a regular system of supports rises from foundations through piers to transverse beams and bookstacks and to windows and roof trusses. This powerful hidden geometry conditions visible and sensible experience of the building … The span of Wren's career saw changes in English architecture comparable to almost three centuries in Renaissance Italy, and in this development Trinity Library is closest to the High Renaissance of Donato Bramante and Jacopo Sansovino.'[6]

Here Downes displays a marked lack of interest in the processes whereby the library was built, which are discussed in detail in its 'biography'; rather his purpose is to affirm Wren's abilities through the design. Downes makes the striking and important point that Wren was not on site to provide close supervision (although we know he visited once) and expected Robert Grumbold, the Cambridge mason who oversaw the work, to go and visit him in London.[7] Downes sets this building in an architectural context by locating it within two traditions ('a traditional European collegiate library' and the 'High Renaissance'). At the same time, he is making claims about Wren's mind – the reference to geometry reminds the reader of Wren's mathematical interests in general and his work in one particular branch of that subject. Wren, we have noted, was far more than an architect; he was a man of wide intellectual interests, a mathematician and astronomer, a founder member of the Royal Society of London, which from 1660 promoted natural philosophy, as well as being attentive to the practical aspects of his designs.[8] Downes is evaluative, for instance, in calling the building Wren's 'most elegant', and is willing to use style terms – 'scrupulously classical', for instance. The whole section on the Wren Library is driven by the author seeking to convey Wren's achievements and quality of mind. Thus the *ODNB* entry

14 Pembroke College, Cambridge, plate 16 in *Cantabrigia Illustrata* (*Cambridge Illustrated*), by David Loggan, Cambridge, 1690, folio, Cambridge University Library. The frontispiece is a portrait of the Duke of Somerset. Loggan had already published a book of engravings of Oxford colleges, *Oxonia Illustrata* (1675) before he embarked on the Cambridge project the following year. He also produced portraits, including one of Isaac Barrow. His work has often been reproduced; there is a *New Loggan Guide to Oxford Colleges*, published in 1932, with fresh engravings and text. Wren's chapel may be seen on the lower right-hand side of the print.

treats buildings in relation to their designer, who is portrayed as brilliant and original.

The entry for the Wren Library, in the Cambridgeshire volume of Pevsner's *Buildings of England* series, starts with the building rather than with its designer. It reminds us that Wren had already designed a chapel, consecrated in 1665, and cloister for Pembroke College.[9] **14** The book's brief is to give an account, as compactly as possible, of its architectural features in the context of the entry on Trinity College as a whole. The discussion of the library alone covers close to three pages, and although it is to the point, it is also lively. For example: 'The library was begun in 1676 and completed internally in 1690. It is 150 feet long, built of Ketton stone with its lovely variety of cream and pink hues, and has an open ground floor with one row of Tuscan columns inside along the centre of its long axis and an upper floor housing the library itself.'[10] When speaking of what I have called Wren's 'trick' with floor levels, he says: 'This conflict between external and internal arrangement, not noticed by many, is a typically Baroque feature. He took it over from Paris.'[11] It was in Paris, which Wren visited in 1665, that he met Gian Lozenzo Bernini, the painter, sculptor and architect, who is discussed in the next essay, and who is closely associated with the baroque style.[12] Pevsner continues, 'The library must have come as a revelation to Cambridge, still used to such fundamentally unclassical buildings as Pepys Building at Magdalene College and Third Court at St John's. Here was sonorous grandeur, without any bragging, simplicity and ease combined with a mastery of the Romance idiom...'[13] There are some tricky concepts here: baroque, unclassical and Romance, for example. None of these is explained in the glossary, although classical is – 'the term for Greek and Roman architecture and any subsequent styles inspired by it.'[14] Baroque is at once a style term and a period term, one furthermore that is extremely hard to define. For Pevsner the library has both classical and baroque elements, at first sight a puzzling combination. Just as striking is the use of metaphor. It is as if the building were a piece of music, or indeed a person. These points not only alert us to the challenges of describing buildings in ways that are accurate and evocative, they also suggest the significance of the use of metaphor and the difficult task of conceptualising a building as a whole.

Kerry Downes and Nikolaus Pevsner come to the Wren Library as architectural historians seeking to provide accounts of the building for a broad readership.[15] As a result they present it as a fine accomplishment by Wren, and as a completed structure. Many authors have noted how techniques that Wren developed for one building were used in later ones.[16] For example, Wren had the novel idea of inverted arches in the foundations for the library at Trinity, and deployed it again for Tom Tower in Christ Church, Oxford. Similarly innovative techniques with respect to roofs were used in making the Wren Library and St Paul's Cathedral. Such comments draw readers to think about the processes through which Wren worked. Since Wren was an accomplished mathematician and natural philosopher, he was skilled in thinking about forms and their physical properties. He developed ideas for buildings that were at once aesthetic and practical. His visual intelligence had to be linked with a practical one if his buildings were to work – that is, not just stand up and last, but completed successfully to the satisfaction of patrons, where price and duration of construction were among the criteria of success.

Architecture is a collaborative venture involving builders and carpenters, as well as patrons and suppliers. Historians such as James Campbell – who explore the relationships between Wren's architecture and his science, looking at the development of building technology in the period – are turning away from a style-based approach, and using archaeological and surveying techniques to understand the building process better. Campbell argues that Wren was interested in the technology of building, and especially in innovative structural carpentry, an interest he shared with other early members of the Royal Society. Although Wren may have had the last word, he collaborated with carpenters, some of whom were more literate and better-off than has been supposed, running what can justifiably be called specialist building firms in the later seventeenth and early eighteenth centuries.[17]

In considering Campbell's scholarship in this context, we move from a detailed, if compact, biography of Wren and a guidebook to original research in a doctoral dissertation – three distinct genres of writing. Campbell's methods, which pay attention to intellectual networks, problem-solving, materials and the division of labour simultaneously, are important for historians concerned to use visual and material culture in an integrative way. He brings together historiographical approaches too often kept apart. Wren was an innovative architectural thinker and designer. He produced the plans for the library at Trinity without receiving a fee, having been invited to do so by Isaac Barrow, Master of Trinity from 1673 until his death in 1677, and an important figure in intellectual circles dedicated to pursuing knowledge of nature. It was to Barrow that Wren wrote the long letter explaining his thinking. Wren loved books and moved in circles where some members had substantial personal libraries.[18] He was also committed to the 'advancement of learning', to use Bacon's phrase, and presumably sought to design a building that expressed the values he and his friends held dear. Thus he could bring first-hand knowledge of libraries and their users to the Trinity designs. These included a simple but clever idea for book-stands in the middle of the tables. **13** In the course of completing the library successfully, he had to solve technical problems, work with those on site – including ensuring detailed instructions reached masons and carpenters – and generate an apt, pleasing structure.[19] For Campbell, then, understanding the physical details of Wren's buildings entailed grasping both his working practices and his networks.

Wren's networks, Trinity's networks

Wren, like those with whom he worked, participated in intellectual circles and patronage networks. Indeed, to build the library at all, the college had to appeal for funds, and those who contributed became patrons. Patronage is made visible in Trinity's library. For example, Charles Seymour, Sixth Duke of Somerset, was a Trinity man.[20] His involvement is evident not just through his statue, but also through his crests and ciphers repeated four times in limewood on the library's west side.[21] In a building such as the Wren Library, affinities between people, ideas and institutions take on material forms. Nowhere is this more evident than in Robert Smith's activities when he was Master of the College. It was through his bequest that the stained-glass window came to the library. As an ardent Newtonian, he ensured that the college made its association with a widely fêted man of genius apparent wherever possible. Both Wren and Newton were presidents of the Royal Society. Wren held prestigious posts – the chair of astronomy at Gresham College, London, the Savilian chair of astronomy at Oxford and Surveyor General of the Royal Works. He came from a family with High Church, Royalist connections and he joined Wadham College, Oxford in 1650, shortly after John Wilkins, divine and natural philosopher, became Master. Wilkins was a significant figure in the early days of the Royal Society, and gathered around him clever men whose interests were in experimental philosophy and often in practical problem solving – people with wide talents and diverse interests. Christopher Wren's architectural practice thus forms one element, albeit a dominant one, of a rich life, during which his wide range of contacts was constantly active.

Thus it is hardly surprising that Wren was extensively portrayed and in a number of media, including marble, ivory, metal, ceramic, print and paint.[22] **15** The Wren Library does not display his likeness, although it uses his name, making the identification between designer and designed particularly close. Portraits of him may be found in the National Portrait Gallery, the British Museum, the Ashmolean Museum, the Royal Society, St Paul's Cathedral and so on. The details of these, as well as their location, provide further evidence of Wren's status, networks and associations. For example, he was painted by Sir Godfrey Kneller in 1711 when St Paul's Cathedral was completed, in a canvas that foregrounds his work there.[23] Kneller also painted Newton, Evelyn and Pepys, and was close to Fellows of the Royal Society, such as the physician Richard Mead. The Huguenot carver David Le Marchand produced an exquisite ivory of Wren around 1723. **16** He too depicted others in Wren's circles: Newton and Locke, for instance.[24] Portraits involve a measure of self-awareness on the part of maker and sitter alike. The goal is to produce a material object that represents someone according to the conventions of the time and embodies an understanding of the sitter's claim to fame. It was frequently said that Wren was a great man, and in producing *Parentalia: or, Memoirs of the Family of the Wrens* in 1750, his son and grandson were well aware of his importance since most of the lavish volume is devoted to him. It is worth noting that the book contains portraits of key people in Wren's life,

15 *Sir Christopher Wren*, by and published by John Smith, after Sir Godfrey Kneller, 1713, mezzotint, 34 cm high × 25 cm wide, National Portrait Gallery, London. John Smith was an important and prolific engraver of mezzotints. The Latin inscription refers to Wren's achievements at St Paul's. Mezzotints, which came into prominence in the second half of the seventeenth century, are particularly effective in conveying subtle tones.

16 *Sir Christopher Wren*, by David Le Marchand, *c*.1723, ivory medallion, 12.7 cm high × 9.2 cm wide, National Portrait Gallery, London. This portrait combines a precious material, skilled, delicate carving and small size, which together produce exceptionally pleasing effects. Le Marchand left France to escape religious persecution and spent most of his career in London.

including John Wilkins, Robert Boyle, Thomas Sprat, Isaac Barrow and Isaac Newton, all of whom were associated with the Royal Society.[25]

Conclusions

The Wren Library may be understood as one of the points where a number of circles intersected. The most obvious way in which it brought people together was by virtue of their membership of the college, and it was through this route that gifts of books, manuscripts and objects arrived. Indeed, we have noted that until the early twentieth century, it was in some ways as much a museum as a library. Today both the display cases and the information leaflet remind visitors, and there are still plenty of tourists coming to marvel at its splendours, that the poet Tennyson, the historian Macaulay, A. A. Milne (author of *Winnie the Pooh*) and Ludwig Wittgenstein the philosopher, were all members of the college. Thus the library quite literally embodies many kinds of affinity. It follows that it can be used as a way of thinking not just about networks themselves but about how they are deposited in material objects, such as the vibrantly coloured window, that possesses, it must be admitted, an element of absurdity, in bringing together people of different times and types, living and mythical. Perhaps it is best described as a secular church window.

To appreciate the cascades of relationships that are present in the library, it has to be seen as a whole and as constantly in the process of change. The library provides evidence that can be brought to bear on a striking array of historical problems. How were libraries conceptualised in the second half of the seventeenth century, especially in the light of claims about the unprecedented advancement of learning? How is the Wren Library like and unlike others built around the same time and does it shed light on the library as a building type?[26] How does it compare with Sir Christopher Wren's other work? How was it viewed, by those who used it, by those for whom it was a 'sight', and by those who analysed it as a building? Did it advance the cause of Newtonianism? Can it help historians to understand the phenomenon of patronage? How have attitudes and approaches to it changed over time? What role has the building and its contents played in the life of the college? How did it impact upon the university and the town at the time it was built? **17**

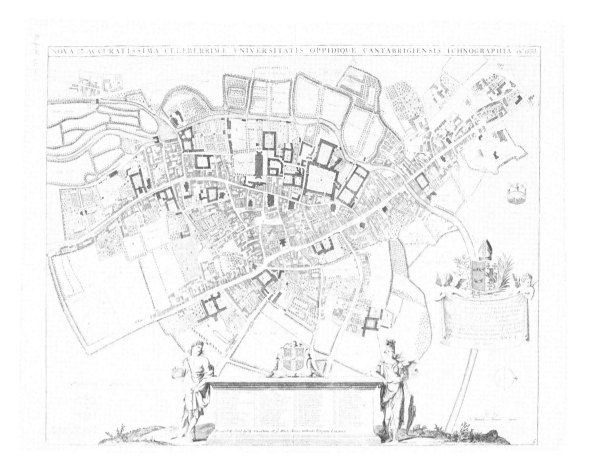

NOTES

1 Quoted in David McKitterick, ed., *The Making of the Wren Library* (Cambridge, 1995), p. 20. Like Wren, and a number of those mentioned in this essay, Evelyn and Pepys were Fellows of the Royal Society, which included many men interested in buildings and indeed visual and material culture generally.

2 Unless otherwise stated, all details about the building come from McKitterick, *The Making*, or from first-hand observation.

3 *Ibid.*, pp. 24, 25, 54, 75–6, 116, 120–4, 129–31 and 135–7.

4 Quoted in *ibid.*, p. 144. Wren's draft letter to Barrow is reproduced on pp. 142–6. Wren is referring to a drawing, reproduced as fig. 34.

5 James Stevens Curl, *Oxford Dictionary of Architecture* (Oxford, 1999), p. 224.

6 Entries are not paginated when viewed electronically; the quotation here, which reproduces most of Downes's comments on the building, comes from the section entitled 'Secular Work of the 1670s', which is pp. 413–14 in the printed version, vol. 60 (2004), see p. 414 for the Wren Library.

7 On this point, see also Adrian Tinniswood, *His Invention so Fertile: a Life of Christopher Wren* (London, 2001), p. 237. Tinniswood sees the Wren Library

17 *Nova & Accuratissima Celeberrimae Universitatis Oppidique Cantabrigiensis Ichnographia Anno 1688 (A New and Most Accurate Plan of the Highly Celebrated University and Town of Cambridge in the Year 1688)*, by David Loggan and reprinted by Henry Overton, 43.5 cm high × 57.7 cm wide, Cambridge University Library. Although dated 1688, this plan was first published in 1690. Loggan's original has been praised by scholars for its precision. Trinity College may be seen in the top half of the map, and to the right, with the Wren Library, then under construction, clearly shown.

as marking a significant point in Wren's career and as one of his greatest works, for example, pp. 239 and 381.

8   James Campbell, 'Sir Christopher Wren, the Royal Society, and the Development of Structural Carpentry 1660–1710', Ph.D. dissertation, University of Cambridge (2000).

9   Nikolaus Pevsner, *Cambridgeshire* (New Haven and London, 2001; first published 1954, 2nd edn 1970), pp.172–5. The entry for the college as a whole is on pp.161–78. On Pembroke Chapel, see pp. 125–6.

10 *Ibid.*, pp. 172–3. The building was not fully completed until 1695. Note too that Pevsner gives the incorrect length.

11 *Ibid.*, p. 173.

12 On Wren's encounter with Bernini, see Tinniswood, *His Invention so Fertile*, pp. 129–30.

13 Pevsner, *Cambridgeshire*, p. 173.

14 *Ibid.*, p. 511.

15 The recent edition was printed after his death in 1983; his name remains associated with the series even where others are listed as authors. The entire project is best thought of as collaborative.

16 For example, Lisa Jardine, *On a Grander Scale: the Outstanding Career of Sir Christopher Wren* (London, 2002), pp. 324–6. Campbell's thesis cited above pays particular attention to Wren's technical advances.

17 Campbell, 'Sir Christopher Wren', Conclusion, pp. 253–5, provides a summary of his claims.

18 Jardine, *On a Grander Scale*, p. 326.

19 Tinniswood claims that Wren was particularly dirigiste in his approach, giving detailed instructions because he did not want workmen 'interpreting' his ideas – p. 238. He then sums up what he sees as innovative in Wren's approach: '[his] professionalism, his holistic approach to design and, most significantly, his need to control every stage of the process, were something new in British architecture'.

20 According to the *ODNB* entry for him, there is no documentary proof that Somerset went to Trinity.

21 David Green, *Grinling Gibbons: His Work as Carver and Statuary, 1648–1721* (London, 1964), p. 81; see also David Easterly, *Grinling Gibbons and the Art of Carving* (London, 1998), pp. 23, 154–62 and 210.

22 The website of the National Portrait Gallery London, www.npg.org.uk, contains illustrations of, as well as information on, a number of portraits of Wren.

23 NPG 113, oil on canvas, purchased 1860, 124.5 cm high × 100.3 cm wide.

24 Ludmilla Jordanova, *Defining Features: Scientific and Medical Portraits 1660–2000* (London, 2000), p. 52, and for portraits of Wren and members of his circle, see Norman H. Robinson, *The Royal Society Catalogue of Portraits* (London, 1980). On Le Marchand, there is C. Avery, *David Le Marchand: 'An Ingenious Man for Carving in Ivory'* (London, 1996), and 'David le Marchand: Precursor of Eighteenth-century English Portrait Sculpture', *British Art Journal*, 1 (1999), pp. 27–34.

25 Christopher Wren, compiler, *Parentalia: or, Memoirs of the Family of the Wrens* (London, 1750).

26 Margarete Bauer-Heingold, *Shöne alte Bibliotheken. Ein Buch vom Zauber ihrer Räume* (Munich, 1972), pp. 55–82, shows the Wren in the context of the other seventeenth- and eighteenth-century English libraries.

FURTHER READING

On the building, the starting point must be David McKitterick, ed., *The Making of the Wren Library* (Cambridge, 1995). For Trinity's library before the Wren was built, see Philip Gaskell, *Trinity College Library: the First 150 Years* (Cambridge, 1980). Guidebooks make clear the library's status as a tourist attraction. For example, William White's *A Visitor's Guide to Cambridge*, 2nd edn (Cambridge, n.d. but possibly 1892), which contains an extended discussion of the library (pp. 182–97) that appreciates its beauty, gives financial and technical details relating to its construction, and provides a detailed description of the building and its contents.

On Wren there are works as diverse as Viktor Fürst, *The Architecture of Sir Christopher Wren* (London, 1956); Raymond Horricks, *Sir Chris, the Architect as Hero* (Worthing, 1998); James Chambers, *Christopher Wren* (Stroud, 1998); and Heywood Gould, *Sir Christopher Wren: Renaissance Architect, Philosopher, and Scientist* (London and New York, 1970), p. 161, which mentions the library in passing. See also Adrian Tinniswood, *His Invention so Fertile: a Life of Christopher Wren* (London, 2001); Lisa Jardine, *On a Grander Scale: the Outstanding Career of Sir Christopher Wren* (London, 2002); and Anthony Geraghty, *The Complete Architectural Drawings of Sir Christopher Wren: at All Soul's College, Oxford: a Complete Catalogue* (Aldershot, 2007).

Most of the figures mentioned in this chapter have entries in the *Oxford Dictionary of National Biography*. The essay on the *ODNB* website 'Royal Society Founder Members', by Michael Hunter, is also useful and reinforces the point about interlocking circles. My essay, 'Portraits, People and Things: Richard Mead and Medical Identity', *History of Science*, 41 (2003), pp. 293–313, explores a prominent Newtonian, also a Fellow of the Royal Society, and the visual and material culture surrounding him in the first half of the eighteenth century. Anthony Geraghty, 'Robert Hooke's Collection of Architectural Books and Prints', *Architectural History*, 47 (2004), pp. 113–25, reveals the architectural interests of another key actor in the early Royal Society.

On Roubiliac, David Bindman and Malcolm Baker, *Roubiliac and the Eighteenth-century Monument: Sculpture as Theatre* (New Haven and London, 1995) is excellent.

On Kneller there is J. Douglas Stewart, *Sir Godfrey Kneller and the English Baroque Portrait* (Oxford, 1983).

The complexities of baroque style come up in the essay on Bernini and in Chapter 3.

John Summerson, *Architecture of the Eighteenth Century* (London, 1986), discussed the freestanding library as a 'new' building type, see pp. 116–22. On the Codrington Library, see Howard Colvin and J. S. G. Simmons, *All Souls: an Oxford College and its Buildings* (Oxford, 1989). See also J. Willis Clark and Arthur Gray, *Old Plans of Cambridge 1574 to 1798* (Cambridge, 1921), part 1: 'Text'; Richard Harraden, *Harraden's Picturesque Views of Cambridge* (Cambridge, 1800), which contains an image of the library; Peter Glazebrook, ed., *Jesus: the Life of a Cambridge College* (Cambridge, 2007), which contains an essay by a historian, Stephen Taylor, on 'Images of the College: Prints', pp. 62–8.

Bridge

We might imagine the Wren Library as the hub of a wheel, and all the historical questions it prompts as radiating out, spoke-like, from it. Equally, we might conceptualise it as one element within a series of comparisons, starting, for example, with the Codrington Library at All Souls' College, Oxford, designed by Nicholas Hawksmoor, who had worked with Wren. **54** Both these buildings involved high levels of craftsmanship and skill as well as exceptional visual intelligence on the part of their designers – these are the themes explored in the next chapter.

2   Craft, skills and visual intelligence

Introduction

In Chapter 1, I considered how historians respond to artefacts by generating descriptions of them. Then, in the first essay, I took a building and discussed ways of describing it and what it might be used as evidence for. There were four distinct stages in the making of the Wren Library: formulating the original idea, which was done by Isaac Barrow, who also raised funds; designing the building, the task of Christopher Wren; execution, undertaken by many hands primarily under the direction of Robert Grumbold; and embellishment, where again numerous people were involved. I noted particularly the contribution of Robert Smith, primarily at the level of ideas, and also with money. The essay hints at the value of thinking in terms of processes and practices, and the importance, not so much of reconstituting them, as of putting effort into imagining them in as much detail as possible. This emphasis on processes and practices is found in many historical fields – developments in the history of science have been particularly influential. It has explored particularly fruitfully many of the themes discussed in this chapter, which also contains a theme – agency – that runs throughout the book. Who did what, in what context and with what historical significance?

Now we address the questions 'How do things come into being?' and 'How can historians conceptualise and interpret processes of production?' Because of the nature of the evidence – work customs and habits, like conversations between makers, patrons and clients, are not necessarily recorded – these discussions are quite general, drawing attention to features of broad historical importance. I also consider the roles of materials, technique, training, patronage, design and so on, and note the interest in the past in charting how things are made. I have just outlined an enterprise that involves diverse fields such as business history, conservation studies and design history. It is helpful, for example, if we can probe both the organisational and the technical elements of making artefacts. Naturally these are diverse, with artisans playing the predominant roles. However, many prized items, the sort of thing that is usually called 'art', were made by people who sought to exercise as much control as possible over the whole process, as, in some periods, did their patrons. This point reminds us that the ways in which images and objects come into being is inseparable from social relationships and that they are embedded in power relations. Accordingly, the theme of hierarchy is inescapable.

Some further preliminary comments are in order. The separation of the study of these matters into distinct fields, while perfectly understandable, is also regrettable; it suggests that more extensive collaboration would be beneficial, as is already evident in material culture studies. Although I often refer to the studio or workshop, we should remember that many of the most significant items of everyday life were made at home. Given the diversity of things themselves, how they were made and how historians understand these processes, is a huge subject. I approach it here in a number of ways in order to suggest some possible avenues. It is worth reflecting upon the languages used to conceptualise making and the need to acknowledge how these have been shaped by myth. This chapter argues for the value of the concept of visual intelligence to describe the constellation of attributes that makers possess. In responding to artefacts, audiences also manifest forms of visual intelligence. By probing the range of skills involved in the generation of artefacts, historians understand them more effectively. Making is about problem-solving and requires specialised forms of intelligence. Some practitioners recorded their ideas about practice and I draw upon their testimony too.

Methods and materials

In 1937, the American artist and designer Hilaire Hiler published *The Painter's Pocket-Book of Methods and Materials*. It is brimming with details and advice about how to proceed with the actual business of painting – tools, types of paint, varnishes and much more. The result is a blend of common sense, recipes, observations about technique in earlier periods, philosophical reflection, chemistry and colour theory, and the author's opinions. The opening words of the 1970 edition are noteworthy: 'Other complicated trades have pocket books containing the essentials of their crafts … in painting a knowledge of the materials used and of the best means of knowing the permanence and quality of the materials … should be the base from which the creative act sets out'.[1] Painting was associated here with trades, crafts and creative acts. This is a striking combination; throughout the volume an understanding of means and methods was linked with both the most practical of considerations – how much colour do you put on a brush? for instance – and a concern with visual effects. The book asserts the 'inseparable relation between materials and expression'. 'An artist thinks and feels in terms of his materials. He must understand them in order fully to comprehend his art'.[2] Processes of making and the final appearance of a work are intimately linked. To understand these processes and their impact, scholars can consider the materials involved, the kinds of skill deployed, the mental operations of makers and the contexts in which they worked.

The issues Hiler discussed, including the most effective forms of training for those who make, with manifest skill, items of visual and material culture, have been debated for centuries. He was particularly concerned with how and what artists learn. *The Painter's Pocket-Book* reveals the complexity of terms such as 'craft' and 'art', how important practical considerations are for practitioners, and the proximity of seemingly mundane matters involving technique to big issues, indeed to entire philosophies of art. Although Hiler claimed that there was an absence of 'pocket-books' for artists, both practitioners and commentators had been tackling questions about skill, technique, materials and making for a long time and in a range of ways.

Relevant writings took many different forms – biography and autobiography, treatises, lectures and discourses, technical manuals and so on. They serve a number of valuable purposes for historians, above all in revealing the languages and idioms through which production is described and analysed and changing ideas about what, precisely, artisans and artists do, or rather what they *say* and *think* they do, or are *thought* to do by others. Written accounts articulate practices, if in selective, highly mediated ways. However, these are not our only route to the processes by which artefacts were made. Things themselves testify to that directly. As a result, restorers and conservators, who work closely with objects at first hand, are able to speak authoritatively about production processes. Commentary and criticism, letters and memoirs also help historians to unlock this topic, as do records of the condition and properties of an object when it changed hands. Inevitably there is the vexed question of documentary evidence, with certain categories of elite artefacts being best served. Yet, even where sources are scarce or elusive, it is worth reflecting upon what paying meticulous attention to the ways and means by which objects are made, contributes to historical understanding.

Keywords

In his influential book *Keywords*, Raymond Williams drew attention to words that did a disproportionate amount of cultural and social work, carrying major historical transformations in their shifting usage. A number of his keywords are used in this chapter, together with others he did not examine. Words, such as 'art', 'genius' and 'skill', are suffused with shifting assumptions about value and social hierarchies. Some keywords are associated with specific disciplines, or used in different ways according to the field in question. This situation, together with the existence of specialised vocabularies associated with processes of making, can appear off-putting to historians. There are, however, challenges to be embraced here, for their potential to contribute to historical understanding.

A number of terms – 'craft', 'design' and 'work', for instance – may appear innocent, but actually belong to value-laden systems of classification that distinguish and rank kinds of making. By that token they also sort types of people. Another cluster – 'inspiration', 'genius', 'intelligence', 'creativity' and 'originality' – imply judgements about makers and their products. The latter are 'internal' words, associated with mental faculties that are highly prized. 'Master' and 'masterpiece' perhaps appear to belong to that group, and are used now in precisely this way, but their origins in guild activities root them in formal practices, designed to judge and police the levels of skill within trade-specific organisations. A masterpiece enabled a journeyman to become a master; its quality was assessed during the rituals of structured communities. In such contexts, including some art academies, the masterpiece or its equivalent was a passport, a letter of credit, a token of recognition by a peer group. Now, severed from that context, 'masterpiece' means either an excellent piece of work in the speaker's opinion, or the best that a given producer achieved, and hence possesses a strong subjective component.

Notions such as 'originality' appear equally subjective. Work that stands out by virtue of exceptional skill – whether in execution or inspiration – has long been desired, in the ancient world as in subsequent times. Accounts of competitions between painters, as told by Pliny, for example, only make sense if producing what was considered uncommonly good was highly prized by patrons, audiences and makers themselves. The criteria naturally vary, and 'originality' is not any one thing: composition, ideas, design and fine handiwork are all involved. To say that something is original is also to make a historical claim, one implying comparison, perhaps with contemporaneous work and/ or with earlier achievements. The making of something exceptional is of deep historical interest; it testifies in a distinctive manner precisely because it is not run of the mill. Originality positively invites contextualisation and interpretation. Note, too, the notion's link with authenticity – 'an original' means the genuine article and invites respect on that account. 'Genius', associated with creativity, invention and inspiration, is closely connected, as its history suggests. Genius was not talent, but signalled an ability that was superior in kind rather than degree to that of others; it assumed its present meaning during the eighteenth century.[3] 'Creative' was also coined in this period. Because of overuse, 'genius' has little analytical bite now, it does not explain anything, implying that a person or phenomenon is beyond explanation by virtue of being extraordinary. In common parlance, 'genius' acts as an intensifier, as the word 'very' does.

Probing terms connected with making and discussing the quality of what is made, is part of thinking critically about past value judgements and the changing contexts in which they were exercised. One such term is 'craft', which has a number of historically specific meanings. The association with skilled making, however, has persisted over many centuries, so that 'craftsmanship', which can be applied to just about any kind of making, implies a positive judgement about skill. Thus, in one sense, craft refers to diverse manual skills. In the present day it also refers to a certain range of products, even if this range resists simple definition. For example, craft fairs are events where goods – such as pottery, wooden items, jewellery, embroidery, knitted garments, leatherwork and batik – are sold. The implication is that these are handmade. In practice the levels of skill manifest in the goods themselves are generally quite varied. So, too, are the people who make them. Some have undertaken long trainings or apprenticeships, others are self-taught. By contrast, the Arts and Crafts movement of the late nineteenth and early twentieth centuries fostered traditional skills, hand printing and furniture-making for example, that were endangered, and sought to make them viable. **18**

'Artisan' is certainly a keyword in Williams's sense – it refers to skilled workers with pride in their products, high levels of articulacy and political awareness, and organisations to defend their interests. We might think of carpenters and bakers, engravers and tanners, instrument-makers and saddlers. Much of what we call visual and material culture was made by artisans. The term shares its origins with 'art', which used to

18 Coffee pot, by Joyce Himsworth, 1926–7, silver with wooden handles, 21.3 cm high × 10.9 cm diameter, Victoria and Albert Museum, London. This is an example of a late Arts and Crafts piece. Designed and made by a woman, it was her first major piece, produced when she was in her early twenties, and bearing her mark. It shows the influence of Celtic designs, which she had studied in Ireland while at the Sheffield School of Art. A detailed description is available on the museum's website. Himsworth was a member of the Sheffield Artcrafts Guild, founded in 1894 to bring together artists and craftspeople. Sheffield remains a centre for making metal goods, especially cutlery, which has been produced there since the late thirteenth century.

mean technical skill; its uses have varied markedly with time, place and vantage point. On the one hand, artisanal work lies at the centre of visual and material culture, through the skilled work involved in paper-making and printing, the production of a wide range of items, such as tools, paints and frames, and the construction of artefacts, such as furniture and clothing, buildings, metalware, crockery, cutlery and so on. On the other hand, those who saw themselves as better educated, using sophisticated ideas in processes of making, rarely wished to be designated 'artisans'. From the sixteenth century onwards, artists and architects were drawn to academies rather than to guilds, and developed explicit cults of individual achievement, which emphasised intellectual insight, inventiveness and originality.

'Art' and 'craft' appear to refer to different enterprises, enjoying different status. This distinction is historically complex, bound up with the intricate, changing sense of the value to be given to the roles of the mind and of the hands. In practice, both types of work require visual intelligence and manual skills. Thus the vexed distinctions between art and craft are bound up with the ways skills are understood. Although not one of Raymond Williams's *Keywords*, 'skill' could well be. Historians can usefully examine skills, asking who possessed and deployed them, how they were spoken about and represented. Damien Hirst is the living artist who, it is claimed, now commands the highest prices in the world. Labels in exhibitions only give his name as the maker. He runs workshops, and many of 'his' pieces are not actually made by him, but by people who could be called craftsmen. Nonetheless the ideas, and arguably the entrepreneurial flair, are his. The people who laboured, however, are not named, nor are they considered artists, yet they are highly skilled. This is hardly a new problem in the visual arts. For any given artefact, we can ask: what skills were involved, who possessed them, and how were they transmitted, valued and represented? We can probe the range of labour processes that 'craft' and 'art' subsumed, the nature of markets and patronage, and the ways in which cultural value is constructed.

Myths of making

There are myths from many periods about how things, especially noteworthy or beautiful ones, are made and about their makers. Myths are simplified, dense stories that concern fundamental questions about human existence, such as the nature of creation. How special artefacts come into being, and the roles of gods and people in the process, are just such questions. Mythic accounts of artistic production frequently involve stereotypes of creativity as a special form of intense, individual

Graveurs en taille douce au Burin et a Leaue forte

Cette au Burin plend vominie son pu de Cie, il Me fe le Cit: pfe de faplache chaude, iuit, le derrene de son hebu comme le Conseruon tres qu'l ne Blenheln qu pu, latuche tire tur la planche prefs lune ponte aqies tert les Cuiteson de fu houvres et fu la trensiton phase l; legrom aequies le Blan sur la Cuit, se exqufant sul prme, sur lail Capiton luc emprmur Tont le Qanice; pius d'on Me la Cire

19 *Graveurs en taille douce au Burin et a Leaue forte* (*Engravers using the burin and etching*) by Abraham Bosse, 1643, etching, 25.9 cm high × 32.1 cm wide, British Museum. The man on the right is working with the tool used to make lines in copperplate engraving. On the left is the etcher, who will immerse his plate in acid to produce the lines. A man and two monks inspect prints hung on the far wall, suggesting the proximity of making and selling. Unusually, the engravers are actually depicted working. Bosse also produced a number of prints of painters and sculptors in their studios, which are available on the British Museum website, but in these the artists display their works to audiences. Bosse was a writer and poet as well as being a major French exponent of engraving, on which he published a treatise in 1645.

energy, which lies outside normal human activities. The idea that a few artists have something of the divine in them has a long history. If such a person is deemed a genius, then attention is easily directed away from processes of making and towards an extraordinary individual, who does not labour, but is inspired. Certainly there is great curiosity about how exceptional objects and images are made, which has been met in a number of ways, such as biography and memoirs. Exceptional makers themselves have an interest in these questions, expressed, for example, in autobiography and self-portraiture. Images of painters and sculptors in their studios are familiar figures, although portraits and photographs rarely show them actually doing anything. **19** In popular discourse, as in some academic publications, romantic notions of mavericks and creative free spirits abound to the extent that eccentricity and bad behaviour are closely associated with designers and architects as well as artists, as if they were a positively expected part of exceptional achievement. People who know little about visual culture have heard the story about Van Gogh cutting off his ear. Although often associated with the early nineteenth-century notion of a bohemian life, these ideas are very much older than that and are remarkably tenacious.

Such notions ignore the often tortuous, protracted, labour-intensive processes through which artefacts come into being. Many of these are utterly prosaic, and involve whole teams of people not a single individual with apparently prodigious powers. This is not to deny the role of inspiration, passion or uncommon drive, but to put such qualities into a more rounded context, including the materials, organisations, social relationships and locations associated with making visual and material culture.

The two paragraphs you have just read do not contain the word 'work'. It is common to say 'art works', but not to describe those who construct items of visual and material culture as 'workers'. Even the most renowned artists worked for a living, some may be said to have laboured; in addition, they were generally operating as businessmen, and also as teachers, collectors, designers, dealers, diplomats or writers. Many artists were and are artisans. **X** Such points might be pursued under the aegis of labour history, a specialism within the discipline of history. 'Work' and its cognates are ideologically fraught, ambiguous terms and have been recognised as such by historians. It can refer to what someone does for a living and in this sense is like 'job', 'trade' or 'occupation', yet it is unlike them in its kinship with physical labour. Professionals and tradesmen, although they may indeed work with their hands, are not generally called 'workers', which carries connotations of bodily activity and low social status. 'Work' can, however, suggest effort that is not manual but intellectual. According to Williams, 'what is now most interesting is [the word's] predominant specialization to regular paid employment',[4] which hardly applies to many forms of art production, although it is more apt for some of today's artisans.

Occupations are notoriously sensitive about how their particular forms of work are described, the status they enjoy, and representations of the forms of labour they entail. These issues go far beyond feelings, aspirations and experiences; they are rooted in institutions, economic relationships, and the power that individuals and groups can command. Since items of visual and material culture are the products of work, they provide rich and direct evidence of all its aspects. Using the language of work in this context helps to signal the importance of market relationships, the skills that makers required, the manner of their acquisition, the significance of raw materials and the processes applied to them, as well as features of the finished things themselves. Most people feel quite comfortable with these moves in relation to artisanal work, less so when it comes to fine art. However, there is quite a cult of studying the 'labour processes' of those deemed great artists so as to shed light on their achievements; for example, through sketches and preparatory work, although these are conceptualised less as 'work' and more as indicative of creative processes. Furthermore, these kinds of activity tend to be conceptualised differently from those of artisans, such as printers and silversmiths. The fact remains that most successful artists possess high levels of manual skill, and that 'artisan' could well be used of them. It may be tempting to buy into and propagate myths of making, but critical historians seek to understand how such myths arose and enquire afresh about diverse processes of production. In no way does this lessen the appreciation of uncommon achievement.

The diversity of work

In this book I mention a range of artefacts, which came into being in correspondingly diverse ways. Some – the Bernini statue, the Renoir portrait – are fine works by artists deemed to be outstanding. They are associated with named individuals, although others may have participated in their construction. In such cases, the roles of some workers are concealed, thereby diminishing our sense of the elaborate social processes involved. Bernini operated a workshop with assistants, for example, yet the use of his name alone implies individual achievement. Sculpture is generally, and for perfectly practical reasons, a collaborative enterprise. The extent to which painting shares that characteristic varies considerably, especially by period, yet when artists buy paint rather than mixing it themselves, send their work to a framer, discuss it with others, elements of collaboration are present. When we look at other categories of artefacts, such as furniture, tableware and dress, problems of attribution become more apparent. Here it is often *designers* rather than *makers* who are named and studied. In such cases it is harder to identify individual producers, to know about the labour processes involved in generating specific articles, and less compelling to see them as works of art made by talented individuals. However, some 'craft' and decorative items have acquired a status comparable to that of works of art – Tiffany lamps, Chippendale chairs and Bernard Leach pots are examples of such artefacts that were made in very different ways. **XI** Commentators claim that they, too, embody creativity – an elusive quality that suggests both originality of conception and design, and high standards of execution.

All forms of making are historically significant. The relatively new field of the history of the book, for example, includes scholars concerned with exactly how paper-making, printing and binding were carried out, as well as with layout and illustrations. There is a great deal of evidence in the very fabric of books themselves. Furthermore, early printing presses have been reconstructed to understand better the processes involved by re-enacting them. The historical role of print culture is now being investigated in considerable depth. While much of this scholarship is concerned with the content of printed works, their dissemination and use, it has also raised awareness of the importance of printers, publishers and booksellers. 'Printer' is a broad category, and includes many distinct activities including typesetting, running a workshop and business, and actually operating the press. Printers were closely allied with other trades, such as booksellers, publishers and engravers, with several roles sometimes performed by a single individual. Some engravers, who might not conventionally be seen as 'artists', are known by name, their work can be traced and understood as an ensemble. Engravers frequently copied existing work, drawings, paintings, buildings and sculpture, for example, and this may in part account for their status. Thus the fine eighteenth-century Scottish line engraver Sir Robert Strange is well known among specialists, while figures in the same period, such as James Gillray, who made original satirical prints, are more likely to be considered 'artists'. **XVIII**

At one level it does not and should not matter whether anyone is designated 'artisan' or 'artist', while at another it is quite crucial. Since these labels are never innocent, occupational vocabularies help us to understand questions around identity, status and income, and to enter into past mindsets. Such terminology tends to shape the ways in which historians think, and to determine which field takes charge of a particular group. In practice, labour history and art history do not overlap very much – artisans 'belong' more to the former, 'artists' to the latter. Yet 'artist', with its complex relationship with 'craftsman', remains a fluid term. Claims that outstanding exponents of fields normally classed as 'craft' should be accorded the status of artists are revealing. The inclusion in art galleries of named potters, such as Hans Coper, who left Germany in 1939, spending most of his life in England, is an example. Who counts as an artist changes over time and with context. Mary Delany, who did embroidery, shell-work, feather-work, cut paperwork and much more in the eighteenth century, is now, as a result of recent, revisionist scholarship, recognised as an 'artist'. If these terms were neutral there would be no need for them to be discussed and negotiated; historians are able to pick up on their shifting meanings and distinctions and investigate the settings in which they were used.

For many centuries, the status of makers bore some relationship to the value and rarity of the materials with which they worked, hence the power and status enjoyed by goldsmiths and silversmiths, compared to those who worked in wood and cheaper metals. While Damien Hirst's gold skull encrusted with diamonds could be seen as an ironic comment on such a state of affairs, it also benefited from it, perhaps exploited it. Similarly, the status of artists, high-profile painters and sculptors, for example, has been related to that of their patrons. Before the seventeenth century only a few such people could operate in isolation from organisations, such as guilds, that were connected with a specific occupation. When there were more art academies, artists clearly valued membership, which gave them recognition, exposure and networking opportunities. Royal appointments and commissions were especially coveted as is evident in Anthony van Dyck's self-portrait with a sunflower, where he flaunts the gold chain given to him by Charles I.

The medieval guild system declined in the eighteenth century, although remnants survive to the present day. It was of exceptional importance in organising work, setting rates for labour, controlling numbers of practitioners, monitoring quality, developing collective cultures, and disciplining members within a hierarchical structure, which could be dominated by a few individuals and their families. Apprenticeship was the principal route to becoming a master craftsman, and it involved not only a didactic relationship between trainers and trainees, but also a moral one. Apprentices lived at close quarters with their masters, who were personally responsible for them and sought to regulate their behaviour. Through the guild system some masters were able to become rich and powerful and in such cases they sometimes operated in a mode more generally associated with 'artists'. In fact, many artists also took pupils into their studios, while academies offered teaching positions for a select few – the texts of their lectures are valuable sources. All these points have implications for the types of evidence that survive. For many artefacts, the particular methods and circumstances of their making are less easy to reconstruct, even if we can chart the types of labour process involved at a general level. The diversity of the types of work that led to items of visual and material culture being produced may also be appreciated from dictionaries of trades or from works, such as Diderot and D'Alembert's *Encyclopédie* (1751–72), which both discussed specific occupations in the body of the work and also illustrated their operations in the plates.

The forms of production mentioned so far were clearly delineated as such in the past and enjoyed more or less structured relationships with organisations and institutions, such as guilds, academies and courts. However, many objects were made more informally, for example, within families, where embroidery, furniture and textiles were produced. Written evidence is always a problem here – sometimes in short supply in the case of elite producers, it is generally extremely sparse when it comes to less prestigious goods. The survival of such items in families and local collections is therefore especially helpful. Business history has an important role to play here in finding and analysing small units of production, especially where records and accounts as well as designs and artefacts survive. In the case of exceptional businesses – the

20 Hat, Women's Land Army, Second World War, brown felt, 29.6 cm long × 28 cm wide × 9.8 cm high, Imperial War Museum, London. During both world wars, women worked on the land to release male agricultural workers to join the armed forces. They were popularly known as 'land girls' and wore a uniform. These women thus became visually distinct. The work was arduous and the pay meagre, but presumably the uniform, like the word 'army', linked them to the forces and helped to affirm their contribution to the war effort.

example of Wedgwood springs to mind – it is possible to find out a very great deal about production processes, for instance about the collaboration between the firm's founder Josiah Wedgwood and the artists he employed to design goods especially at the luxury end of the business.

There are three analytical levels involved when we consider processes of production. At the most general one, we are interested in types of work: printing, silversmithing, dress-making, for instance. At the second level we are concerned with the actual processes involved – how a book was printed, a chalice made or a chemise produced at a given time and place. Then, at the most specific level, named makers and particular objects they produced are the focus. It is relatively rare to find all these levels attended to by a single historian, and art historians especially tend to focus on the last, which gives priority to the connections between the appearance of the finished article, the manner of its making and the maker him or herself.

Hats

I now turn to a particular category of object: the hat. For much of human history, hats have played a central role in mediating social relationships, eliciting commentary and analysis. Hats are visually eloquent; the contexts in which they were made, how and by whom, together with the precise ways in which they were used and worn, were full of meaning. They were an important element of past economies – items that could be taxed and their import controlled.[5] The intricate relationships between hats and social etiquette are well known. That men and women, particularly from the early eighteenth century onwards, wore distinct types of hats, suggests their importance for the articulation of gender as well as other forms of social difference. Some hats carried occupational significance, a point that applies particularly to armies, navies and airforces, and also elsewhere. **20** One example is the association of both scholars and artists with a range of smallish, soft headgear from the so-called Titian cap to the beret, including turbans, and 'night caps'.[6] Occupations in direct relationships with the public have also paid careful attention to headwear – the police with protected helmets, nurses with hats, initially made of fabric and then from paper that lasted about three weeks, and English barristers with expensive eighteenth-century-style wigs still made from horsehair by artisans, for example.[7] Collections of hats, as of other accessories, help to document the main changes in the production and uses of hats, which are indicative of taste, fashion and style. The appearance of hats is sensitive to period and social status.

The analysis of actual surviving hats tends to be undertaken by costume historians. This is sometimes combined with a discussion of production methods. For example, the connections between hats and felt-making were particularly close.[8] Where records of specific businesses survive, it is possible to move to a more detailed level of analysis. The London hatters Lock and Co., can be traced back to 1765 in their current London location; this business developed from an earlier one, which began in 1676.[9] Hats that appear in paintings are also historically eloquent. With the advent of photography it can be possible to tie matters down even further. For example, the very hat worn by Heather Firbank, a young society woman, in a photograph from about 1910, is in the Victoria and Albert Museum, London.[10] Hats associated with other named individuals have also been preserved.[11] They alert us to changing materials and techniques of production. Materials and methods of making are reasonably well documented, and the hats themselves provide direct evidence on such matters. A few individual hatters have become particularly well known and their works treated as *objets d'art*, as has happened to the English hatter David Shilling, who might, by that token, be considered an artist. Initially, Shilling made hats for his mother to wear at a fashionable horse race, and then ran a business, becoming a designer of hats rather than making them himself.

Hatters, like many early modern trades, were active in defence of their rights; as a result, there is evidence about the organisation and culture of the trade and about the political culture in which it was embedded. Hatmakers participated in broader trends, economic and social as well as political – evident in the use of beaver hair, which became increasingly scarce as supplies from North America, turned to when European ones became depleted, also began to run out. At this point in the late eighteenth century, top hats began to be made of silk plush.[12] The history of milliners, who were women, tells a different story, since they possessed no traditional skills or guild organisation when they came into their own during the eighteenth century. Milliners were businesswomen, who were craftspeople, shopkeepers and trendsetters. By the nineteenth century, the occupation had some structure as there is evidence of apprentices making miniature hats as part of their training. Yet 'milliner' remained a fluid category, sometimes combined with dress-making and haberdashery. It is possible to name some makers, especially from the nineteenth and twentieth centuries. Yet here again, such individuals were designers rather than makers, and the hats themselves remain the most powerful testimony to materials and methods of making. Straw hats could easily and cheaply be customised by the wearer, and were commonly worn by a wide range of the population over several centuries.

Making hats for men and women was a highly skilled activity, undertaken by distinct occupations – hatters were separate from milliners, felt-making was different from straw-plaiting and so on. These were crafts, but they could also be forms of art. Hats, such as simple caps, were made at home, and trimmed to suit individual budgets and taste. At the highest levels, those who made hats received elite patronage and worked in ways similar to painters and sculptors, even if the status they and their creations enjoyed was somewhat less elevated. Detailed analysis of the finished products gives historians access to an array of social and cultural issues, including etiquette and decorum. Undertaking such an analysis depends upon a grasp of the materials, their costs, and of the relationships between makers and purchasers. Since hats were made, and worn, to be interpreted according to their look, as well as their use, we might say that visual intelligence – that is, an understanding of visual effects and of how they may be knowingly created – is integral to their production.

How to...

Fully documented processes of making are relatively rare. What incentives were there for makers to record their production processes, even assuming this was possible? In any case, many wanted to keep the tricks of the trade to themselves. Furthermore, some skills are so ingrained in the body that practitioners would be hard pressed to put them into words. As a result, many processes remain unarticulated, best understood either by direct observation or first-hand experience, hence the interest in re-enacting now obsolete forms of production. For many centuries, however, there has also been a drive to reveal such 'secrets', to explain how things are done, and to share techniques and practice. 'How to' books, like other advice books, need to be treated with scepticism, yet they are revealing in what they make explicit for their intended audiences. In the fields of art and material culture such works abound, they go back a long way and continue to be popular.

In the 1940s, the American sculptor Jack Rich wrote *The Materials and Methods of Sculpture*, designed for both the student and the professional. **21** He drew attention to the materials of modern sculpture – including wax, plaster, metals, stone and wood – and the methods that can be applied to them – such as casting, carving and hammering.

1. Making a preliminary series of drawings prior to carving the wood.

21 Illustrations from Jack C. Rich, *The Materials and Methods of Sculpture* (New York, 1988), plates 50 and 51, each page 16.5 cm wide × 23.5 cm high, Cambridge University Library. These pictures are designed to illustrate the actual processes involved in wood-carving. The work was first published in 1947.

2. Chaim Gross selecting a block of lignum vitae at the lumber yard.

3. Drawing the design upon the log with chalk.

4. Close-up showing the use of a large gouge for roughing out the masses.

5. Entire mass roughed out.

PLATE 50 DIRECT SCULPTURE IN WOOD

Numerous plates show people at work, tools, and finished pieces. Rich included technical information and a glossary. His work is partly a manual, but he also engaged with modern and contemporary sculpture, showcasing trends he considered significant. Yet readers could never learn to be sculptor from the book. As Rich says 'perpetual practice or application is the only way in which an art or craft may be mastered'.[13] His focus is neither autobiographical nor biographical but on techniques themselves.

21 (*cont.*)

6. The forms emerging from the block after use of a smaller gouge.

7. Front view of work at same stage.

8. Clarifying the forms by use of the rasp.

9. Application of beeswax for polishing, after the surfaces have been worked smooth.

10. The completed work, BALANCING, now in the collection of the Philadelphia Museum of Fine Arts.

PLATE 51   DIRECT SCULPTURE IN WOOD (*Continued*)

By contrast, the ideas of another American artist, William Thon, were published in a more personal book. **22** *The Painter and his Techniques* suggests that a 'how to' manual was intended. There are detailed photographs with captions, showing his manner of working, for instance, in watercolour. Over eight pages, Thon's way of making a watercolour is depicted in twenty photographs and described in the captions. No glossary or diagrams are needed; his tools are his fingers, a jug, sponge, tissues, brushes, quill pen and razor blades. Readers see him making a specific watercolour, illustrated in colour in its finished state. It would be

22 Illustration from Alan Gruskin, *The Painter and his Techniques: William Thon* (London, 1964), pp. 106–7, each page 20 cm wide × 28.5 cm high, Cambridge University Library. Thon is shown working on a watercolour.

possible to treat the painter's reflections as advice, and practising artists might get ideas from the book, but it remains an account of one man's practice and ideas. The photographs convey a sense of the intense physicality of the processes involved.

Descriptions of practices and processes have their limitations. One is the sheer difficulty of being explicit about what is done and known. Another is conveying what are essentially subjective judgements. According to Alan Gruskin's caption to the last set of photographs depicting Thon making a watercolour,

> Thon stands back from the watercolour to judge what still needs to be done with it. With larger paintings he often uses a stepladder in order to view his work from the proper distance. Then, working with pen and ink, sponge or brush, he reinforces the painting here and there, before he places a mat around it, and sets it aside to dry. He will study it intently, sometimes for weeks, before deciding it is finished. And he may take it back to the studio later to rewet the surface and make changes to gain the effect he wants.[14]

The pictures plus caption cannot explain the mental processes involved in deciding a work is 'finished'. How does Thon judge what still needs to be done? Presumably he uses his visual intelligence. Is the decision affected by the timing of an exhibition, the wishes of potential purchasers, and the practicalities of storing works? Judgements about timing and degree of finish may be about relations with a client, or about money, as well as 'aesthetic' judgement.

Visual intelligence

I use 'visual intelligence' both to refer to the skilful processes involved in making items of visual and material culture, and as a prompt to consider the mental activities involved in designing and producing artefacts and thinking them through. Some of these activities are not fully conscious, and their precise nature may be close to impossible to examine except through inferences from the end result.

Visual intelligence is readily discernible in the operations called 'design'. Although a set of recognised professional practices only since the nineteenth century, 'design' may be used to suggest the array of processes whereby images and objects come into being, excluding their physical production. Artefacts do not come into being by accident; they arise from deliberate human action, frequently to solve a specific problem. In a range of senses, they are designed. 'Design', a noun and a verb, has multiple meanings. It can refer to a physical object, Wren's drawn plans for the library, for example; to the ideas that lie behind specific plans; to a whole field; to distinct professions, such as graphic design or theatre design; and to the process of thinking through how something should function and look.

Design history is now a developing field in its own right, one with many disciplinary allies, and a focus on recent times, although as a process design is as old as human societies. Its specialisation is historically important; in its broadest meaning, 'design' shapes every aspect of our lives, and necessarily forms a major element within visual and material culture. Design history has a great deal to offer other types of historians, and for four principal reasons: the links between producers and consumers are frequently examined; much design involves collaboration, the precise nature of which is conceptualised and charted; it is open to other disciplines and shares much with fields such as business history; and it focuses on the design *process*, on materials and on modes of production in contexts, often industrial ones, where these can be documented with relative ease.

The *concept* of design has a long history. In the seventeenth and eighteenth centuries, many educated Europeans and Americans thought of God as the designer of the universe, and the 'argument from design', recently revived by creationists, sought to prove the existence of God from evidence of his designing hand in nature. This encouraged the detailed inspection of both natural and man-made objects and refined existing frameworks for conceptualising the nature of visual experience. The stakes in 'design' were high. This applied to the art world too. For example, 'In the official doctrine of [French Royal] Academy the priority of design was asserted to uphold the status of painting as a liberal art against the rival institution of the guilds. Line was associated with that part of painting which involved "invention" and the production of an "idea". It showed that the artist was working with his mind or intellect rather than merely with his hands.'[15] Founded in 1648, the Royal Academy of Painting and Sculpture in Paris was attentive to 'theory', that is to explicating and discussing the nature of the visual arts, and members drew on earlier debates about the relative merits of design and colour. Since it bore so directly on the status of artists, the concept of design was of fundamental importance for them. We might see design as the conscious, mental effort to solve a two- or three-dimensional problem, often followed by specific designs for an artefact.

Visual intelligence can also be understood in terms of the ability to respond to a situation, to speak to and move viewers. Talent and experience play a part, but the key is mental processes that are at once social, diplomatic, aesthetic, technical and so on, through which the actions of the hand are mediated. The essays in this book explore examples of visual intelligence in operation. We have observed Christopher Wren designing a new library for Trinity College, Cambridge, both solving technical problems and working out how to produce a beautiful building, fit for purpose, to a budget and suited to the site. The ability to re-present an event or story in a fresh manner is another example of visual intelligence in operation. Jacques-Louis David's famous depiction of the death of Jean-Paul Marat in 1793 is a case in point. Painted at the behest of the French revolutionary leadership immediately after his murder by Charlotte Corday, David found a visual idiom that both displayed and brought into being Marat's martyrdom exceptionally effectively. This effectiveness may be analysed in terms of distinct components of the canvas – composition, skill in handling paint, and choice of palette, for example. The ensemble works powerfully and memorably in its striking simplicity.

By 1793, David had been in the public eye as an artist for close to two decades. As Thomas Crow shows, the painting, especially when compared with other depictions of Marat, provides valuable ways of thinking about the visual culture of the Revolution. Because David was a prominent painter, it is possible to analyse in considerable depth, not only his political activities and commitments, but also his manner of working. Libby Sheldon has demonstrated the insights that can be generated by a careful study of the canvas itself using, among other techniques, infrared reflectography, and comparison with related works. David himself did not like talking about methods and materials. Nonetheless, she has been able to marshal evidence for all the stages of making the portrait – preparatory drawings, composition, choosing the canvas, its preparation, underdrawing, the *ébauche* or coloured sketch, the selection of colours and painting the final layers of oil paint – and interprets it in the light of a wide range of evidence about David's training, his own methods of teaching, his recorded ideas, his self-portrait of 1794, and the availability of tools and materials. She concludes, 'all these technical decisions have shown David's careful management of the spectator through the orchestration of his materials'.[16]

By tracing the processes through which people such as David worked, it is possible to think in a more rounded way about their visual achievements in a precise context. There are insights into visual intelligence to be gained from those who left a lot behind; paying attention to processes yields ideas that can be adapted and used more generally, even when the type and level of detailed evidence is of a different order.

An artist and his materials

I close this chapter with a well-documented case: the long-standing relationship between one artist and the firm that supplied his materials. It involves craft, skills and visual intelligence. The intimacies of the relationship are evident in the extensive correspondence between the Victorian artist George Frederick Watts and his supplier, Winsor and Newton, about paints, oils, varnishes, brushes and canvases. **XII** It lasted from 1860 until the artist's death, after which his widow stayed in touch. The firm had been founded in 1832 by William Winsor, a chemist and artist, and Henry Charles Newton, who was also an artist. Firm and artist exchanged samples of paint, discussed colours and finishes; Watts gave them feedback and sought advice. The letters suggest a genuine collaboration. The materials directly affected both the look of the works and Watts's techniques. For example, on 26 July 1878, the artist wrote to Newton:

Dear Sir,

I am in the habit of rubbing my pictures before painting on them with Potatoe [*sic*] or Onion and leaving moisture which forms a pleasant surface. Please tell me if there is any thing in this likely to affect the colours – it occurs to me that what is left from the Potatoe is a sort of starch and may be injurious.

I hope you are well. I suppose it is too far for you to come or I would ask you to favour my studio with a visit.

Yours very truly,

G. F. Watts

Two days later Newton reassured him that this practice would not adversely affect the performance of oil paint, although it might have an impact on the varnish, illustrating the point with a story about a 'Decorative Painter'. At this time Newton was seventy-four, in poor health and unable to travel significant distances, so he declined the invitation to visit Watts's studio: 'Thanks for the kind privilege of entering your sanctum, it has always possessed an unusual interest for me, from the circumstance of your evidently strong desire that your pictures should possess the enduring qualities that we find in the Old Masters – qualities that most artists desire, but few will take the care and go through laborious efforts to attain'.[17]

Newton ends his letter: 'Permit me now (as I may not have another opportunity) to thank you individually and in the name of my firm for the constant support and patronage you have bestowed on us for so many years and permit me also to say that should there be any technical matters wherein I can be of any service, pray command me unreservedly.' At one level these were indeed 'technical matters', at another they informed Watts's whole approach to painting.

I used the word 'intimacies' to convey how close these matters were to Watts's heart, a point discernible from the content, care and frequency of his letters, and to those who ran the business, and to emphasise how central the matters discussed were to artistic practice. I also meant it to suggest the candid sharing of experience and expertise between practitioner and supplier. The scholarly function of such documents is not just to help us chart specific collaborations, but to offer historians models of working relationships between producers of visual and material culture and their collaborators.

Conclusions

This chapter has been concerned with process and practice, which can be brought to the fore in accounts of the visual and material past in a variety of ways. Paul Hogarth does so, for example, in his study of the 'artist as reporter', where he examines how news entered the public domain in visual form. Technologies and skills played decisive, if complex, roles:

it was not until around 1905 that photography was routinely used to cover major news stories, for example.[18] Hogarth sees the advent of the box camera in 1889 as the beginning of the end for artist-reporters, not the much earlier introduction of the technique of photography itself in 1839. Until the late nineteenth century, the visual intelligence of artists who could sketch fast and select key elements of what they observed was crucial, but so was the way in which their work was translated into print by others. After the 1880s, while outstanding photographers could achieve extraordinary coverage and shape opinion, long-established art techniques did not die, as is apparent from the role of war artists in both world wars, and in current conflicts. Satirical commentary also continued, for example, in early twentieth-century magazines, such as *L'Assiette au Beurre* (1901–12), which encouraged visual flair.[19] Once again skills, techniques, materials and visual intelligence can be shown to be intimately blended.

NOTES

1 Hilaire Hiler, *The Painter's Pocket-Book of Methods and Materials*, 3rd edn (London, 1970), p. 9. Hiler died in 1966. This edition was edited by Jan Gordon, and revised by Colin Hayes. Hiler also published *Notes on the Technique of Painting* (London, 1934), as well as books on abstraction and expressionism.

2 *Ibid.*, pp. 224–6.

3 Williams, *Keywords: a Vocabulary of Culture and Society*, rev. and expanded edn (London, 1983), pp. 143–4.

4 *Ibid.*, p. 335.

5 Fiona Clark, *Hats* (London, 1982), pp. 86 and 84.

6 *Ibid.*, p. 70; Hilda Amphlet, *Hats: a History of Fashion in Headwear* (Chalfont St Giles, 1974), pp. 152–5.

7 Amphlet, *Hats*, pp. 166–7 and 172.

8 Clark, *Hats*, p. 84.

9 Frank Whitbourn, *Mr Lock of St James's Street: His Continuing Life and Changing Times* (London, 1971).

10 Clark, *Hats*, pp. 46–7.

11 *Ibid.*, pp. 58 and 59.

12 *Ibid.*, p. 85.

13 Jack Rich, *The Materials and Methods of Sculpture* (New York, 1947), p. viii.

14 Alan Gruskin, *The Painter and his Techniques: William Thon* (London, 1964), p. 110.

15 Charles Harrison *et al.*, eds., *Art in Theory, 1648–1815* (Oxford, 2000), p. 17.

16 William Vaughan and Helen Weston, eds., *Jacques-Louis David's Marat* (Cambridge, 2000), p. 124.

17 *G. F. Watts Letters*, Heinz Archive, National Portrait Gallery, London, vol. 7, pp. 17–21.

18 Paul Hogarth, *The Artist as Reporter* (London, 1967), pp. 40–1.

19 This phrase, literally 'the buttered plate', is difficult to translate adequately into English. Published between 1901 and 1912, the magazine specialised in attacks on the establishment and bourgeoisie. See Paul Hogarth, *The Artist as Reporter*, expanded edn (London, 1986), pp. 84–5.

FURTHER READING

Works relevant to the themes of this chapter include Nicholas Penny, *The Materials of Sculpture* (New Haven, 1993), and Marjorie Trusted, ed., *The Making of Sculpture: the Materials and Techniques of European Sculpture* (London, 2007), which contains a useful glossary. She covers wax, terracotta, bronze and lead, medals and plaquettes, marble and stone, alabaster, ivory and bone, wood, semi-precious materials and plaster; ch. 1 outlines working practices and the principal ways in which they have changed. See also Antony Griffiths, *Prints and Printmaking: an Introduction to the History and Techniques*, 2nd edn (London, 1996), which has an extensive glossary and brilliantly conveys the processes of print-making; Philippa Abrahams, *Beneath the Surface: the Making of Paintings* (London, 2008), is by an artist and restorer, who tries to understand past techniques and media (drawing, illuminated manuscripts, miniatures, fresco, egg tempura, watercolours and acrylics) by trying them out. The book contains useful information on pigments. The series Art in the Making is helpful, for example: David Bomford *et al.*, *Rembrandt* (London, 1988); David Bomford *et al.*, *Impressionism* (London, 1990). Then there are works by those art historians who seek to fully integrate detailed analyses of making into their work. Outstanding examples are Katie Scott, *The Rococo Interior: Decoration and Social Spaces in Early Eighteenth-Century Paris* (New Haven and London, 1995), and Anthea Callen, *The Art of Impressionism: Painting Technique and the Making of Modernity* (New Haven and London, 2000); see also Callen's, *Techniques of the Impressionists* (London, 1982).

On craft, see Edward Lucie-Smith, *The Story of Craft: the Craftsman's Role in Society* (Oxford, 1981); Peter Dormer, *The Art of the Maker* (London, 1994); Peter Dormer *et al.*, *Arts and Crafts to Avant-garde: Essays on the Crafts from 1880 to the Present* (London, 1992); Peter Dormer, ed., *The Culture of Craft: Status and Future* (Manchester, 1997); Richard Sennett, *The Craftsman* (London, 2008), who addresses myths of making; and Glenn Adamson, ed., *The Craft Reader* (Oxford, 2010), which is extremely wide ranging and a brilliant introduction to the complexities of 'craft' as a concept; it covers the nineteenth century onwards. The *Journal of Modern Craft* (2008 onwards) includes much of historical interest and pays attention to 'practice'. On the Arts and Crafts movement, there is Rosalind Blakesley, *The Arts and Crafts Movement* (London, 2006), and Anthea Callen, *Angel in the Studio: Women in the Arts and Crafts Movement, 1870–1914* (London, 1979). On Tiffany, see Martin Eidelberg *et al.*, *The Lamps of*

Louis Comfort Tiffany (London, 2005). For dragonfly lamps, see pp. 34–5, 64–5 and 186–98.

On practice in the history of science broadly defined there is Simon Schaffer and Steven Shapin, *Leviathan and the Air Pump: Hobbes, Boyle and the Experimental Life* (Princeton, 1985); Pamela Smith, *The Body of the Artisan: Art and Experience in the Scientific Revolution* (Chicago and London, 2004); and Celina Fox, *The Arts of Industry in the Age of Enlightenment* (New Haven, 2009). Fox is in fact an art historian who is working with recent trends in the histories of science and technology in compelling ways. Her book speaks eloquently to many of the themes of this chapter. Anthropological insights can also be useful, for example, Cristine Grasseni, ed., *Skilled Visions: Between Apprenticeship and Standards* (Oxford, 2007).

In addition to Raymond Williams's *Keywords*, there is also Tony Bennett *et al.*, eds., *New Keywords: a Revised Vocabulary of Culture and Society* (Malden, MA, 2005), see also the reference works on concepts listed on pp. 234–5.

On artisans, an excellent introduction is James Farr, *Artisans in Europe, 1300–1914* (Cambridge, 2000); see also Geoffrey Crossick, ed., *The Artisan and the European Town, 1500–1900* (Aldershot, 1997); and Francesco Filangeri, *Artigianni* (Rome, 2010) (texts in English and Italian).

On work more generally, see Patrick Joyce, ed., *The Historical Meanings of Work* (Cambridge, 1987); Jan Lucassen, *Global Labour History: a State of the Art* (Bern and Oxford, 2006); Richard Donkin, *The History of Work* (Basingstoke, 2010); William Sewell, *Work and Revolution in France: the Language of Labor from the Old Regime to 1848* (Cambridge, 1980). And specifically on hatters, Michael Sonenscher's *The Hatters of Eighteenth Century France* (Berkeley, 1987), gives a wonderfully rich sense of a trade. See also the journal *Labour History* (2003 onwards). For the theme of work in art, there is T. J. Barringer, *Men at Work: Art and Labour in Victorian Britain* (New Haven and London, 2005). Giles Waterfield, *The Artist's Studio* (London, 2009), contains many relevant examples of artists in their working environments.

On 'genius', there is Penelope Murray, ed., *Genius: the History of an Idea* (Oxford, 1989); David Cropley *et al.*, eds., *The Dark Side of Creativity* (Cambridge, 2010); and Rudolf and Margaret Wittkower, *Born Under Saturn: the Character and Conduct of Artists* (London, 1963).

On design, a good place to start is John Heskett, *Design: a Very Short Introduction* (Oxford, 2005); see also the *Journal of Design History* (1988 onwards) and *Design and Culture* (2009 onwards); David Pye, *The Nature and Aesthetics of Design* (London, 1978); Penny Sparke, *An Introduction to Design and Culture in the Twentieth Century* (London, 1986); and Kjeitil Fallan, *Design History: Understanding Theory and Method* (Oxford, 2010), which is especially relevant and is itself designed in a particularly interesting manner. Patrick Cramsie, *The Story of Graphic Design: From the Invention of Writing to the Birth of Digital Design* (London, 2010), chs. 6–10, is excellent.

The plates to the *Encyclopédie* are well known, but William Sewell's thoughtful article puts them in a fresh context: 'Visions of Labour: Illustrations of the Mechanical Arts before, in and after Diderot's *Encyclopédie*', in *Work in France: Representations, Meaning, Organization, and Practice*, ed. Steven Kaplan and C. Koepp (Ithaca, 1986), pp. 258–86. Geraldine Sheridan, *Louder than Words: Ways of Seeing Women Workers in Eighteenth-Century France* (Lubbock, TX, 2009) draws heavily upon the *Encyclopédie*. Her article 'Recording Technology in France: the *Description des Arts*, Methodological Innovation and Lost Opportunities at the Turn of the Eighteenth Century', *Cultural and Social History*, 5 (2008), pp. 329–54, contains wonderful material on images of artisanal activities, drawing practices and collaboration. See also *Technology and Culture* (1959 onwards).

Laurel Thatcher Ulrich's *The Age of Homespun: Objects and Stories in the Creation of an American Myth* (New York, 2001), which discussed objects made in the home, has been enormously influential. See also Mary Beaudry, *Findings: the Material Culture of Needlework and Sewing* (New Haven and London, 2006).

On the myriad processes surrounding books, see Mirjam Foot, *Bookbinders at Work: their Roles and Methods* (London, 2006); Simon Eliot and Jonathan Rose, eds., *A Companion to the History of the Book* (Malden, MA, and Oxford, 2007); James Raven, *The Business of Books: Booksellers and the English Booktrade, 1450–1850* (New Haven and London, 2007); Marjorie Plant, *The English Book Trade: an Economic History of the Making and Sale of Books* (London, 1939 and subsequent editions); Alan Bartram, *Making Books: Design in British Publishing Since 1945* (London and New Castle, DE, 1999); Sigfrid Steinberg, *Five Hundred Years of Printing*, rev. edn (London and New Castle, DE, 1996); Geoffrey Glasiter, *Encyclopedia of the Book*, 2nd rev. edn (London and New Castle, DE, 2001).

On hats, see Penelope Corfield, 'Dress for Deference and Dissent: Hats and the Decline of Hat Honour', *Costume*, 23 (1989), pp. 64–79; this is a lively piece that touches on many themes in this book.

On Winsor and Newton, see the entry in the *British Artists' Suppliers, 1650–1950*, 2nd edn, by Jacob Simon, which may be found on the website on the National Portrait Gallery, London. It also summarises Watts's relations with the firm. On Watts himself, see Veronica Gould, *G. F. Watts: the Last Great Victorian* (New Haven and London, 2004).

The activities of the working group Art Technological Source Research (ICOM-CC) is relevant to this chapter and may be followed on their website, which also contains short essays. On conservation, the *National Gallery Technical Bulletin* (1977 onwards) is illuminating and many volumes are now available online. A number of major galleries operate conservation studios and publish in this area. Starting with their websites is best.

Finally, I recommend Danny Gregory, *An Illustrated Life: Drawing Inspiration from the Private Sketchbooks of Artists, Illustrators and Designers* (Cincinnati and Newton Abbott, 2008), which brilliantly illustrates visual practices through 'illustrated journaling', which, he argues, allows 'you [to] see ideas unfold and deepen' and to appreciate how 'by the simple act of drawing' people can see 'their world for the first time by sketching it on a page' (pp. 1 and 3).

Bridge

In the following essay we examine a medium – sculpture – where scholars have demonstrated these points particularly effectively, and consider Gian Lorenzo Bernini, about whose working processes a certain amount is indeed known. He was the recipient of forms of patronage that have left traces; he was so renowned in his lifetime that accounts of his activities have remained, and he operated a workshop with assistants, for whom he made terracotta models, known as *bozzetti*, to help them carve in just the way he wanted. Some of these fragile objects have survived. Bernini was a fine draughtsman and painter as well as an architect, writer and theatre designer. He also sketched out ideas on paper. Bernini mediated contemporary cultural currents in a manner that, while it has not always found aesthetic favour, was both moving and intellectually acute.

ESSAY

'The Jewel of the Church': Bernini's *Ecstasy of St Teresa*

Introduction: a church in Rome

XIII Santa Maria della Vittoria was built between 1608 and 1620 by Carlo Maderno. Its best-known feature is a statue by Gian Lorenzo Bernini depicting the mystic Teresa of Avila, life size and resting on a bank of clouds with an angel holding a golden dart smiling down upon her. This extraordinary piece of sculpture is located in a chapel dedicated to the Cornaro family. An established tourist attraction in Rome, it, like the entire church, is taken to epitomise the baroque style with which Bernini was so closely associated. The settings, chapel and church, the maker, the patron, the subject matter, the style, and the figures themselves, all invite historical attention, and are productively seen as an ensemble.

According to a popular guidebook, the church's interior is 'almost shockingly excessive to modern eyes, its ceiling and walls are pitted with carving, and statues crammed into remote corners as in an over-stuffed attic'. It describes the chapel in which Bernini's work is located as sepulchral:

> [it] continues the histrionics: a deliberately melodramatic work, it features a theatrically posed St Teresa of Avila against a backdrop of theatre-boxes on each side of the chapel, from which the Cornaro cardinals murmur and nudge each other as they watch the spectacle … Bernini records the moment when, in 1537, she had a vision of an angel piercing her heart with a dart. It is a very Baroque piece of work in the most populist sense: not only is the event quite literally staged, but St Teresa's ecstasy verges on the worldly as she lays [*sic*] back in groaning submission beneath a mass of dishevelled garments and drapery.[1]

Both the setting and the central figures are indeed dramatic. **23** This is one of Bernini's most celebrated works; it is widely considered to be his finest religious image. Teresa and her angel have been photographed frequently, and hence aspects of the sculpture are familiar to wide audiences, yet all too often it is divorced from its context of chapel, church and patron. It is difficult to capture the whole chapel in a single photographic shot, and postcards sometimes eliminate any trace of the immediate setting in which St Teresa is located.

23 Photograph of Bernini's statue of Teresa and the angel, in the Cornaro Chapel, Santa Maria della Vittoria, Rome, by Francesco Filangeri, 2011. To get a sense of how these figures fit into the chapel as a whole, compare this image with **XV**, using the candlesticks and cross as reference points.

Her position inside a chapel, named for its patron Federico Cornaro, which is in turn located inside a church with a particular history, is worth stressing.

Santa Maria della Vittoria owes its name to an image of the Virgin with her child and three other figures, worn around the neck of a Catholic army chaplain during the Battle of the White Mountain on 8 November 1620. The success of his side was attributed to the miraculous image, which had previously been damaged. Of the five figures depicted, all apart from the Christ child have lost their eyes. After it entered the church in 1622, the name Santa Maria della Vittoria was used following a rededication service. The chaplain in question was a Discalced Carmelite, the order founded by Teresa of Avila. The church is not large but possesses many small chapels: the patronage of one was acquired by the Venetian Cardinal Federico Cornaro in 1647. Bernini designed the chapel, unveiled in 1652, as an integral whole, although much of the work was executed by others. Opposite the Cornaro Chapel is one dedicated to St Joseph, which also features a recumbent saint with an angel, sculpted by Domenico Guidi and inspired by St Teresa across the aisle. The bearded sleeping saint is having a dream when an angel appears to him; he is shown with glorious golden rays behind him, and rich marble surrounds him. According to its own guidebook, 'this church constitutes one of the most representative monuments of the Baroque style'.[2]

The relationships between church, chapel, St Teresa's life and the sculpture are, chronologically speaking, tight. Less than half a century separates the initiation of the whole building and the completion of the Cornaro Chapel. In 1608, when building on the church started, Bernini, then aged ten, had been living in Rome for three years, and was well acquainted with his father's sculpture workshop and its activities. The woman he depicted had died in 1582, was beatified in 1614, and canonised in 1622 by Gregory XV, whom Bernini knew and portrayed.[3] Thus Teresa was 'present', and in multiple ways, in Bernini's world. Her presence was, however, complex and contentious – this was a woman whose life was marked by struggle. Female mystical experience was hardly uncontroversial in post-Tridentine Rome; what such women saw and whether their visions were authentically divine was subjected to close critical scrutiny.

The saint

Teresa of Avila was born in 1515 and became one of the Catholic Church's most famous mystics. She continues to have an exceptional presence in Christian communities as internet searches immediately reveal. Look in library catalogues and numerous works associated with her come up. In her own lifetime, she was well known and provoked much debate; she was a formidable administrator as well as a prolific writer. Teresa was a reformer who wanted to change the nature of her order, re-endow it with simplicity and religious focus, turn nuns away from worldly matters and frequent contact with their families, embrace poverty, and develop fresh approaches to prayer and meditation, which stressed inner, mental processes requiring considerable discipline. While she gained support from those who were interested in the ideas of Catholic renewal, she also encountered opposition, for example, to the austerities she advocated.[4]

The scene that Bernini depicted comes from her *Life*, written between 1562 and 1565, but not published until the first edition of her complete works in 1588. One of many later editions appeared in Naples in 1604, when the Bernini family was still living there. Teresa's life was active as well as meditative, and the powerful accounts of her spiritual experiences were specifically written at the behest of her confessors precisely because her claims were controversial. Thus the context in which her visions were recorded was quite specific – the product of a striking meticulousness, which resulted in an account of her spiritual life that was as accurate as she could make it in order to meet the scepticism and hostility she encountered. She was attentive to broader discussions within the church about the nature of religious experience, discussions that could hardly have been more highly charged politically, emotionally and diplomatically. Teresa was an astute writer. An example of her precision comes in *Spiritual Relations*, written after the *Life*, and in some ways a continuation of it. In Relation V, from 1576, she explains:

> Rapture and suspension of the faculties, in my opinion, are one and the same thing ... The difference between it and rapture is that rapture lasts longer and is more readily perceptible from without, for little by little breathing diminishes, so that the subject cannot speak or open the eyes ... When rapture is deep ... the hands become as cold as ice and sometimes remain stretched out as though they were made of wood ... If rapture lasts, the nerves, too, are affected.[5]

Although she is primarily concerned in her writings with her experience of God's presence, she acknowledges what can be seen 'from without', while dreading, she confesses, being observed in the grip of ecstasy.

According to her editor and translator, the visions to which Bernini makes reference occurred in the 1560s.[6] Teresa's descriptions are vivid and physical – arrows thrust into entrails, the soul wounded and in pain, the feeling of being burned up by fire. The statue looks rather tame by comparison. Commentators on the statue customarily cite a particular passage, which I provide here in full.[7]

> It pleased the Lord that I should sometimes see the following vision. I would see beside me, on my left hand, an angel in bodily form – a type of vision which I am not in the habit of seeing, except very rarely. Though I often see representations of angels, my visions of them are of the type which I first mentioned. It pleased the Lord that I should see this angel in the following way. He was not tall, but short, and very beautiful, his face so aflame that he appeared to be one of the highest types of angel who seem to be all afire. They must be those who are called cherubim: they do not tell me their names but I am well aware that there is a great difference between certain angels and others, and between these and others still, of a kind that I could not possibly explain. In his hands I saw a long golden spear and at the end of the iron tip I seemed to see a point of fire. With this he seemed to pierce my heart several times so that it penetrated to my entrails. When he drew it out, I thought he was drawing them out with it and he left me completely afire with a great love for God. The pain was so sharp that it made me utter several moans; and so excessive was

the sweetness caused me by this intense pain that one can never wish to lose it, nor will one's soul be content with anything less than God. It is not bodily pain, but spiritual, though the body has a share in it – indeed, a great share. So sweet are the colloquies of love which pass between the soul and God that if anyone thinks I am lying I beseech God, in His goodness, to give him the same experience.[8]

Teresa visualises the angel with precision – he is short rather than tall. She describes her experiences so vividly that an artist such as Bernini could visualise them in turn. To be exact, Bernini revisualised them in the medium of stone, mediating them for his patron and for others using the church.

By 1647, when Cornaro took up the task of decorating the chapel, Teresa had been a saint for twenty-five years, having been canonised at the same time as Ignatius of Loyola, in whom Bernini had a particular interest, and whose spiritual exercises were widely employed. Her works had been published in a number of editions and countries; her order, the Discalced (reformed) Carmelites, was established in 1593, and thereafter spread rapidly, eventually all over the world. Images of Teresa proliferated with her order; most, however, were not taken from life, so it would be a mistake to understand Bernini's statue as a *portrait* of the saint.[9] Other artists, for example Peter Paul Rubens, also depicted her, enabling historians to consider the ways in which Teresa was imagined and reimagined – her visual afterlife is a rich historical subject in its own right. **XIV**

The patron

Federico Cornaro came from an ecclesiastical dynasty: he was ambitious, a wily diplomat, in every sense a prince of the church. The most comprehensive account of him and his art patronage, by William Barcham, refers to his 'careerism', his strategic approach to his life, and emphasises his strong desire to be elected to the papacy. This never happened, although there is evidence the possibility was discussed by others – perhaps Federico's patronage of the chapel was motivated by this ambition.[10] Cornaro had made his way in the church as an administrator, rather than as a theologian or a moral leader; indeed, he was weak on the pastoral side. He possessed, however, an exceptionally strong sense of his family's legacy and position. On each side of the chapel is a row of busts, of Cornaro himself, and of high-ranking, deceased members of his family – one doge (his father) and six cardinals. **XV** It is simply wrong to interpret them as looking at Teresa as if in a theatre. Barcham insists none of the figures could have 'seen' the figure of Teresa from the position in which they are placed, and that Bernini would not have been careless on such a matter.[11] His suggestion is that they are discussing church policy and that Bernini had both depictions of the Council of Trent and Venetian group portraits in mind when designing this part of the chapel, which is admittedly hard to interpret.

The Cornaro men are in naturalistic settings, four on either side, behind structures that could be draped pews, with carved columns and ceilings suggesting sumptuous interiors behind them. The figures are not looking at Teresa herself, but praying, talking and reading. One commentator, Howard Hibbard, suggests they are meditating upon Teresa's vision: 'we may even assume that their study and devotion have conjured up the vision'. He continues, 'If this is so, the *Ecstasy of St Teresa* is an artistic re-evocation of an actual event as it is imagined by the Cornaro cardinals who, though all but one were dead, appear before us in the vigour and animation of life'.[12] On this reading, Bernini's work is part of the miracle, whereas on Barcham's the groups are primarily an inventive form of commemoration, but are not, except for Federico and his father, portraits – 'none of the men is individually recognisable'.[13]

When Bernini received this generously funded commission, he was not overwhelmed with jobs, and his reputation had become somewhat fragile owing to a controversy about his architectural work at St Peter's. It is possible that Cornaro and Bernini, both closely involved in the papal court, had known each other for decades. Cornaro had spent the years 1602 to 1623 in Rome, and Bernini was fêted at the papal court while still very young. His biographer Filippo Baldinucci stated that when 'he had scarcely completed his tenth year [the pope] wished to see the youth … Paul V was very anxious that the genius of Giovan Lorenzo, still young and tender, be sustained by an authoritative hand … Therefore, he entrusted Bernini to Cardinal Maffeo Barberini, a great devotee and patron of the noblest arts…'.[14] Although Cornaro was not close to this particular pope, he can hardly have been unaware of Bernini especially since he was devoted to the Barberini family – some of the bees that signified them are present in the chapel. Cornaro had attended the canonisation of Teresa, and was present, near the pope, when Santa Maria della Vittoria was rededicated; as an ambitious priest, he kept his finger on the pulse of developments in the church, including among the Discalced Carmelites, to whom, in fact, he had no particular affinity.[15] In terms of personal spirituality, there is no evidence that Cornaro was drawn either to Teresa herself or to her order; rather, he seems to have been attracted by this particular church and the status it had acquired by virtue of other distinguished cardinals, Gessi and Vidoni, having monuments there. He wished to draw public attention to himself and to his family, and gave Bernini plenty of scope and lavish resources in designing an extraordinary ensemble. The relationship and negotiations between Cornaro and Bernini are not known in detail, but it is plausible that they discussed all aspects of the enterprise, and that nothing was done without a three-way conversation, which included the Discalced Carmelites, who received a magnificent monument to their founder, just as Cornaro memorialised himself and his family in a manner made possible by the exceptional verve and originality of Bernini, who, in turn, benefited from the acclaim the chapel received.

The maker

A child prodigy, Bernini's abilities were early and widely recognised and he received patronage from the highest levels. He served many popes, visited Paris to work for Louis XIV, undertook a commission for Charles I of England and was admired by Queen Christina of Sweden. Bernini exhibited a striking array of talents: he was a writer, painter, architect and theatrical designer as well as a sculptor and draughtsman. **24** He was polymathic and prolific. In his later years, Bernini was also devout. During his months in Paris in 1665, his 'minder', Paul Fréart de Chantelou, kept a diary, which revealed Bernini's spiritual attentiveness, in regular prayers, participation in services and frequently receiving the sacraments. In Rome, he was close to the Jesuits. He was widely read in religious literature and gave drawings of sacred subjects as gifts when he left Paris. By 1647, Bernini had executed many figures of male and female saints, portrayed a number of popes and cardinals, and worked with a range of sacred buildings.

　　In presenting Bernini as the maker or 'author' of the Cornaro Chapel, two further points need to be borne in mind. The son of an artist who ran a workshop, he himself possessed a substantial team. **25** To execute the chapel many trades and numerous individuals were involved. The ceiling painting depicting scenes from Teresa's life, for example, was undertaken by Guido Ubaldo Abbatini, working from a sketch by Bernini; other sculptors besides Bernini received payment for work in the chapel, and stonemasons, silversmiths, carpenters, glaziers and

24 *Giovanni Lorenzo Bernini*, ascribed to Salvator Rosa, 1630–73, pen and brown ink on light brown prepared paper, 22.9 cm high × 17.8 cm wide, British Museum. The drawing is inscribed 'Berninus Pittor, Sculptor, et Architectus'. Rosa was a great favourite among eighteenth-century British collectors. This portrait was bequeathed to the museum by the well-known antiquarian and collector Richard Payne Knight.

25 *The Ecstasy of St Teresa*, by Gian Lorenzo Bernini, terracotta *bozzetto*, 1640s, 47 cms high, Hermitage Museum, St Petersburg, Russia. Bernini made *bozzetti* in terracotta or wax to express his initial ideas and help his assistants. The equivalent of drawings, studies, sketches and architects' models, they reveal the maker's ideas as they develop. They could also be used to indicate to patrons how an expensive, large-scale work was progressing.

metalworkers also worked on it.[16] It would perhaps be most accurate to call Bernini the designer of the chapel, who participated in its execution, and is most closely associated with its central feature. And yet, in a profound sense, the Cornaro Chapel belongs to Bernini: 'Bernini himself used to say that this was the most beautiful work ever to come from his hand', Filippo Baldinucci claimed shortly after Bernini's death.[17] He took elements from Teresa's accounts and imagined them afresh in his own fashion.

His mode of address has hardly been uncontroversial. The popular guidebook mentioned earlier is not alone in considering the figure of

Teresa altogether too 'worldly' for its subject matter; that is to say, her ecstasy could be interpreted as pertaining to the flesh rather than to the soul. I consider it inconceivable that Bernini intended her to be seen as experiencing orgasm. Rather there is an inevitable and understandable overlap of the idioms, verbal and visual, in which intense and passionate religious and sexual love were expressed. The idea of rapturous, loving union between beings is present in her writings; the existence of such shared languages is perfectly plausible.

Given what is known about the artist, as well as about the patron and the church, it could hardly be the case that, at a *conscious* level, the statue contains sexual allusions. I suggest that claims it does actually reveal a concern about Bernini's approach, his 'style', which appears flamboyant, elaborate and highly expressive, manifest as much in the handling of drapery as of Teresa's face and body. In this context we must remember how complex Bernini's legacy has been, how contested his artistic achievements by later generations. This much was clear in Richard Norton's 1914 book. The opening section, 'An Estimate of Bernini', addresses the 'disregard' and 'false judgements' from which the sculptor has suffered – 'His style is said to be extravagant and artificial and his violent material effects are said to show he was unable to express thought.' Norton's defence of the statue of Teresa reveals that comments about its allegedly sexual nature had indeed been made. He insists upon the artistic quality and decorum of the statue, while being critical of the angel, 'with [his] tilted nose and silly smile'.[18]

Bernini's oeuvre, and the religious figures in particular, suggest his responsiveness to prevailing sensibilities. This was part of his job and integral to his success. He designed the entire chapel into which Teresa and the angel were set; now, the figure of Teresa, and especially her face, is frequently presented out of context. Photography and digital techniques can show artefacts in ways that were unavailable in the past. **26** Hence it is all the more vital to turn to the works themselves and consider their original settings.

The spectator

Teresa is high above the person who stands or kneels in front of the chapel, while the angel is more prominent than the saint herself. Most noticeable are the billowing folds of her gown, her bare protruding foot, the cloud on which the figures are placed and the golden rays behind them. The light is particularly striking. Above the figures is an oval window, transparent in the centre, with yellow glass around the perimeter. The light on the statue changes constantly and is dappled

26 Photograph of the statue of Saint Teresa in the Cornaro Chapel, Santa Marie della Vittoria, Rome, by Nina Thune, 2006. This close-up shows the saint's face in a way that is not available to ordinary visitors. There has been much discussion about her facial expression and its interpretation. Compare this image with **XV** and **23**.

on her face. It is possible to pay for a few minutes of artificial light, when the illumination is more even and flatter. In designing the window, Bernini clearly had natural and candle light in mind. Kneel in front of the chapel and you can make out her head, although one fold of drapery obscures her left eye, but you are not looking into her face. Rather, the angel is the active figure, and she is his foil. Holding the arrow in his right hand, he is much higher than her, looming over her, catching the light more easily. In this position the spectator is aware of the images of Cornaro and his family, of the coloured marbles, church furniture and decorated ceiling, but the details of the painted scenes of Teresa's life are not easily visible. The colour of the marble statues is sometimes warm, evocative of amber. In just the time it took to write my notes, the light changed markedly, bringing effects like those that candlelight produces.

Present-day visitors are aware of the visual conversation between Teresa and Joseph in the chapel opposite. They may be equally aware of how difficult it is to re-create past viewing experiences. The window, for example, was damaged in the late eighteenth century – how similar are the hues of the replacement? The oral, aural and olfactory supplements to viewing Teresa and her angel are missing. Even the sense of texture that accompanies the observation, especially of sculpture, is shaped by spectators' own tactile experiences, and hence differs between people and periods. Noting these elements helps call to mind the array of factors that shaped the look of the past. Looking never happens in isolation from other senses, and in a place of Catholic worship in the seventeenth century, speech, music and incense, like bodily movements, were integral to religious experience. Our goal is to pay as close and thoughtful attention as possible to the nature and contexts of past worlds of sight.[19]

The style

It is customary to rely upon style terms to evoke what we might term cultural packages from the past. What is meant by 'baroque', which is inseparable from Bernini, and is increasingly being used by historians? In her recent textbook, Merry Wiesner-Hanks observes that it was used as a term of criticism in the eighteenth century 'to describe art that was exaggerated, emotional, confused, twisted and theatrical', in contrast to classicism. 'Dramatic art would glorify the reformed and reinvigorated Catholic Church, appealing to the senses and proclaiming the power of the church to all who looked at paintings or sculpture or worshipped in churches'.[20] Thus baroque art is linked by Wiesner-Hanks, as by numerous historians, not just to a particular manner and period, but also to an institution – the Roman Catholic Church – and its 'Counter-Reformation' agendas. While 'baroque' is often used as if its meaning were self-evident, those who do attempt to define it generally emphasise a number of key points, such as drama, manifest deep feeling, excess, uninhibited, ostentatious display, and a close association with the aspirations of a renewed Catholic Church and ambitious, absolutist states.

A number of issues arise from the ways in which 'baroque' is used, which come up in relation to other style terms. Four stand out. First, 'baroque' is frequently used to include just about everything in a given era, with the exact chronological boundaries varying from one writer to another. This use risks circularity: phenomena from the period in question are 'baroque' because they come from an era that has already been labelled 'baroque'. In such cases, unspecific assumptions about drama, excess and so on are mobilised. Perhaps we should be more sceptical about whether notions, such as 'the baroque era', are useful, since they appear to promise a particular purchase on an equally particular period, but fail to do so in practice. Arguably, the complexities of the Cornaro Chapel are not illuminated by being called 'baroque'. Second, terms such as 'baroque' are interpreted through the prism of what is generally called 'taste'. 'Baroque' is peculiarly vulnerable to criticism or neglect by those who espouse simplicity as an aesthetic norm. Many writers on Bernini have felt the need to defend their choice of subject matter. Yet on *historical* grounds, that is to say, because of his public role and significant contributions, he needs no special defence. It is inappropriate to express distaste for the manner in which Teresa is displayed or to use 'baroque' as a term of abuse. Third, when 'baroque' is opposed to other styles, such as 'classicism', unfortunate, sometimes false polarities are created. Bernini, for example, was also a classicist, and was seen as such during his lifetime. The espousal of what were understood by actors in the past as ancient aesthetic values was compatible with many styles and not limited to specific eras. It is worth searching for ways of describing and analysing artefacts that eschew the habitual reflexes style terms prompt. They may, at one level, be convenient shorthand, but they can also impede fresh approaches.

Fourth, and most challenging, is the question of causality. Wiesner-Hanks is not alone in presenting 'baroque' art and architecture as an expression of the values of the Catholic Church, a way of proclaiming its power. Such a formulation implies that those values initially arose and were articulated within an institution, whose members disseminated them via their patronage relationships and the commissioning of artists, who, in turn, rearticulated them. On such an account, the Catholic Church was the cause, 'baroque' style the effect. Is it not likely that the relationships were more intertwined, messy and intimate?[21] I am not suggesting that the causality simply be reversed, but rather that the institutional changes and the shifts in the look of visual and material culture were mutually reinforcing, constantly playing off each other over substantial periods of time. 'Conversation' may be a useful concept here. We might think figuratively in terms of close, sustained conversations, of types of cultural exchange where forms of expression arise in a context of mutual interaction. Probably conversations, literally speaking, occurred in the case of the Cornaro Chapel, between makers, patrons and custodians of the building. As the order that presided over the church and the legacy of their founder as represented in it, it is unlikely much was done without their consent.

The dramatic look of Bernini's statue thus prompts further reflection on a number of historical and historiographical questions. How did the reputations and imagery of saints evolve? How did public expressions of spirituality shift over the sixteenth and seventeenth centuries? Which aspects of reformed Catholicism were given visual form and for which audiences? How did ecclesiastical dynasties operate? What sorts of culture did new orders generate? What visual idioms were deemed appropriate for the intense religious experience of women in a context where their spiritual authority was far from assured? Why has Bernini's reputation been so varied and contested? How does taste, in matters of religion as of art, shape scholars' views of the past?

Bernini, himself close to the centre of Catholic power and latterly a profoundly religious man, was, from his childhood, a participant in Roman culture. He helped to shape, rather than passively reflect, religious sensibilities. In the particularities of a given commission, it is possible to discern the array of historical forces at work, to appreciate the range of actors involved and to generate a form of integrated history. Although a well-established topic, the complex roles of images and artefacts in all the reformed churches are only beginning to be understood. Teresa herself was appalled by iconoclasm. According to Bilinkoff, she was a 'lover of religious images and pictures', who was unable to see why those who loved the Lord would not want to look at portraits of him.[22] Yet, since her ecstasies were intensely private, it is difficult to imagine Teresa would have felt at ease with Bernini's representation of her. Furthermore, her emphasis on interiority moved beyond visualisation as a device in prayer. By the middle of the seventeenth century in Rome, Bernini's statues of her and the angel expressed, to general approbation, an interpretation of her that has reached vast audiences and provoked a range of responses among people who have little or no knowledge of her achievements and ideas.[23] The name Cornaro has indeed been kept alive through Bernini's work, but ironically through a controversial evocation of a woman with whom Federico himself had little religious affinity.

NOTES

1 Martin Dunford, *The Rough Guide to Rome* (New York, 2007), p. 131; note that the claim about the date is wrong, while the description of the onlookers is misleading. However, these comments give clear expression to common reactions. Guidebooks vary in the dates they give for the construction of the church; I assume that the church's own guidebook, cited below, is correct. Cf. Anthony Blunt, *Guide to Baroque Rome* (London, 1982), pp. 122–3, and Georgina Masson, *Companion Guide to Rome*, 6th edn (London, 1980), pp. 257–8.

2 *The Church of St Mary of the Victory* (Rome, 2007), p. 5.

3 Filippo Baldinucci, *The Life of Bernini* (University Park, PA, and London, 1966), pp. 14–15 (trans. Catherine Enggass, first published 1688, eight years after Bernini's death).

4 I take the phrase 'Catholic renewal' from R. Po-chia Hsia, *The World of Catholic Renewal, 1540–1770*, 2nd edn (Cambridge, 2005).

5 E. Allison Peers, ed. and trans., *The Complete Works of St Teresa of Avila* (London and New York, 2002; first published 1946), vol. 1, p. 328.

6 *Ibid.*, p. 187.

7 For example, Charles Avery, *Bernini Genius of the Baroque* (London, 1997), p. 144.

8 Peers, *Complete Works*, vol. 1, pp. 192–3.

9 Jodi Bilinkoff, *The Avila of Saint Teresa; Religious Reform in a Sixteenth-century City* (Ithaca, 1989), p. 138, is, presumably, a portrait strictly speaking, as it was made in 1576 when Teresa was still alive. According to the caption it is by Fray Juan de la Miseria. Alison Weber, *Teresa of Avila and the Rhetoric of Femininity* (Princeton, 1990), p. 164, mentions other depictions of her.

10 William Barcham, *Grand in Design: the Life and Career of Federico Cornaro, Prince of the Church, Patriarch of Venice and Patron of the Arts* (Venice, 2001), on the papacy see pp. 380–91; figs. 49–56 concern the chapel.

11 *Ibid.*, p. 368.

12 Howard Hibbard, *Bernini* (Harmondsworth, 1975; first published 1965), p. 130.

13 Barcham, *Grand in Design*, p. 368. For another reading, centred on the Eucharist, see Irving Lavin, *Bernini and the Unity of the Visual Arts*, 2 vols. (New York, 1980), vol. 1, part 2. See also Jennifer Montagu's review in the *Burlington Magazine*, 124 (1982), pp. 240–2, which challenges Lavin's interpretation. Lavin's concern is with Bernini's revolutionary conceptions of the interrelations between art, architecture and sculpture.

14 Baldinucci, *Life*, p. 9. On the Barberini, see Peter Rietbergen, *Power and Religion in Baroque Rome: Barberini Cultural Policies* (Leiden, 2006).

15 Barcham, *Grand in Design*, esp. p. 112.

16 *Ibid.*, ch. 5, marshals all the evidence about the construction of the chapel, including details of payments where known.

17 Baldinucci, *Life*, p. 35.

18 Richard Norton, *Bernini and Other Studies in the History of Art* (London, 1914), contained, for the first time, images of Bernini's *bozzetti*, the small terracotta models that he made, of which only a few have survived, to help him think through his ideas in three dimensions and to guide his assistants. Quotations from pp. 7 and 32. Barcham, *Grand in Design*, fig. 56, shows Bernini's *bozzetto* for the relief on the left wall.

19 This is why photographs from angles that could never have been seen by pedestrians in the church are so misleading. A serious offender is Lavin, *Bernini*, see vol. 1, p. xiii, for an explanation of how the photography was carried out. Scaffolding was used to photograph the statues. In

vol. 2, plates 147–97 relate to the Cornaro Chapel. Plate 167, for example, is mounted on the page, portrait style, so that the viewer is looking at Teresa's (vertical) face.

20 Merry Wiesner-Hanks, *Early Modern Europe, 1450–1798* (Cambridge, 2006), p. 352.

21 O'Malley raises such questions in David Luebke, ed., *The Counter-Reformation: the Essential Readings* (Oxford, 1999), p. 75.

22 Bilinkoff, *Avila*, p. 75.

23 k r buxey, *Requiem* (2002), a thirty-nine-minute video of the artist experiencing orgasm, showing only her head, perhaps suggests the impact of Bernini's work.

FURTHER READING

Guidebooks to Rome are one place to start, and the Cornaro Chapel is generally discussed. The church has its own guidebook in English.

On Rome in the period, see Peter Rietbergen, *Power and Religion in Baroque Rome: Barberini Cultural Politics* (Leiden, 2006). The book is not illustrated, however. He discusses the concept 'baroque' and argues for it being seen as 'the culture that was the expression of life in European society in the decades following the Council of Trent' (pp. 11–12).

On the patron, William Barcham, *Grand in Design: the Life and Career of Federico Cornaro, Prince of the Church, Patriarch of Venice and Patron of the Arts* (Venice, 2001), is comprehensive.

Baroque is a vexed notion. For a basic introduction, see Flavio Conti, *How to Recognise Baroque Style* (London, 1978), who presents Bernini as 'one of the main creators and exponents of Roman Baroque' (p. 11). See also José Antonio Maravall, *Culture of the Baroque: Analysis of a Historical Structure* (Manchester, 1986; first published in Spanish in 1975); Erwin Panofsky, *Three Essays on Style* (Cambridge, MA, 1995), contains 'What is Baroque?'; Aidan Weston-Lewis, *Effigies and Ecstasies: Roman Baroque Sculpture and Design in the Age of Bernini* (Edinburgh, 1998); and Helen Hills, ed., *Rethinking the Baroque* (Farnham, 2011), which is extremely wide ranging, especially in its engagement with theoretical issues. See also Rémy Saisselin, *The Enlightenment against the Baroque: Economics and Aesthetics in the Eighteenth Century* (Berkeley, Los Angeles and Oxford, 1992).

An example of the use of 'baroque' in a new context is Brian Nance, *Turquet de Mayerne as Baroque Physician: the Art of Medical Portraiture* (Amsterdam, 2001); Turquet's dates are 1573–1654/5. It is more common to find it associated with a period as in Marc Foster, *Catholic Revival in the Age of the Baroque: Religious Identity in Southwest Germany, 1550–1750* (Cambridge, 2001); cf. Lyndal Roper, *Witch Craze: Terror and Fantasy in Baroque Germany* (New Haven, 2004).

The secondary literature on Bernini is vast, but the following represent a range of approaches: Richard Norton, *Bernini and Other Stories in the History of Art* (London, 1914); Irving Lavin, ed., *Gianlozenzo Bernini: New Aspects of his Life and Thought* (University Park, PA, 1985); Rudolf Wittkower, *Gian Lorenzo Bernini: the Sculptor of the Roman Baroque*, 4th edn (Oxford, 1997); Charles Avery, *Bernini: Genius of the Baroque* (London, 1997); Maarten Delbeke, Evonne Levy and Steven F. Ostrow, eds., *Bernini's Biographies: Critical Essays* (Philadelphia, 2006); Andrea Bacchi, Catherine Hess and Jennifer Montagu, eds., *Bernini and the Birth of Baroque Portrait Sculpture* (Los Angeles, 2008).

There is also a huge body of work on Teresa, some of it by devotees: for example, Shirley du Boulay, *Teresa of Avila: an Extraordinary Life* (London, 2004); Rowan Williams, *Teresa of Avila* (London, 1991), is a useful introduction from a theological perspective; Robert Petersson, *The Art of Ecstasy: Teresa, Bernini and Crashaw* (London, 1970), which adopts a comparative literature approach; Jodi Bilinkoff, *The Avila of Saint Teresa: Religious Reform in a Sixteenth-century City* (Ithaca, 1989); and Alison Weber, *Teresa of Avila and the Rhetoric of Femininity* (Princeton, 1990), for an analysis of the complexities of her writings and the controversies they prompted from a gendered perspective.

On images of Teresa there is Jean de la Croix, 'L'iconographie de Thérèse de Jésus Docteur de l'Eglise', *Ephemerides Carmeliticae*, 21 (1970), pp. 219–60, which provides seventy-nine plates. On Rubens's depictions of her, see Hans Vlieghe, *Saints II* (New York and London, 1973), pp. 163–8. The painting in the Fitzwilliam Museum is discussed on pp. 163–4. This volume is part of the series Corpus Rubenianum Ludwig Burchard.

The broader historical issues alluded to in the essay have been extensively debated by historians. See, for example, David Luebke, ed., *The Counter-Reformation: the Essential Readings* (Oxford, 1999); John O'Malley, *Trent and All That: Renaming Catholicism in the Early Modern Era* (Cambridge, MA, and London, 2000); A. D. Wright, *The Counter-Reformation: Catholic Europe and the Non-Christian World* (Aldershot, 2005; first published 1982), see the Preface to the revised edition, ch. 7, Conclusion and Revised Bibliography; and R. Po-chia Hsia, *The World of Catholic Renewal, 1540–1770*, 2nd edn (Cambridge, 2005), which are, in their different ways, effective introductions to the much-debated phenomenon of the 'Counter-Reformation'.

Also relevant are Simon Ditchfield, 'Of Dancing Cardinals and Mestizo Madonnas: Reconfiguring the History of Roman Catholicism in the Early Modern Period', *Journal of Early Modern History*, 8 (2004), pp. 386–408, and 'Thinking with the Saints: Sanctity and Society in the Early Modern World', *Critical Inquiry*, 35 (2009), pp. 552–84 (part of a special issue on saints); and Stuart Clark, *Vanities of the Eye: Vision in Early Modern Europe Culture* (Oxford, 2006), esp. ch. 6 'Apparitions: the Discernments of Spirits', on Teresa, see p. 223.

Bridge

My discussion of baroque style leads directly into the next chapter, which concerns periodisation. Although recognised as exceptional, Bernini and his work are taken to typify a time, as so many makers and artefacts have been. Chapter 3 examines the dense, sometimes tangled relationships between the appearances of things and the times in which they were produced, and reflects upon the ways in which they are conceptualised, for example, through the notion of 'style'.

3   Periodisation

Introduction: a feel for the past?

The word 'periodisation' refers to a set of processes without which history as a discipline could not function. Through them the past is divided up and named, ideally in a meaningful manner. Assumptions about continuities and shifts are, often tacitly, incorporated into historical language. Thus, periodisation furnishes historians with ideas about periods, their characteristic qualities and possible modes of explanation. It also speaks to the nature of historical change and involves reflection, however implicitly, upon time. This definition of the term gives priority to the work of contemporary professional historians, yet distinctions between eras were made in the past too. Hence periodisation is a long-established phenomenon. Names were used to separate one age from another, and terms coined to point up differences and similarities between one time and another. Some historical actors experienced an intense awareness of the particular features of their own times and both attraction and repulsion for earlier, different times. Thus 'periodisation' comprises a number of operations, experiences and beliefs, some more explicit than others. Objects and images are integral to processes of periodisation. So how do visual and material culture, used in a self-aware manner, help historians think about the constellation of issues subsumed under this term? Might artefacts assist in fresh thinking about change and its conceptualisation and offer new insights into the ways periods were experienced in the past?

This chapter examines several facets of periodisation, discussing its deployment, for example, in art history through the notion of style, and in the work of Michael Baxandall, who wrote of a 'period eye'. We consider which analytical terms are likely to be of most use in the practice of history. Period specificity, historians' approaches to writing about and analysing the links between objects and eras, and the challenge of explaining change are also discussed. It is possible to use things in order to think about a period and to use a period as the context through which to interpret artefacts, although we need to avoid circularity in the process. Taking the consciousness of periods that existed in the past, together with a range of objects made and used at a given moment, sheds light on an era. Historical research aims to make coherent connections between phenomena in the past. Exceptionally high levels of academic specialisation can militate against this because contemporaneous artefacts tend to be categorised and set apart from one another, and studied separately – furniture from dress, porcelain from silver, medals from portraits. Reunited, artefacts can generate a more holistic sense of a period.

Objects and images are commonly used to generate period 'feel', without a scrupulous analysis of how they shed light upon the characteristics of the time in question. We recognise that a reconstructed room, shop or street gives visitors a sense of period, but it is harder to see exactly how its contents bear upon historical understanding. **XVI** Period 'feel' resembles both historical 'background' and the use of illustrations primarily as decoration, in that the precise role of artefacts in comprehending an era is under-conceptualised. Yet there is more to period 'feel' than this. A careful look at the spectrum of artefacts produced at a given time can prompt a number of questions. What attitudes, values and patterns of production and consumption do they suggest? What sensibilities, knowledge and practices do they presuppose? What kind of historical account makes sense of their range, in terms of style, materials, scale, craftsmanship and content? How are these artefacts connected with other aspects of their originating society? Since it can be difficult to verbalise our responses to objects, speaking of a period 'feel' may be the closest it is sometimes possible to get to the contribution non-written sources make. This 'feel' depends on historians engaging with as wide an array of items as possible, which is why museums and galleries, churches and cathedrals, indeed all historic buildings, have the potential to play a generative role in the practice of history, provided we bring a critical framework to them. 'Feel' can feed historians' imaginations and prompt analysis.

Given the centrality of periodisation for historical practice, it should follow that historians spend time reflecting critically upon it. Many clearly do, and important revisionist work frequently argues for new chronologies, reveals the inadequacies of prevailing assumptions about when periods begin and end, and considers how specific periods, and change more generally, are best conceptualised and documented. At the same time, we operate with conventionalised and institutionalised ideas on these matters, especially when teaching. It is worth asking who generates ideas about periods, how they work and what nurtures a strong and widespread sense of their defining features?

Periods and public culture

People commonly say that they *like* some periods while finding little appeal in others. When someone is drawn to, or repulsed by, an era in this way, the issues are rarely purely intellectual. Rather, periods touch those who engage with them, partly through strong historical characters, dramatic events or the literature of the time. Attraction always has an aesthetic component, and the appeal of chunks of the past is no exception. It would be surprising if artefacts and the sense of sight did not play their part. Hence it is worth reflecting upon these matters and feeding the resulting insights back into historical practice. Thinking about public culture is one way of doing so.

Many forms of public culture encourage us to see artefacts as signs of their times. Museums and galleries, films and television, the internet and widely read publications generate and disseminate popular ideas about past times through their uses of images and objects. While the media do not invent the names for periods or their major characteristics, they circulate and promote them, keeping them before the public eye. Since all these forms of culture need support and resources, they tend to trade on easily recognisable terms and ideas about periods. There is constant interaction between consumer goods, such as clothing, furniture and household accoutrements, and widely held sentiments about historical periods. Cultural institutions reinforce these trends through the display and sale of items that are readily associated with specific eras. Successful television series, films and exhibitions spawn related consumables, and those who purchase them recognise their affinities with the period in question. Hairstyles, jewellery and book design function similarly. The processes whereby a thing and a period become associated for viewers are hardly fully conscious: they involve associations, made by eye and brain, which result from established visual habits. Thus in everyday life, most people, largely unawares, deploy skills that allow them to connect artefacts with certain periods. Through visual and material culture, periodisation – an abstract matter for historians – is present in quotidian existence, such as home decoration.

Working historically with objects and images depends upon specialised visual habits that assess artefacts in terms of periods, places them in their originating times, and recognises subsequent appropriations. Historians seek and pay attention to signs of period specificity. The broad public culture in which we operate helps to shape the presuppositions about periods held by professionals, students and general audiences. Bringing such matters up for conscious, critical attention brings with it the need for a distinctive type of focus on artefacts. It is precisely because there are no clear boundaries between a diffused sense of periods that invade a given culture, and the ways in which historians approach the question of periodisation, that it helps to be meticulous, reflective and self-aware. Historians, like everyone else, are subject to the imaginative tugs, aesthetic drives and emotional preferences, which manifest themselves in reactions to objects and images, especially in contexts that are supercharged with consumables referring to past times. In producing and disseminating ideas about periodisation, the roles of public history, the media, business and industry need to be borne in mind. Educational institutions operate with assumptions about periods that are also shaped by political imperatives. Curricula and textbooks not only reinforce images of specific times, but also affect which are deemed the most significant. In all these processes, visual dimensions are operating.

Whether in public culture or in more specialised contexts, artefacts are taken to carry and express their times in their appearance, hence it is worth considering how links between periods and objects work. Many disciplines, such as art history, with its sustained engagement with the concept of style, grapple with this issue. There are diverse ways of studying and conceptualising such links. Our environment trades on their existence, providing the setting in which we deploy forms of periodisation, while experiencing it in myriad ways.

Periods and objects

The links between artefacts and periods are present in historical practice in a number of forms. Historians might start with a specific period and examine its diverse material manifestations. Thus, when thinking about colonial America – that is, the Thirteen Colonies between 1607 and 1776 – it is possible to turn to dress, portraiture, furniture and architecture as material manifestations of that era. To gain some historical advantage by doing so, it is necessary to provide an account of them and explain their characteristics in terms of other features of that society, such as the availability of materials, skills and markets, religious beliefs and practices, and attitudes towards European culture. Plain, austere forms and designs have been linked to certain kinds of religion, such as the Shakers, whose furniture, produced from the late eighteenth century onwards, remains

27 Photograph of original Shaker wooden furniture in a dining room of Hancock Shaker Village, Pittsfield, Massachusetts, by David Lyons, 2001. Shaker furniture is famous for its simple clean lines and thoughtful, functional designs, which express and reinforce the sect's spiritual values and way of life, the rejection of ornament, and the beauty of the wood. Although the Shaker movement developed in the United States in the later eighteenth century, most of the surviving pieces were made somewhat later. It is still possible to buy books of Shaker designs for woodworkers to copy. A single small community has survived, while the visual style associated with Shakers is recognised worldwide. This photograph evokes the visual economy of their furniture.

a byword for simple, unpretentious elegance. **27** Sometimes austerity is associated somewhat more broadly with 'Puritanism', on the grounds that its alleged core beliefs, such as hostility to imagery and showiness, shaped the look of what was made, allowing it to become a sign of an era. In practice matters were never so simple – Oliver Cromwell, the seventeenth-century political leader who espoused a style of Puritanism, loved 'high' art, for example. This type of argument, in which visible traits are linked to a period through values and beliefs of which they are supposedly an expression, is common enough. It relies on matching a given feature with some other element known to exist at the time artefacts were made, and gathers plausibility as further examples accumulate and links are demonstrated in greater detail.

In an analytically distinct move, historians can start with a range of objects to build up a richer picture of a given period. However, these will not necessarily look similar, a point that reminds us that different styles and visual modes co-exist. This approach to visual and material culture can be extremely generative, for example, in thinking about the ways in which ideas are expressed in different media; it is especially effective when used in conjunction with big themes. Attitudes towards death are a case in point. **28** Written sources certainly exist, but artefacts related to death are plentiful, diverse and eloquent – mourning dress and jewellery, funerary accoutrements, *memento mori*, monuments and headstones, for example. Likewise in gender history, since so many artefacts are gendered, it is worth considering as wide a range as possible of visual and material manifestations of femininity and masculinity. The gendered nature of work can usefully be considered in relation to the gendered nature of dress at a given time, for instance. In such cases the patterns and associations may be complex, but they are worth pursuing, for example, in order to test claims about periods by using fresh categories of sources. Looking across distinct types of contemporaneous evidence helps historians both to build up a fuller picture of a specific period and to track and conceptualise change.

When objects seem striking, unusual or puzzling, they prompt questions about how to explain them. The lifelike wax anatomical models produced in later seventeenth- and eighteenth-century Italy are intriguing examples. The vogue for objects in wax was highly specific historically. Although crude waxes went on being used in popular peepshows, and Madame Tussaud's continues to this day, the role of wax in high culture is relatively limited by period. Possibly this phenomenon appears more marked than it actually was due to poor survival rates given the fragility of the material, but there is good reason to suppose that the luxurious models coveted by elites, like the gruesome wax scenes of death and dying, were only made for a restricted period. **XVII** Why did wax models appeal to the privileged? The vogue for some wax models has been presented in terms of the need for practical substitutes for cadavers

28 *Lydia Dwight*, by John Dwight's Fulham Pottery, 1674, grey stoneware, hand-modelled and salt-glazed, 25.5 cm high × 20.5 cm wide, Victoria and Albert Museum, London. Lydia Dwight was six when she died, and this piece was commissioned by her father, who was not himself a modeller, but someone who was interested in developing materials and in running a business. It is not known precisely how this piece was intended to be used; any kind of formal display seems unlikely. The date of her death is inscribed on the figure and it is evidently intended to memorialise her. It invites historians to reflect upon ways in which it might be interpreted.

in anatomy teaching, which explains neither their collectability nor the astounding efforts to make them beautiful. How in such cases might artefact and era be linked convincingly, and might the answers suggest the need to reappraise other phenomena, such as 'realism', attitudes to the body and disease, and the nature of medical education?

Another type of starting point for historical research is relevant here. It is possible to begin with phenomena, rather than with objects or periods. Cross-dressing, the cultures of sport, heroism, and the cult of motherhood, are all good examples, where, by paying close attention to visual and material culture, questions of periodisation can be focused more precisely. In these cases the visual component is evident – the roles of medals and portraits in sport, for instance. Arguably all historical phenomena possess such dimensions, hence rethinking issues of periodisation using visual and material evidence could well be constructive more generally.

For connoisseurs, curators, dealers and collectors, the precise dating of objects is crucial. This is partly a matter of monetary value, and partly of establishing as accurately as possible what the item in question actually is. Highly specialised skills are involved, which depend upon making secure links between what is seen and touched, and the date of production. These skills hinge on experts knowing and remembering characteristics, such as shape and colour, the manner in which details are represented, the nature of the materials, including types of paper, tools, paint and so on. It is rare to come across an artefact so decontextualised and lacking in clues that nothing hints at its origins. Even in an archaeological context where evidence can be sparse, the materials and shapes, as well as location, if known, help with dating. Materials and medium, genre, colours and contours, scale and subject matter offer clues about the period in which a given object was made. Sepia photographs, sculptures made from plastic, video installations, and watercolours of market scenes, apparently do so. However, present-day photographs can be made to look 'Victorian', and watercolours may require close attention to dress and watermarks on paper, to be dated with precision.

The need for accurate dating is connected with concerns about authenticity. When dates and makers are reliably established, for which provenance, if known, is central, the object has been 'authenticated'. Authenticity – a complex idea – is prized for both economic and scholarly reasons. Attributions change, and misattributions abound. Fakes – objects made in one period to deceive viewers into believing they originated in another – abound. Techniques for dating materials exist, while methods of making leave discernible marks. It should be possible to distinguish between a man-made and a machine-made product, for instance from tool-marks, hence an understanding of implements and equipment is worthwhile. Frames, pedestals and other mountings also provide clues. Nonetheless, the overall look of something remains a major consideration when linking artefacts and periods. Period detail may be found in hairstyles or body shapes. When the human figure is represented, period effects are especially prominent because the types of costume, and of overall shape, are chronologically specific. The content of an artefact bears testimony to its moment of production, as do its formal properties, the methods and techniques and the manner of its making. It is significant that, viewed in hindsight, fakes and pastiches often betray themselves by inadvertently revealing the actual period in which they were made.

Style

The concept of 'style', which is notoriously hard to define, offers one way of analysing the overall look of something. 'A system of signs used to embrace meaning', according to one reference book, it is 'a distinctive, recognisable pattern or form' for another.[1] Susan Sontag wrote, 'to speak of style is one way of speaking about the totality of a work of art', adding, 'like all discourse about totalities, talk of style must rely on metaphors. And metaphors mislead.'[2] Her comments should not distract us from the central point that periodisation, like style, relies on metaphor, which may indeed 'mislead', but is nonetheless indispensable.

Jas Elsner, an art historian, tackled the matter rather differently: 'the basic stylistic reflex', he suggested, 'is the grouping of like with like and the disjunction of unlikes, on the basis of morphological or formal analogies.' For the philosopher Nelson Goodman, 'subject is involved with style ... I cannot subscribe to the received opinion that style depends upon an artist's conscious choice among alternatives'.[3] So, 'style' has a number of meanings and is used in a variety of ways, while remaining metaphorically rich and evocative. It has been central to art history since its inception as a discipline, although its star has risen and fallen at various times. Musicology, literary studies, design and architecture, for example, also deploy it. Furthermore, 'style' has prompted considerable philosophical debate, while it is used freely in everyday discourse.

We can think of 'style' as meaning the distinctive manner with which something is executed, no matter whether the medium is drama, art, poetry, interior decor or clothing. Style is related to performance: we speak of styles of acting, singing and speaking, and 'stylish' and 'in style' reinforce the point that style is about practices in which manner and content are closely connected. A concept that can be used of individuals, of movements (such as Art Nouveau or Expressionism) and schools, of visual similarities where there was no shared group dynamic (Gothic) and of whole eras (modernism and post-modernism) is certainly complex. 'Late style' refers to artists, such as Rembrandt and Titian, who go on creating, and doing so distinctively, into old age. In formulating the phrase, a general phenomenon is posited concerning the relationships between style and stage of life – a type of biographical periodisation.

In the preceding essay, we noted Bernini's designation as a 'baroque' sculptor.[4] He had a style or styles taken both to be characteristic of him and shared with others practising at the same time. To say that Bernini is theatrical and concerned with movement might link him to other manifestations of the baroque style, but does not indicate what is distinctive about his individual manner of sculpting. Such understanding is built up through repeated visual engagement with his works, and then expressed verbally – to the extent this is possible – by specialists, using his works in support. The only way to speak convincingly of Bernini's style(s) is through systematic examination and comparison. It is possible to say that his portraits are particularly lifelike, but that is a matter of judgement. It is also possible to draw attention to specific virtuosic pieces of carving, such as the fabric upon which the blessed Ludovica lies in San Francesco a Ripa, Rome. But Bernini's distinctive style is a complicated ensemble, where content and manner are blended. Similar arguments apply to Wren's architecture and Renoir's painting. Renoir is sometimes designated an 'Impressionist' painter, who was influenced by 'the great Rococo masters', and used 'feathery brushstrokes characteristic of his Impressionist manner' and 'a softer and more supple kind of handling'.[5] Such comments show how accounts of a painter's style move easily from large-scale phenomena, such as Impressionism, to specific ones, such as brushstrokes.

Style has been fundamental for connoisseurship. It may be possible to identify the work of a given hand by characteristic ways of dealing with small details: ears, fingers or noses, for instance. These are matters of *individual* as opposed to *collective* style. In cases where little is known of an artefact, especially when costume and other obvious elements are absent, viewers consider the ensemble, including materials, techniques, subject matter and presentation, putting them together in their minds in order to date the item in question and perhaps identify a possible maker. Thus, 'style' refers to a range of phenomena, operates at a number of levels, and provides a sense both of historical and individual specificity, and of coherence. It does so through individuals, movements and institutions located in, and sometimes seen as definitive of, a particular era. This is achieved through attention to minute particularities and overall appearance. But periods are complex phenomena, and even within one style, there can be many forms, just as in a single period distinct styles co-exist. Style terms help us navigate visual intricacies, and their explicit use in the past provides valuable historical evidence.

The concept of style has occasioned elaborate theoretical debates among literary critics, art historians and philosophers. While they can hardly 'solve' the problem of style by removing its ambiguities, they are helpful in promoting a critical vantage point upon style terms and demonstrating their baggage. Historians might well consider which phenomena the concept can legitimately be applied to and why. How valuable are distinctions between levels and types of style, such as individual style and period style? It is vital to think about the diverse forms of agency implied by languages of style, and to differentiate, between, say, conscious choices made by individuals, the shared practices of workshops, and statements made by movements, especially those reacting against pre-existing styles.

Close analysis of artefacts invites reflection upon 'style'. The moves made in formal stylistic analysis, which can be done in a number of ways, demonstrate to historians precisely how visual thinking operates. This is why disciplines in which meticulous visual commentaries are routine are so valuable for historians. Some discussions of specific styles, such as Svetlana Alpers's impassioned account of the differences between Italian and Northern European art, set out the core assumptions underlying these styles – their different use of perspective, for example. She links such differences with other features, such as ways of generating knowledge.[6] Thus 'style' may be connected with a worldview, with ways of seeing. The self-aware use of style and style terms alerts historians to their metaphorical resonances, the need to avoid using them thoughtlessly as labels, and encourages reflection upon the links between periods, patterns and forms.

In some quarters, however, the concept of style has had a bad press. First, it has been associated with an evolutionary approach to visual and material culture, which presents styles as a type of genealogical tree, one leading to another, like the generations of a family. As George Kubler pointed out, it is a 'great defect in the loose concept of style … to lay upon the past the burden of an evolutionary line that was never known to participants as a necessity'.[7] This would imply a kind of internal logic that is unhistorical.

Second, style terms often carry an unhelpful moral charge through elaborate associations and their metaphorical potency. Arguably style terms always carry values, the point is to be aware of them. 'Rococo' is one example – the name was coined at the end of the eighteenth century after the phenomena to which it refers had ceased to be common, and initially expressed distaste for the *ancien régime*, its perceived frivolity and self-indulgence, as manifest in the fine and decorative arts. It stood in contrast to austere, high-minded, and frequently reformist neo-classicism. For some nineteenth-century collectors and connoisseurs, such as the Goncourt brothers, the values were reversed, with rococo appearing civilised, delicate, elegant and refined. Armed with an awareness of these cultural resonances and linguistic intricacies, we find the history of such ideas worth studying in their own right. In the case of rococo, historical actors contributed to a sense of the distinction between periods in the past. They were, in fact, periodising in a self-conscious manner. Thus, however morally suspect style terms appear, we can treat them historically and learn a great deal from the cultural processes through which they were forged, contested and deployed.

A third reservation about the notion of style concerns the mechanistic way in which it is used as a label, which fails to do conceptual work, and may actually impede analysis by removing incentives to probe more deeply. It is tempting to assume that a category can somehow explain an artefact. Such classification may fail to take the object itself sufficiently seriously and to facilitate interpretation. There are similar problems with labelling whole periods using style terms, such as 'colonial'. If we add to these points the ambiguity of the term itself, it is easy to appreciate why some have turned their backs on it. Yet, as Jas Elsner has argued, it remains valuable for art history, and accordingly should be considered carefully by historians of visual and material culture.[8] 'Style' still lies at the centre of debates about how to talk coherently about the appearances of things.

Words and things

Much evidently hinges on the languages used to describe, evoke and analyse periods, styles, and items of visual and material culture, and to conceptualise the links between them. There are considerable challenges here for the craft of historical writing. We have noted that terms used to describe periods are suffused with metaphor, values and associations, as phrases such as 'the Great Depression' reveal. Historians' prose betrays presuppositions about the relationships between artefacts and periods and what constitutes plausible explanations of them. The language of reflection, for example, arises from the assumption that the historical conditions of a given period are primary, and the qualities of artefacts secondary. This position has been attributed to the Victorian architect Augustus Pugin, who 'pioneered in the idea that building was a statement of value, reflecting the ethic of the builders'.[9] Accordingly, buildings in the Gothic style *reflect* a charitable conception of order, classical ones legalistic and repressive ideas. Hilda Amphlet wrote that caps in domestic service *reflected* hierarchy, although it could equally plausibly be argued that they helped to create and reinforce it. For Fiona Clark, turbans, '*reflect*[ed] the oriental influence conveyed through the Ballets Russes' in the early twentieth century.[10] But surely oriental styles were actively embraced, and the impulse for doing so came from many quarters. Similar claims are made for eighteenth-century satirical prints *reflecting* public opinion.[11] I would argue that artefacts generated and helped to shape ideas and practice in such fundamental areas as religious belief, political power and kinship. We need as clear a sense as the evidence permits of who is exercising agency and by what means, as well as languages adequate to expressing intricate, dynamic interactions.

A congenial language derives from ideas of mediation. The term implies that artefacts are in creative conversation with the contexts in which they are made and used, rather than mirroring them. Each cultural product may be understood in terms of transformation, because it has passed through a human mind or minds. As a result, made things may be treated as commentaries upon and interventions in specific situations.[12] The idea that any item passively mirrors its time is inherently implausible, precisely because the characteristics of particular settings have to pass through makers, who necessarily re-present them. Spectators similarly pass what they see through their bodies and minds. Transformations occur at every stage. Specific, detailed case studies help to generate the most plausible languages for connecting artefacts, settings and periods. Links can then be made in a highly focused manner through patron–client–producer–collector–user relationships, institutions, skills, habits, materials and so on.

The connections between objects and periods are sometimes conceptualised in a more general, abstract manner, for example by using the notion of a *Zeitgeist*, a spirit of the time, discernible in artefacts, and to which they therefore testify. Although many scholars now find this idea imprecise, and evocative of a philosophy of history that no longer commands wide assent, echoes of it remain. Generally we expect a matching between times and cultural products, a match that phrases such as 'spirit of the age' express. It is frequently observed how phenomena cluster together in ways that are hard to explain, and thus to say that something is 'in the air' can be a useful holding operation, until a more convincing account can be given. In fact, 'spirit of the age' implies a stronger claim than 'in the air', since the former refers to something *inherent* in a past period, even constituent of it, whereas the latter simply assumes it is around. Thus reconsidering the concept *Zeitgeist* may put constructive pressure on scholars to think harder about what the defining characteristics of a given era actually were.

Two further terms are relevant to thinking about periodisation in relation to visual and material culture: 'fashion' and 'influence'. Although frequently used of dress, fashion can refer to any phenomenon, from technology and music to food and ideas. Fashion refers to what is current at a particular time: the miniskirt in the 1960s, for example. In practice, only a small proportion of women actually wore such short skirts, thus to say they were *the* fashion or *in* fashion simply means that they were in favour among trendsetters and their followers. It is essential to distinguish between what most people think of as fashionable, which one dictionary defines as 'prevailing custom', and what designers, celebrities and others in the public eye are wearing, which could be called 'high' fashion. Others may know about, envy, disdain or look up to high fashion. They may not adopt it themselves for reasons of practicality, preference or cost. The ubiquity of cheap versions of designer clothes reveals the power of emulation, thereby reinforcing a more general point about how fashion is tied up with social hierarchies and attitudes towards them as well as with economic resources.

In a distinct usage of the term, if we say that a person acts in a particular fashion, the word indicates a style, manner or pattern in their behaviour. When applied to objects, a make or shape is implied, as in the evocative phrase, now archaic, 'fully-fashioned stockings'. 'Fashion' can be used of any trend or mode, and carries connotations of impermanence. Fashions react to and succeed one another, and are frequently used to characterise an era, making them pertinent to periodisation. The word 'fashion' is sometimes used pejoratively, to suggest a trivial fad, something that is *merely* modish. Historians are likely to be interested in ways of integrating fashion(s) into broader accounts of the past. Two aspects of 'fashion' are helpful. First, the *content* of fashion appears meaningful, offering clues about prevailing preoccupations, aesthetic preferences, gender assumptions and so on. The simplicity of short hairstyles, such as the bob in the 1920s, associated with a more independent lifestyle for women, eloquently communicated and contributed to the shift away from stuffy, conventional and time-consuming activities and an embrace of self-consciously modern styles and behaviour. **29** Simple lines recurred across clothing, jewellery, furniture, buildings and so on, which implies that such trends, being broadly shared, are historically significant. Such an approach compares a wide range of artefacts and attends to reactions against previous fashions as well as the development of innovative materials and techniques, and new groups of consumers.

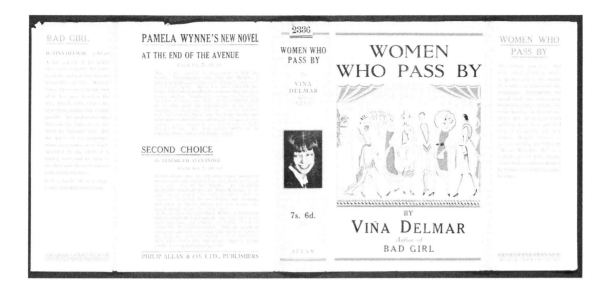

29 Book jacket of *Women Who Pass By* by Viña Delmar (London, 1929), designer not known, 43.5 cm wide × 19.3 cm high, Cambridge University Library. Note the stylised illustration, showing, as does the photograph of the author, simple short hair, and the book blurbs, which highlight the complications attendant upon women having more freedom.

Historically, fashions have changed at a variety of paces from one period, and medium, to another, and it remains extraordinarily difficult to explain precisely why and how such variation occurs, although attempts, for example, by sociologists and marketing specialists, have been made. Costume historians have written extensively in this area, charting distinct shifts in male and female attire, and noting the advent of new substances – rayon, rubber, nylon, Lastex and Lycra, in the case of women's underwear. Critical reflection on periodisation and the nature of change is invited. For example, Elizabeth Ewing challenges the common view that the First World War was a major turning point with respect to dress, and argues that key shifts, such as ordinary dress becoming everyone's dress, occurred much earlier.[13] Men's and women's fashions changed at different paces and did so at variable rates according to period, although full explanations of these complex phenomena appear elusive.[14]

A second way in which the concept 'fashion' helps historians is through its use in charting complex changes in the domains of visual and material culture and suggesting social patterns and relationships for further study. It is significant that fashion has attracted sociologists of the stature of Georg Simmel. Fashion, adornment and style – he wrote about them all – played an important role in his sociological thinking as a whole. His work, like writings by other social scientists, have put into play ideas, vocabularies and theories that historians may find inspiring.

The connections between 'fashion' and 'influence', the second term to consider, are close. Small numbers of people usually initiate and support trends in fashion, which take hold, at least in part, because of their social prominence – setting trends in material and visual culture is a significant form of influence, as we know from the case of Amelia Bloomer, the nineteenth-century feminist advocate of dress reform. The role of individuals in periodisation is complex. Some eras are named after powerful individuals, generally rulers, thereby asserting their exceptional impact. Sometimes style-cum-period terms, such as Georgian, Regency and Victorian, result. Such people have impressed themselves upon a place and time in a particularly insistent manner, or are deemed to have done so by others, a phenomenon that can generate a facile sense of coherence. 'Victorian' is a case in point, since it is sometimes used of countries over which Queen Victoria herself did not reign. However dominating a figure she may have been, 'Victorian', either as a period or a style, embraces phenomena of such diversity that historians should be sceptical.

Yet a small number of people undeniably have exercised extraordinary levels of influence, and not only rulers, but writers, artists, designers, architects and so on. Although we could say that they possessed talents that enabled them to stand out, matters can hardly be so simple. How is it possible for a small number of people to articulate something that is apt for the moment, for this is surely an important component of 'influence'? Examples include the Bauhaus movement, creators of the New Look after the Second World War, Mary Quant in the 1960s, and the designers of Apple computing products. Admittedly, 'influence' is difficult to track precisely, hence detailed case studies are an attractive option. These help historians to explore the ways in which names get associated with periods and come to symbolise them, a phenomenon that can occur either at the time or retrospectively. When exceptionally influential figures come from the visual arts, architecture and design, they actively shape what later becomes 'the look of the past' and thereby contribute to forms of periodisation.

I turn now to three examples in order to explore further the challenges of periodisation in relation to visual and material culture. First, I discuss the so-called 'age of revolutions' and its relevance for work on images and objects. The second example is 'modernism', a concept that implies the centrality of artefacts, including buildings, for understanding a particular period in the late nineteenth and early twentieth centuries. Finally, I discuss the approach of Michael Baxandall, and the book in which he uses the idea of a 'period eye'.

Revolutionary ages

We do well to keep reminding ourselves that historians are above all wordsmiths, who have vocabularies, shared with other disciplines, through which to discuss period specificity. Periodising terms are forms of shorthand that expedite discussion. But more than this, they frequently imply interpretations and explanations of change, give weight to some phenomena over others, and are metaphorically charged. Some of the problems of periodisation can be appreciated through a familiar historical example, the so-called 'age of revolution(s)'. Commonly used by historians, it does not map at all easily onto movements in art and architecture, for example. Characteristically, there is little agreement on its chronological boundaries, while the very term 'revolution' is laden with moral, emotional and political values. Mostly 'age of revolution(s)' refers to the period between the 1770s and about 1850, and has been used by Europeanists and those who want to link the American Revolution with the Old World. It can, however, be employed with greater geographical breadth. 'Revolution' is an evocative idea, not an innocent description. It is generic rather than specific, invites the use of comparison to assess each case and analyse shared features, and refers to shifts that are deep and significant. The word itself contains no direct implications for material and visual culture. Thus associating an era with revolution and denoting it by a style term, such as 'baroque', are different types of operation, although both involve periodisation. The conceptual burden in the case of 'revolution' is of a different order when historians seek to integrate artefacts into their accounts.

Revolutions are commonly seen as markers of such general significance that they divide one era from another. The American Revolution, it has been argued, was a major turning point for both the United States and the mother country, while the French Revolution is taken to signal the demise of the *ancien régime*. Some surveys of early modern history stop in 1789, when the Revolution in France is conventionally deemed to have started. Others continue until 1815, and the final defeat of Napoleon at Waterloo. The revolutionary 'epidemic' in 1848 is commonly taken to mark the end of the 'age of revolutions'. Such judgements about the nature and boundaries of periods have entailments for historical explanation. Would any of these accounts look different, and if so how, were artefacts to be integrated into them? There is some evidence that they would, since studies of the culture of the French Revolution that have engaged with objects and images have shifted historiographical emphasis away from the minutiae of political events and towards practices, beliefs and identities. The examination of public life – in which clothing, symbols, festivals and processions played a major role – has been central to this shift. Studies of artefacts, such as porcelain, clocks and furniture, have not yet been fully integrated into these accounts.

The decorative arts produced during the Revolutionary period broadly defined are sometimes assigned the style term 'empire', associated particularly with Napoleon Bonaparte. It remains in use for clothing – most women know what an empire-line dress looks like. This use of 'empire', which includes the period before Napoleon actually became emperor, does not speak directly to broad historical trends, but implies that artefacts expressed such trends. Bonaparte, like so many authoritarian leaders, was attentive to the visual and material manifestations of his rule. The degree to which these manifestations are incorporated into historical accounts of him varies considerably. Historians' sense of the period has certainly been shaped by high art, even when they do not study it explicitly.

Painters such as Jacques-Louis David and his pupil Jean-Auguste-Dominique Ingres have left powerful visual legacies through their receipt of major commissions and the reception of their work. Since David himself was a public, politically active figure, it has been possible to explore the precise relationships between the regimes under which he worked and the mediations his works performed. This is partly because patronage relationships were well documented – commissions for portraits of members of the political elite, for example. David's long career spanned many regimes, he adopted a number of visual styles, while his portrait practice encompassed sitters of diverse political persuasions. As a result, conceptualising the forms of periodisation involved is tricky, and terms such as 'revolutionary' and 'neo-classical' hardly help. They do not convey the ways in which he contributed to the shaping of public culture. Like his master, Ingres painted powerful figures of his time (Bonaparte, Charles X and Pope Pius VII), subjects from French history (The Dauphin entering Paris, the Vow of Louis XIII, and Joan of Arc at the Coronation of Charles VII) as well as other works set in distant times and places. It is revealing that one contemporary critic saw his image of Napoleon I on his imperial throne as containing 'gothic' elements.[15] In Ingres's work there is considerable potential for examining the specificity of early nineteenth-century France; his canvases also reveal his historical and aesthetic awareness of other periods.

Influential historians who work on the main phase of the French Revolution, 1789–99, and its impact, have turned to prints, caricatures, costume, and everyday items such as pottery, which were highly responsive to short-term change. **XVIII** Their approach is underwritten by the emphasis, during a time of political instability, on appearances betokening political affiliation and by the use made in successive regimes of public display. Such scholarship, however, tends to differ from the close readings of paintings by David and Ingres undertaken by art historians. Whatever research style is adopted, a sense of period specificity is most easily generated when there are tight, direct links between objects and contexts, for example through biography.

The French Revolution is an instructive example because sources are plentiful, its visual and material aspects have received considerable attention, and its status as a major transition is not in doubt. Writings about it occupy a range of registers, and many if not most works on the subject actually display little interest in artefacts, while those that do foreground them tend to have turned away from conventional historiographical issues. The high degree of academic specialisation is one reason why different types of history are not more integrated. Another reason concerns disparate levels of abstraction, which constitutes a significant conceptual problem for integrative forms of history: historical periodisation often works at levels of generality that do not mesh easily with accounts of specific items of material culture.

These issues emerge clearly when considering another type of revolution. Changes in the nature of artefacts are driven by a number of factors, such as fashion and taste, the availability of disposable income, the organisation of labour, supplies of materials, and patterns of patronage. 'The Industrial Revolution', which has been a major periodising idea for a very long time, touches all of them. It is a contested concept, which can be approached through a figure such as the famous British potter and entrepreneur Josiah Wedgwood and his highly distinctive products. Already we have three conceptual levels: a period term, an individual of major significance at the time, and artefacts closely associated with both period and person. Much periodisation operates at a general level, and making convincing connections between period terms and artefacts can be difficult when not enough intermediate phenomena are brought into play. In this case, an influential figure and his products act as bridges. Wedgwood products can be put in the period category 'the (early) Industrial Revolution', while the Industrial Revolution can be illuminated by paying attention to them. Phenomena possessing different levels of embrace are connected through the figure of Wedgwood himself and through his business. Wedgwood was a pioneering industrialist, who was close to other innovators in science, technology, business and design. His company made a range of products that are visually distinctive. We still speak of 'Wedgwood blue'. **XIX** It can be highly effective, then, to link general period terms with specific artefacts by turning to biography, networks, personalities, patrons and business history. This human scale grounds what would otherwise be vague connections, and provides evidence for the mediating processes between historical processes and objects.

In considering the 'age of revolutions' we should turn briefly to another period term, 'the Enlightenment', which is mainly deployed in intellectual and cultural history, and commonly seen as integral to critiques of the *ancien régime*, indeed as inseparable from revolution. This concept has no clear correlate among visual styles, and it sounds odd to speak of Enlightenment furniture or dress, although not of Enlightenment science or medicine. During the period when the Enlightenment is generally agreed to have occurred, from the late seventeenth to the end of the eighteenth century, there were many styles, including classicism, baroque, rococo, neo-classicism and romanticism, which hints at some of the difficulties of linking historical periods to visual and material culture in this case. Nonetheless, innumerable artefacts speak to the major themes of the Enlightenment, and there is huge potential, little realised so far, for further historical scholarship. This would explore the generation of convincing links between the conceptually dense notion 'the Enlightenment' and specific items of material and visual culture.

Such integration is more easily achieved when period terms already contain aesthetic implications. Historians of the late nineteenth and early twentieth centuries are familiar with the idea that 'modernism' acts as a bridge between aspects of visual and material culture and other contemporary phenomena such as urbanisation, engagement with non-Western cultures, psychoanalysis, physics and the impact of new media, such as photography and film.

Modernism

'Modernism' is one of a cluster of terms, together with the adjectives 'modern' and 'modernist' (which can also be used as a noun), the verb 'modernise', and two abstract nouns, 'modernity' and 'modernisation', which epitomise the concerns of this chapter. According to Raymond Williams, 'modernism and modernist have become more specialised [than modern], to particular tendencies, notably to the experimental art and writing of *c*.1890–*c*.1940'.[16] In the present context, two features of 'modern' phenomena stand out. First, the nature of modernity, which is a state or condition, has elicited a great deal of interest in recent decades, and, precisely because of the importance of 'modernism', a cultural and aesthetic phenomenon, considerable attention has been paid to its visual manifestations. Different chronologies are deployed: significant shifts in 'modern' art have been located earlier in the nineteenth century, while the origins of 'modernity' have also been found in the Enlightenment. Debates about the relative merits of the 'ancients and moderns' took place in seventeenth century. Hence 'modern' has a long history, and the nature and timing of 'modernity' could hardly be more contested. We can readily appreciate the complexities of periodisation in the case of modernity and their relevance to the project of incorporating visual and material evidence into historical accounts.

Second, in the case of modernism, a movement in which the visual arts played a central role, there is a rich historiography upon which to draw, largely by literary critics and art historians. Furthermore, because modern times are so strongly associated with processes of urbanisation, topics such as modernist architecture, town planning and the visual spectacle of the city have played a particularly prominent role in writings in a number of fields, including in the social sciences. These provide examples of ways of connecting periods to man-made items.

'Modern' has two ranges of meaning – one relative, the other absolute. The common polarity in social thought between 'modern' and 'traditional', for example, is relative in that each term is defined by comparison with the other; the pair can be applied to any epoch. When anything is promoted as being 'modern', there is an implied contrast with what went before. This is an old trope, which is not period specific. By contrast, 'modern' can refer to a particular period. Christopher Bayly's magisterial *The Birth of the Modern World* covers the period from 1780 to 1914, thus in this context 'modern' is absolute and specific. Inevitably historians disagree on when modern history began, although the period around the French Revolution is frequently taken as a starting point. Another candidate is 1500, following the 'discovery' of the New World. 'Modernity' refers to the state of being modern, and numerous scholars from a range of fields and perspectives have attempted to analyse and interpret its most salient features, such as the formation of a proletariat, industrialisation, the dominance of science and technology, and the rise of nationalism. All of these themes are present in visual and material culture. In addition, we might want to pay attention to fields such as photography and technologies for efficiently producing multiple copies of an image, which ensured that, by the early twentieth century, news could be effectively and cheaply illustrated. The *processes* whereby societies became 'modern' are known as 'modernisation'.

'Modernism' is a distinct notion, as its suffix tells us: '-ism' and '-ist' usually denote a commitment to something, such as a body of thought inviting allegiance, a movement with devoted participants.[17] Thus 'modernism' refers to the espousal of self-consciously innovative, anti-traditional ways of writing, designing buildings, composing music, making art and so on in the late nineteenth and early twentieth centuries. It covers an enormous range of phenomena, produced in diverse places and over many decades. Precision in its use is difficult to achieve.

Scholars acknowledge its reactive qualities, its rejection of established, bourgeois and academic values. Self-consciously innovative movements between about 1880 and 1920 may therefore be dubbed 'modernist'. Most commonly the term implies aesthetic movements, but it can be used more broadly. For example, Carl Schorske, in exploring 'the passage to modernism' in Austria, discussed Sigmund Freud, whose medical training was thoroughly characteristic of his time, but whose development of psychoanalysis as a body of theory and a set of practices profoundly shaped modernist culture. While it is meaningful to ask 'when was modernism?', especially if cultural and geographical zones are specified, the answers cannot be straightforward. Modernism remains an important period category for our purposes because the links between visual and material culture and broad historical trends have been extensively explored.

Schorske focused his study of modernism through the theme of history and its changing role over the late nineteenth and twentieth centuries in Austria. His explanation of the project merits close attention:

> In an era of growing nationalism, collective identities were redefined as a summa of convergent cultures of the past. The architecture of cities appropriated the styles of bygone times to lend symbolic weight and pedigree to modern building types from railway stations and banks to houses of parliament and city halls. The cultures of the past provided the decent drapery to clothe the nakedness of modern utility. Historicism in culture arose as a way of coming to grips with modernisation by marshalling the resources of the past. Conversely, at a later stage, modernism in culture arose in reaction to this effort as intellectuals attempted to confront modernity in its own terms, free from the manacles of mind that history and historicism were now thought to impose.
>
> To master modernity by thinking *with* history, to master modernity by thinking *without* history: these then are not simply antitheses, but rather successive phases in the same effort to give shape and meaning to European civilisation in the era of industrial capitalism and the rise of democratic politics.[18]

Schorske considers modernisation (the process), modernity (a condition) and modernism (a cluster of cultural movements), examining the relationships between them. He presented architecture, for example, as a vehicle for values, beliefs and strategies – that is, as an active force – and assumed that specific styles carried widely understood meanings: 'the choice of style related sometimes to the function of the building and always to show forth the values of its patrons'.[19] While he charts a clear change from thinking with history to thinking without it, he was alive to continuities, as his phrase 'the same effort' indicates.

Schorske identified two main traditions, which he saw as preceding and contributing to modernism – the Baroque and the Enlightenment. For example, 'the Baroque tradition of grace, exalting the life of feeling and beauty, fed the sensitivity and sensuosity of fin-de-siècle aestheticism'.[20] I am interested in the form of Schorske's argument, which presented traditions and movements in such a way that their aesthetic, social and political dimensions are blended. Architectural projects take their natural place within other changes, which might be regarded as more conventionally historical, such as the role of the court and the position of professions. He treats problems of periodisation holistically, without seeking special explanations for architectural change that are separate from those for town-planning or the shifting status of the army, both of which are relevant to his study.[21] In his discussion of late nineteenth-century public buildings, including a monument to the eighteenth-century ruler, Maria Theresa, Schorske traced the relationships between tradition and modernity in cultural politics: 'imperial power expresses itself in aesthetic culture, and the liberal élite … honours the Baroque dynastic tradition'.[22] **30** He assumed that architectural style and town-planning decisions carried meaning visually, not only for those who undertook them, but also more generally, although he does not specify how widely legible they were. Schorske further assumed that buildings and monuments, including their spatial arrangements, were zones through which relationships between interest groups, classes, competing institutions, and professions were negotiated. Hence items of visual and material culture offer ways of understanding those negotiations. They expressed the values of those involved in their own distinctive, i.e. visual manner – for example, through the choice of style – and are essential for understanding the passage to Viennese modernism.

This account of a work by an influential cultural historian illustrates the centrality of visual and material phenomena for modernism, a category that refers to a period, a cluster of styles and a set of values. At a time when *post*-modernism is widely and loosely invoked, critical reflection upon modernism is worthwhile. The extensive existing literature on modernism provides a wealth of examples for the integrated use of images and objects in explorations of an era. One notable feature of modernism was the self-consciousness of participants as critics of existing cultural and social arrangements, and as innovators who embraced

30 Postcard of the Monument to Maria Theresa in Vienna, date and photographer unknown, 13.8 cm high × 9 cm wide, Cambridge University Library. The inscription names the designer, the German sculptor, Kaspar von Zumbusch, and indicates the date the monument was unveiled. The date of the statue is usually given as 1887. Zumbusch was responsible for other monuments in Vienna, where he was Professor in the Academy, Berlin and Munich. Maria Theresa was Holy Roman Empress between 1745 and 1780; Zumbusch has surrounded her with key figures from her reign – military, cultural and political. Commissioned by her descendant Franz Joseph I, it engages with the world of a century before in multiple ways, including through its eighteenth-century 'feel'.

new knowledge and insights generated by technology, philosophy, science and medicine. As a result we may speak of 'period consciousness'.

Period consciousness

I have already mentioned various forms of period consciousness, such as the coining of 'rococo' and its changing resonances. Knowing when period terms were formulated and why, and understanding the contexts in which this occurred helps us to develop a critical understanding of both past and present forms of periodisation. The relatively recent notion, 'early modern', was developed by historians, but is too broad to serve the interests of specialists on artefacts, and has only gained ground since the Second World War. We do not speak of early modern furniture, for example. 'Early modern' is an imposed idea, not an actors' category. By contrast, there were writings on 'the Renaissance' during the eighteenth century, although the term is often associated with the nineteenth-century Swiss historian Jacob Burckhardt, and it implies the integration of images and objects. The sense of rebirth during the time designated 'the Renaissance' is a matter of considerable historical interest. 'Renaissance', then, involves successive layers of period consciousness.

There is another reason for historians to engage with period consciousness, one aspect of which was mentioned earlier. We derive our sense of periods from items in books, shops, television and film, as much as from museums, buildings and galleries. I argued for a critical understanding of public culture to assist historical reflection upon periodisation by clarifying our own forms of period consciousness. Period consciousness was also a phenomenon in the past, deposited in numerous ways in artefacts and available, if selectively, to later generations. Varying degrees and forms of such consciousness existed. Something of their originating period is inevitably present in artefacts, which is why historians over many centuries have indeed used them, as Francis Haskell demonstrated in *History and its Images*. However, the phrase 'period consciousness' implies a stronger claim: that some people in the past were actively aware of distinctions between, and the qualities of, their own and other times. Artefacts provide supporting evidence.

To probe the look of the past, we use the specifically visual and material forms of period consciousness. When makers seek to innovate, to set themselves apart from, perhaps marginalise, earlier styles, they manifest period consciousness. When they use visual ideas from other times or strive for a look that is futuristic, then they may again be said to express period consciousness. Similarly, when they capture phenomena that seem to typify the moment, a form of period consciousness is involved.

Thus artefacts are an exceptionally rich source for historians interested in period consciousness. Artists, architects, artisans and designers constantly reflected on these issues, and style terms played a major role in many such endeavours.

Sometimes period consciousness was both intense and widely experienced, as was the case following the First World War. That event – generally understood to be an unprecedented catastrophe – focused entire populations on the contrasts between the era that preceded it, the war itself, their present, and future possibilities. The war and its aftermath can be understood and made vivid through artefacts, such as the work produced by official war artists, as well as by documents. It was experienced by contemporaries in diverse ways, many of which found expression in visual and material culture. Posters are particularly well known, and postcards are becoming increasingly so. The phenomenon of 'trench art', such as carved shell cases, arguably manifests a special type of period consciousness. Professional artists responded to the war and its aftermath quite directly. We can use such materials to assess period consciousness in the past.

Manifestations of period consciousness, then, provide an opportunity for those interested in periodisation to probe the ways in which historical actors themselves contributed to this complex phenomenon. Many artefacts were made with posterity in mind – portraiture, for example. Portraitists are likely to be keenly aware of past, present and future while they are working. This does not necessarily mean that specific signs of the times are included, it can mean just the opposite, as in the case of Sir Joshua Reynolds. In his quest to elevate the status of portraiture in eighteenth-century England, he sometimes used female dress that was to some degree generic: an allusion to classical costume and a way of ensuring his portraits did not date too quickly. He hardly lacked period consciousness, rather he deliberately and strategically suppressed *contemporary* detail on occasion. Portraits are designed to bring out what is most noteworthy in sitters, who, regardless of their degree of prominence, like artists, possess forms of period awareness that are not necessarily pulled into full consciousness. Period consciousness is especially likely to be evident when rulers, and others who 'make' periods, are depicted. This gives elite portraiture a special historical interest, a point touched on earlier in relation to Napoleon Bonaparte.

Self-portraits offer further evidence of period consciousness: Richard Cosway and Joseph Wright of Derby showed themselves in seventeenth-century dress, or as it is tellingly called 'Van Dyck' costume. Cosway was paying homage to Rubens whom he admired and whose works he collected. Wright's oeuvre contains many paintings set in earlier times and places. Cosway and Wright were sensitive to period-specific looks. James Northcote wore a Titian cap in one self-portrait, making visible his affinity with a master whose biography he wrote. Reynolds included a bust of Michelangelo. Such work, which explores nostalgia, admiration, tradition and heritage, like so much art, helps historians think about periodisation more broadly. When movements are organised around revivals, such as the nineteenth-century Gothic revival, the phenomenon is even more striking.

We have seen how historians, using their visual skills, can find both period specificity and period awareness in many aspects of artefacts, including style, medium and subject matter. They are also to be found in the relationships that produce artefacts, that commission, display and use them, in the social and psychological characteristics of audiences, and in attitudes and beliefs. Such an approach is most effective when it is built on an understanding of the past visual habits and skills upon which artefacts were premised. Habits and skills – whether possessed by makers, patrons or audiences – have varied markedly over time and existed at diverse levels of awareness. One of the most compelling accounts of visual conventions and skills is by Michael Baxandall.

The period eye

In *Painting and Experience in Fifteenth-Century Italy*, Baxandall explored the visual assumptions embedded in pictures of the time. Artists deployed colours, gestures, perspective, bodily movements and so on that were recognisable and meaningful to the social groups that employed them. To establish what these habits and conventions were, he examined social practices requiring visual skills, such as dancing, making calculations based upon visual inspection as merchants needed to do, and religious activities, including preaching. His subtitle 'a primer in the social history of pictorial style' reveals in the word 'primer' a desire to make his arguments widely accessible, while 'social history' suggests an interest in context. 'Pictorial style' alludes to the ways paintings looked, and were looked at, in the period. Baxandall was also interested in 'cognitive style', which he took to be period specific. He attached considerable importance to understanding ways of thinking, which happen in particular social contexts and may be traced in pictures.[23] To make the links between images and social history as tight, direct and convincing as possible, Baxandall used a range of texts, such as contracts, treatises, manuals, dramas, poems, sermons, devotional and theological works, and contemporary observations. He argued for a period-specific eye, which deployed equally specific skills, themselves comprehensible in terms of the religious, educational and economic contexts in which they were exercised. The kinds of visualisation that formed part of instructions on how to pray explained the 'general, unparticularized, interchangeable types' of people who are shown by 'painters specially popular in pious circles, like Perugino'. While praying, specific faces known to the worshipper could be imagined; hence, Baxandall suggested, 'the pious beholder could impose his personal detail' on the images.[24]

There is no suggestion that everyone at a given historical moment possessed this period eye, rather it was socially specific. Indeed, Baxandall was reluctant to generalise at all from the particular forms of looking that he traced. Nonetheless, because his arguments are so meticulously conceptualised, it is worth considering how his insights may be turned to good effect in the practice of history, including how they help us to think about periodisation and style. He only discussed painted pictures in an era when patronage was the major structuring relationship in the visual arts. Thus Baxandall tied artists not just to their products, but also to the settings in which these were viewed. *Painting and Experience* affords general insights into the ways in which items of visual culture are linked to their contexts and hence about the ways in which scholars can reconstruct the connections. His insights prompt the following questions. What assumptions, practices, beliefs and knowledge do artists build into their work? What contract, explicit or otherwise, do producers make with clients and audiences? What intermediaries exist between the worlds of audiences and those of makers? 'Intermediaries' could be zones (such as religion), institutions (such as schools and universities) or media (such as publishing). What cultural resources and specific vocabularies are available to audiences in responding to visual and material culture? What are the main historical variations in such resources? What are the key visual conventions at a given time and place? How were images used? What sorts of conversations and debates were they designed to prompt? What skills did beholders need? Which areas of life are connected most directly to artefacts? What forms of behaviour and bodily posture do specific works invite?

I derived these questions from my reading of *Painting and Experience*, but they are raised by a great deal of excellent work. Baxandall was not alone in claiming that art is integrated into life, albeit life of certain, specific kinds, that there are perpetual exchanges between the looking skills of ordinary existence, and the more specialised skills of looking at paintings. Baxandall wanted to know what painters, patrons and beholders brought with them: 'fifteenth-century pictorial development happened with fifteenth-century classes of emotional experience'.[25] Thus he constantly and inventively explored period specificity and distilled his insights so that they would be accessible to undergraduates.

Painting and Experience emphasises 'that the forms and styles of painting respond to social circumstances', and 'bits of social practices or convention ... may sharpen our perception of the pictures'. At the very end, he 'revers[es] the equation – to suggest that the forms and styles of painting may sharpen our perception of the society'. 'A pictorial style gives access to the visual skills and habits and, through these, to the distinctive social experience. An old picture is the record of visual activity'.[26] Baxandall thus offered one model for a synthesis of history and art history, for a reciprocal relationship between the two. His vision that the direction of analysis can go either way is important: 'approached in the proper way ... the pictures become documents as valid as any charter or parish roll'.[27] It is a strikingly integrative approach, applicable beyond painting in its concern with the appearances of things, with ways of seeing and with how specialists use their visual intelligence to produce visual effects – all key components of the look of the past. What Baxandall did not address was the nature of change.

Old-fashioned approaches to style offered one solution to the problem of change by positing the development from one style to another as an almost inexorable process, hinting at a kind of internal logic. Scholars are critical of these notions of style, and there is still debate about its precise meanings, uses and limitations. This has not prevented style terms, like 'style' itself, from being treated as if their meanings were self-evident. An alternative is to engage with scholars, such as Baxandall, to see what hints they contain for the explanation of change. There are plenty of openings in his approach. He took a limited number of domains – gauging, preaching and praying, and dancing – showing how they provided access to paintings in his period. He also explored patron–client relationships, the uses and costs of coloured pigments and an understanding of perspective. It would be feasible to track back and forth between changes in these domains and shifts in visual and material culture in other contexts, while using the overall method that lies at the heart of *Painting and Experience*. The importance of preaching in reformed churches, for example, offers such an opportunity. Arguably different experiences and skills came into prominence in sixteenth-century art – Baxandall's approach helps to reveal such change. What characterises this approach is a dual interest in visual habits, skills and conventions, and in the social relationships out of which artefacts arise. Historians can explore how all these changed, especially when institutions, such as the Church, underwent profound alteration. For any given historical moment it is possible to ask what the visual habits were, how they were socially distributed, and how they were different from or similar to those of other times and places.

NOTES

1 Shearer West, ed., *Guide to Art* (London, 1996), p. 826; Jonathan Harris, *Art History: the Key Concepts* (London, 2006), p. 305.

2 Susan Sontag, 'On Style', in *Against Interpretation* (London, 1994), pp. 15–36, at p. 17.

3 Jas Elsner, 'Style', in *Critical Terms for Art History*, ed. Robert Nelson and Richard Shiff, 2nd edn (Chicago and London, 2003), p. 102, and Nelson Goodman, 'The Status of Style', *Critical Inquiry*, 1 (1975), pp. 799–811, at p. 799.

4 Ian Chilvers *et al.*, *The Oxford Dictionary of Art* (Oxford, 1994), pp. 52–3.

5 *Ibid.*, p. 418.

6 Svetlana Alpers, *The Art of Describing: Dutch Art in the Seventeenth Century* (London, 1983), and her 'Style is What You Make It: the Visual Arts Once Again', in *The Concept of Style*, ed. Beryl Lang, rev. and expanded edn (Ithaca, 1987), pp. 137–62. For Alpers's preference for 'modes', see pp. 145, 147, 155, 158 and 162.

7 George Kubler, 'A Reductive Theory of Visual Style', in *Concept of Style*, ed. Lang, p. 165 – he is discussing the ideas of James Ackerman here.

8 Elsner, 'Style'.

9 Carl Schorske, *Thinking with History: Explorations in the Passage to Modernism* (Princeton, 1998), p. 76.

10 Hilda Amphlet, *Hats: a History of Fashion in Headwear* (Chalfont St Giles, 1974), p. 164, and Fiona Clark, *Hats* (London, 1982), p. 50, emphasis added.

11 For a critique of such claims, see Ludmilla Jordanova, 'Image Matters', *Historical Journal*, 51/3 (2008), pp. 777–91.

12 See Robert Nelson, 'Mediation' in *Critical Terms*, ed. Nelson and Shiff, pp. ix–xii, esp. p. x where he talks about 'the ways in which knowledge is constructed, conveyed, replicated, instilled and maintained … and [the] creation, patronage, and social function of works of art'. Thus 'mediation' draws attention to social processes. Cf. Harris, *Art History*, pp. 193–4, and Jordanova, *History in Practice*, 2nd edn (2006), where 'mediation' is defined in the glossary.

13 Elizabeth Ewing, *Dress and Undress: a History of Women's Underwear* (London, 1978) and her *Everyday Dress, 1650–1900* (London, 1984), p. 137.

14 For example, Clark, *Hats*, p. 7.

15 Robert Rosenblum, *Jean-August-Dominique Ingres* (London, 1990), p. 60; all the paintings mentioned are reproduced in this book.

16 Raymond Williams, *Keywords: a Vocabulary of Culture and Society*, rev. and expanded edn (London, 1983), p. 208.

17 *Ibid.*, pp. 173–4.

18 Schorske, *Thinking*, pp. 4–5, emphasis in original.

19 *Ibid.*, p. 9.
20 *Ibid.*, p. 11.
21 *Ibid.*, ch. 7, 'Museum in Contested Space: the Sword, the Scepter and the Ring'.
22 *Ibid.*, p. 121;, pp. 117–21 discuss the statue of Maria Theresa.
23 Michael Baxandall, *Painting and Experience in Fifteenth-century Italy: a Primer in the Social History of Pictorial Style*, 2nd edn (Oxford, 1988), p. 108.
24 *Ibid.*, pp. 46–7.
25 *Ibid.*, p. 56.
26 *Ibid.*, pp. 151–2.
27 *Ibid.*, p. 152.

FURTHER READING

Periodisation is discussed by Penelope Corfield, *Time and the Shape of History* (New Haven and London, 2007): pp. 150–7 consider 'Times Names'. See also Michael Bentley, ed., *Companion to Historiography* (London and New York, 1997), esp. chs. 13, 25, 35 and 38 and pp. 395–506, and the special issue of *New Literary History*, 1/2 (1970), 'A Symposium on Periods', which includes material on art. Chapter 5, 'Periodisation', in my *History in Practice*, 2nd edn (London, 2006), sets out my basic position on this theme.

On public culture, see David Brigham, *Public Culture in the Early Republic: Peale's Museum and its Audience* (Washington DC and London, 1995); Ivan Karp *et al.*, eds., *Museums and Communities: the Politics of Public Culture* (Washington DC and London, 1992); Aaron Cohen, *Imagining the Unimaginable: World War, Modern Art & the Politics of Public Culture in Russia, 1914–17* (Lincoln, NE, 2008). On public history, the following collections focus on the United States, but raise general issues: Barbara Howe and Emory Kemp, eds., *Public History: an Introduction* (Malabar, FL, 1986), and James B. Gardner and Peter LaPaglia, eds., *Public History: Essays from the Field* (Malabar, FL, 1999); cf. W. J. T. Mitchell, ed., *Art and the Public Sphere* (Chicago and London, 1992).

Richard Middleton, *Colonial America: a History, 1565–1776*, 3rd edn (Oxford and Malden, MA, 2002; previous edns, 1992 and 1996), weaves visual and material culture into a broad historical account, while Robert Blair St George's edited volume *Material Life in America, 1600–1860* (Boston, 1988) starts with material culture and does not foreground 'colonial' as a category.

On the visibility of religious values there is Louis Nelson, *The Beauty of Holiness: Anglicanism and Architecture in Colonial South Carolina* (Chapel Hill, 2008), and Kenneth Fincham and Nicholas Tyacke, *Altars Restored: the Changing Face of English Religious Worship, 1547–1700* (Oxford, 2007). More specifically on Shakers, see William Ketchum, *Simple Beauty: the Shakers in America* (New York, 1996), and Edward Andrews and Faith Andrews, *Religion in Wood: a Book of Shaker Furniture* (Bloomington and London, 1966).

There is now an extensive literature on the visual and material culture of death. Nigel Llewellyn's work is especially relevant, see his *The Art of Death: Visual Culture in the English Death Ritual c.1500–c.1800* (London, 1991) and his chapter on monuments to dead children in Gillian Avery and Kimberley Reynolds, eds., *Representations of Childhood Death* (Basingstoke, 2000), pp. 52–64. See also Philippe Ariès, *Images of Man and Death* (Cambridge, MA, and London, 1985).

Recent work on wax anatomical models includes Rebecca Messbarger, *The Lady Anatomist: the Life and Work of Anna Morandi Manzolini* (Chicago and London, 2010) and Anna Maerker, *Model Experts: Wax Anatomies and Enlightenment in Florence and Vienna, 1775–1815* (Manchester, 2011).

On fakes, see Otto Kurz, *Fakes: a Handbook for Collectors and Students* (London, 1948), Preface and Conclusion, for his more general reflections on fakes. For example, p. 317: 'Every forgery will – unconsciously – show symptoms of the style of the epoch which produced it. Contemporaries may not discern it but, seen from a distance, the signs of the period of origin gradually become apparent.' Thus for Kurz, 'style must always remain the essential criterion' for recognising fakes (p. 318). See also Mark Jones, ed., *Why Fakes Matter: Essays on Problems of Authenticity* (London, 1992); David Phillips, *Don't Trust the Label: an Exhibition of Fakes, Imitations and the Real Thing* (London, 1986); and Julia Poole, *Plagiarism Personified? European Pottery and Porcelain Figures* (Cambridge, 1986). Bernard Berenson's *Essays in Appreciation* (London, 1958), contains a short essay on 'The Importance of Fashion for Dating Pictures', pp. 39–43; he is often taken as an archetypal connoisseur.

The literature on style is formidable both in extent and complexity. One strand goes back to the founding fathers in art history, for example, Alois Riegl, *Problems of Style: Foundations for a History of Ornament* (Princeton, 1992; first published 1893); Heinrich Wölfflin, *The Principles of Art History: the Problem of the Development of Style in Later Art* (London, 1932; first published 1915). Beryl Lang, ed., *The Concept of Style* (Ithaca, 1987), revised and expanded edition is useful, esp. chs. 2, 4, 5 and 7. The chapter on style by Jas Elsner in Robert Nelson and Richard Shiff, eds., *Critical Terms for Art History*, 2nd edn (Chicago, 2003), is also worthwhile. A diverse, interdisciplinary collection is Caroline van Eck, James McAllister and Renée van de Vall, eds., *The Question of Style in Philosophy and the Arts* (Cambridge, 1995). It focuses on the eighteenth and nineteenth centuries and claims that an important transition occurred around 1800 in the ways philosophy and the arts were understood. A number of the essays are, however, quite general, see, for example, chs. 2 and 9; chs. 4 and 7 are also helpful. The field called 'stylistics' is pertinent here, see Katie Wales, *A Dictionary of Stylistics*, 3rd edn (Harlow, 2011). Although an element of language studies, and hence distinct from the use of style in relation to visual and material culture, since there is no 'translation' problem between media to contend with, it provides a valuable sense of analytical terms and possibilities. On 'late style', see, for example, Edward Said, *On Late Style* (London, 2006), his last book, which uses mainly literary and musical examples. Said credits Adorno with coining the phrase, which has appealed to musicologists. Cf. Thomas Dormany, *Old Masters: Great Artists in Old Age* (London, 2000); Philip Sohm, *The Artist Grows Old: the Aging of Art and Artists in Italy, 1500–1800* (New Haven and London, 2007); and Nicholas Delbanco, *Lastingness: the Art of Old Age* (New York and London, 2011).

The literature on specific styles is highly diverse; there are writings at many levels, including the most basic one of how to recognise this or that style. I find these particularly interesting because they reveal common assumptions not just about periods in the past and their defining characteristics, but about the connections between the appearance of things and the times in which they were made. For example, Maria Gozzoli, *How to Recognize Gothic Art* (London, 1978). At a more sophisticated level, José Antonio Maravall, *Culture of the Baroque: Analysis of a Historical Structure* (Manchester, 1986; first published in Spanish in 1975), is an attempt to reflect on period specificity and style in ambitious, comparative terms. On Bernini in particular, Charles Avery, *Bernini: Genius of the Baroque, with Special Photography by David Finn* (London, 1997), provides an overview of his oeuvre. On rococo, there is Katie Scott, *The Rococo Interior: Decoration and Social Spaces in Early Eighteenth-Century Paris* (New Haven and London, 1995), and Michael Snodin, ed., *Rococo: Art and Design in Hogarth's England* (London, 1984). See also the further reading for the essay on Bernini.

For a range of approaches to fashion, see Gordon Wills and David Midgley, *Fashion Marketing: an Anthology of Viewpoints and Perspectives* (London, 1973); Elizabeth Wilson, *Adorned in Dreams: Fashion and Modernity* (London, 1985); Aileen Ribeiro, *Fashion in the French Revolution* (London, 1988), and *Dress in Eighteenth-century Europe, 1715–1789*, 2nd edn (New Haven and London, 2002); Bonnie English, *A Cultural History of Fashion in the Twentieth Century: From the Catwalk to the Sidewalk* (Oxford, 2007); Rachel Worth, *Fashion for the People: a History of Clothing at Marks & Spencer* (Oxford, 2007); and Christine Ruane, *The Empire's New Clothes: a History of the Russian Fashion Industry, 1700–1917* (New Haven and London, 2009).

On Simmel: David Frisby and Mike Featherstone, eds., *Simmel on Culture* (London, 1986), include his writings on fashion, art and so on; for a general introduction to Simmel, see David Frisby, *Georg Simmel*, 2nd edn (London, 2002; first published 1984). Lou Taylor, *The Study of Dress History* (Manchester, 2002), sets out the main approaches.

A good example of the impact of an individual designer is Alec Issigonis: Laurence Pomeroy, *The Mini Story* (London, 1964).

For the age of revolutions see, for example, Christopher Bayly, *The Birth of the Modern World, 1780–1914: Global Connections and Comparisons* (Malden, MA, and Oxford, 2004). Classic texts using the idea include Eric Hobsbawm, *The Age of Revolution* (London, 1962) and many subsequent editions, and R. R. Palmer, *The Age of the Democratic Revolution* (Princeton, 1959), vol. 1, and (1964), vol. 2. Work that gives particular attention to visual and/or material culture during the French Revolution of 1789 includes: Mona Ozouf, *Festivals and the French Revolution* (Cambridge, MA, and London, 1988; first published 1976); Lynn Hunt, *Politics, Culture, and Class in the French Revolution* (Berkeley and London, 1984); David Bindman *et al.*, *The Shadow of the Guillotine: Britain and the French Revolution* (London, 1989); Richard Wrigley, *The Politics of Appearances: Representations of Dress in Revolutionary France* (Oxford and New York, 2002); and Rolf Reinhardt and Hubertus Kohle, *Visualizing the Revolution: Politics and the Pictorial Arts in Late Eighteenth-century France* (London, 2008). See also Albert Boime, *Art in an Age of Revolution, 1750–1800* (Chicago, 1987), which is part of his series, A Social History of Modern Art.

On the Industrial Revolution, S. D. Smith, 'Determining the Industrial Revolution', *Historical Journal*, 54 (2011), pp. 907–24; E. A. Wrigley, *People, Cities and Wealth: the Transformation of Traditional Society* (Oxford, 1987); Neil McKendrick *et al.*, eds., *The Birth of a Consumer Society: the Commercialization of Eighteenth-Century Britain* (London, 1982); and Maxine Berg, *The Age of Manufactures, 1700–1820: Industry. Innovation and Work in Britain*, 2nd edn (London and New York, 1994), are useful. On Wedgwood, see Brian Dolan, *Josiah Wedgwood: Entrepreneur to the Enlightenment* (London, 2004).

In relation to 'empire', see Martyn Lyons, *Napoleon Bonaparte and the Legacy of the French Revolution* (Basingstoke, 1994), who devotes one chapter to art, propaganda and the cult of personality. By contrast, Robert Asprey, *The Rise and Fall of Napoleon Bonaparte*, 2 vols. (London, 2001–2), uses illustrations, mostly portraits, in a conventional way to give visual relief and pays no particular attention to visual and material culture. It is aimed at a general audience. Philip Dwyer, *Napoleon: the Path to Power, 1769–1799* (London, 2007), uses illustrations in a similar way. By contrast, in art-historical work, 'empire' and art are shown to be entwined: David O'Brien, *After the Revolution: Antoine-Jean Gros, Painting and Propaganda Under Napoleon* (University Park, PA, 2004). The currency of style terms and ideas is revealed in Melanie Fleischmann, *In the Neoclassic Style: Empire, Biedermeier and the Contemporary Home* (London, 1996; first published 1988). Todd Portersfield and Susan L. Siegfried, *Staging Empire: Napoleon, Ingres, and David* (University Park, PA, 2006), is superb. See also Susan Siegfried, *Ingres: Painting Re-imagined* (New Haven and London, 2009).

Dorinda Outram, *Panorama of the Enlightenment* (London, 2006), is extensively illustrated. See also Celina Fox, *The Arts of Industry in the Age of Enlightenment* (New Haven, 2009).

The secondary literature on modernism is vast and diverse. In addition to works cited elsewhere, see Scott McQuire, *Visions of Modernity: Representation, Memory, Time and Space in the Age of the Camera* (London, Thousand Oaks and New Delhi, 1998); Robert Nelson and Richard Shiff, eds., *Critical Terms for Art History*, 2nd edn (Chicago, 2003), ch. 13, 'Modernism', by Charles Harrison; Charles Harrison and Paul Wood, eds., *Art in Theory, 1900–2000: an Anthology of Changing Ideas*, 2nd edn (Malden, MA, 2003); Stephen Kern, *The Culture of*

Time and Space, 1880–1918 (London, 1993). See also Corfield, *Time*, ch. 5, 'Mutable Modernity'. T. J. Clark's *The Painting of Modern Life: Paris in the Art of Manet and his Followers* (London, 1985) has been hugely influential. Richard Brettell, *Modern Art 1851–1929: Capitalism and Representation* (Oxford, 1999), carefully explains his choice of dates and reviews alternatives in his Introduction, see also his brief comments on p. 11 on Modern Art Movements, and the Timeline, pp. 240–9. This volume is part of the Oxford History of Art Series, all of which contain timelines. Cf. the timeline in Graham Clarke, *The Photograph* (Oxford, 1997), pp. 234–7, which covers 1500–1990.

Modernisation has been a contested concept in the social sciences, see, for example, A. D. Smith, *Social Change: Social Theory and Historical Processes* (London, 1976).

On Vienna, see Carl Schorske, *Fin de Siècle Vienna: Politics and Culture* (New York, 1979). Schorske may usefully be compared with William Johnston, *The Austrian Mind: an Intellectual and Social History, 1848–1938* (Berkeley, 1972), who uses style terms extensively. Charles Ingrao, *The Habsburg Monarchy, 1618–1815*, 2nd edn (Cambridge, 2000), provides an excellent introduction. See also the more popular Gordon Brook-Shepherd, *The Austrians: a Thousand-Year Odyssey* (London, 1996), who describes Maria Theresa as ruling with 'motherly absolutism' in the non-paginated captions. Guidebooks to Vienna are useful. The collection of essays in honour of Carl Schorske touches on many topics central to this book: Michael Roth, ed., *Rediscovering History: Culture, Politics, and the Psyche* (Stanford, 1994).

On World War I as a major transition, see *Art from the First World War* (London, 2008); David Peters Corbett, ed., *Wyndham Lewis and the Art of Modern War* (Cambridge, 1998); Nicholas J. Saunders, *Trench Art: a Brief History & Guide, 1914–1939* (London, 2001); Nicholas J. Saunders, *Matters of Conflict: Material Culture, Memory and the First World War* (London, 2004); Samuel Hynes, *A War Imagined: the First World War and English Culture* (London, 1990); and Paul Fussell, *The Great War and Modern Memory* (Oxford, 2000; first published 1975). Although predominantly about literature, Fussell's book has had an enormous impact on approaches to the war. In terms of 'futures', there is Didier Ottinger, ed., *Futurism* (London, Paris and Milan, 2009); Dick Jude, *Fantasy Art Masters: the Best in Fantasy and SF Art Worldwide* (London, 2002); and Vincent Di Fate, *Infinite Worlds: the Fantastic Visions of Science Fiction Art* (London, 1997).

Francis Haskell, *History and its Images: Art and the Interpretation of the Past* (New Haven and London, 1993), and *Past and Present in Art and Taste: Selected Essays* (New Haven and London, 1987) are relevant to the themes of this chapter.

On self-portraiture, see Anthony Bond *et al.*, *Self Portrait: Renaissance to Contemporary* (London and Sydney, 2005); and John Peacock, *The Look of Van Dyck: the Self-Portrait with a Sunflower and the Vision of the Painter* (Aldershot, 2006).

In addition to *Painting and Experience*, see Michael Baxandall's *Patterns of Intention: On the Historical Explanation of Pictures* (New Haven, 1985). Cf. Svetlana Alpers and Michael Baxandall, *Tiepolo and the Pictorial Intelligence* (New Haven and London, 1994). Margarita Dikovitskaya, for example, discusses Baxandall in her *Visual Culture: the Study of the Visual after the Cultural Turn* (Cambridge, MA, and London, 2005).

Bridge

Sometimes a medium, a style, a subject, a technique or forms of display comes to sum up an era. In such cases, items of visual and material culture express, reinforce or challenge received ideas about periodisation. In the next essay I turn to one such case: black and white photography of hardship during the American Great Depression. A few photographs are capable of evoking that era for viewers. I consider these powerful and familiar images through an exhibition in the 1950s, an era of prosperity and confidence for the United States. The ways in which *The Family of Man*, a book as well as a successful exhibition, was 'of its time', is an intriguing question.

ESSAY
Photographing 'the Family of Man'

Photography: treachery and seduction

In 1955, the Museum of Modern Art in New York (MoMA) staged an exhibition created by the renowned photographer, Edward Steichen, entitled *The Family of Man*. It contained 503 photographs from sixty-eight countries, as the front cover of early editions of the published version proclaimed. **XX** The exhibition was followed by an international tour, and it has been said that the volume is the best-selling photographic book of all time.[1] The book and the exhibition are indicative of the ubiquity of photography in the modern world. Photographs of all kinds are used in historical works, while some historians are also photographers. Most people in the developed world now own at least one camera, for instance on a mobile phone. Perhaps we are all photographers now.

The role of cameras in everyday life is historically significant. People generate an abundance of images, which record, communicate and act as triggers for remembering an array of occasions in quotidian existence. Photographs are indeed historical documents, although the concepts 'document' and 'documentary' require careful handling. Photographs taken by non-professionals, as well as by those paid to do so, are rich sources for historical research and writing. In being so widely accessible, photography is unlike many techniques for producing images or objects. It is because most historians are photographers in their non-professional lives that it is helpful to reflect carefully and critically on their use of photographs in an academic context.

Photography stands apart from other media in some further respects. It is simply everywhere: on websites and in advertising, newspapers and magazines. As a result it is common to *see through* photographs, and to do so in two ways. First, spectators place a special kind of trust in what photographs depict, although it is well known now, and has been since the invention of the medium, that manipulation is easily done. Those reporting the news use photographs in just this way, to – apparently – tell it as it was. Thus we are prone to see through the representation to an original scene, and to engage with that scene as if it were immediately before us. Advertisers and journalists know this perfectly well, and especially when charities are raising funds to help in disasters, they rely on such directness.

The people in openly emotive images are often haunting; their faces become spuriously familiar when an iconic photograph is reproduced many times. Second, viewers see through photographs because, since there are so many of them, they have long ceased to be remarkable, except in certain highly specific circumstances, such as photographic exhibitions, where attention is drawn to the artistry of photographs. The experience of looking at photographs produced expressly to elicit careful inspection, framed and spaced out on a white wall with captions, accounts for only a minute proportion of the time most people spend with photographs. When we walk along the street, photographs exist in our visual field; they may be glanced at, seen, but rarely registered as artful constructions. It follows that photographs are exceptionally hard for historians to use well, that they possess a distinctive treachery as sources. If they are to be deployed as evidence and not merely as illustrations, their constructed nature has to take centre stage, even when they seem to be merely 'snaps'. Nothing can be taken for granted; in other words, photographs need to be seen as artefacts. 'Photographs can speak to us only after we have mistrusted and challenged them.'[2]

One form of this treachery arises from the capacity of photographs to be manipulated. Photographs are routinely altered by professionals, who choose an overall look along with size. This is why, when it comes to 'art' photography, prints made and signed by the photographer are highly valued – the cropping, the paper, the tones, the size have generally been selected either by the person who operated the shutter or in close consultation with them. In practice, photographers rarely work alone and there is a spectrum of degrees of control from more or less total, as in the case of the pioneering American art photographers Edward Weston and Alfred Stieglitz, to virtually none at all, for photographers who send their pictures to newspapers. Photographs, then, are treacherous because, for the most part, viewers do not know exactly what they are seeing and how it has been doctored. The point is easier to understand, at least in principle, in the era of digital photography, with the widespread use of computer programmes, such as Photoshop.

Photographs are, however, treacherous in other ways, which Steichen exploited in *The Family of Man*. He stated that the book 'was conceived as a mirror of the universal elements and emotions in the everydayness of life – as a mirror of the essential oneness of mankind throughout the world'.[3] The emotional impact of photographs is both treacherous and seductive, a phenomenon that many writers have explored. The capacity of photography to work on the emotions has been growing since the middle of the nineteenth century. The medium has always been in conversation with other forms of representation, including those that preceded it. Photography is currently an integral part of the psyche of most people in

31 *Paul and Virginia*, by Julia Margaret Cameron, 1865, albumen print on gold-edged cabinet, 11.7 cm high × 9.6 cm wide, National Portrait Gallery, London. The title of this small photograph refers to a famous French novel from the end of the eighteenth century about two children growing up together in an idyllic tropical setting. Bernardin de Saint-Pierre's work enjoyed huge popularity. The names of the children who posed for Cameron are known – William Frederick Gould and Elizabeth ('Topsy') Keown, both of whom appear in other photographs by her. This is not a portrait of two Victorian children, but a fantasy image based on a work of fiction.

those parts of the world where cameras and the mass media are commonplace and the worldwide web has further intensified its reach. People shape their feelings through their uses of, and responses to, photographs. Even when the photographs in question are formalised and bureaucratic, as in the case of identity cards and passports, they are woven into the fabric of our existence, into our senses of ourselves. Photography is powerful and pervasive, which renders it at once an alluring and also a dangerous historical source. Used self-consciously, however, it offers enormous potential for thinking about the past.

Photographs, then, are commonly treated by historians as images that give direct access to the scenes they represent. They serve to illustrate a putative something out there, and since there are so many of them, we are apt to treat them carelessly, to take them for granted. Perhaps the fact that most historians also take photographs, whether for personal or professional use, enhances the tendency to treat them as simple records. But clearly, like all artefacts, they arise, are deployed and then redeployed in specific social situations. In the case of *The Family of Man* exhibition, a great deal is known about its context and how it was viewed. Despite its popularity among mainly middle-class visitors and favourable press comments when it opened in New York, it elicited hostility from some professional photographers, critics and commentators, who thought it crudely manipulative, pushing a phoney universalist humanism that ignored social, political and economic realities.[4] *The Family of Man* was certainly ideologically charged – in its espousal of an anti-nuclear position, for example – a point that enhances its historical interest.

The exhibition reveals another key feature of photography: its flexibility and diversity as a medium. Photography has operated in the main genres found in paintings and prints, such as still life, landscape, the nude and portraiture, and is extensively used in religious contexts – on gravestones, for example. It has played a central role in avant-garde art movements, such as surrealism, and continues to be closely associated with cutting-edge work. In the nineteenth century, carefully staged photographs, for example by Henry Peach Robinson and Julia Margaret Cameron, functioned rather like history paintings and grand manner portraits. **31** The medium appealed particularly to practitioners of science, medicine and technology, who championed and practised it, and used it in their publications. Anthropologists and social scientists also deploy it. Photography is a recognised and long-established research tool in its own right. Its professional forms are strikingly diverse, with studio and wedding photography being quite distinct from advertising, journalistic or art photography. Advocacy photography, practised by journalists, social commentators and artists, was born out of a desire to espouse a cause and convey commitments. This tradition is part of documentary photography. 'Documentary' implies the desire both to record a state of affairs and to comment upon, and perhaps change, it. *The Family of Man* contained pictures by leading exponents of photo-reportage, such as Dorothea Lange and members of the Magnum group, which had been formed in 1947 and included Robert Capa and Henri Cartier-Bresson, both of whom were represented in the exhibition. It also included photographs from *Vogue*, which are visually quite distinct in their calm elegance. Although dominated by American photographers and subjects, major practitioners from other areas were selected, such as Bill Brandt and August Sander from England and Germany respectively.[5] **32**

Edward Steichen: maestro

Edward Steichen, the driving force behind *The Family of Man*, organised the exhibition while working for MoMA. The museum, founded in 1929, was a strong advocate for contemporary art, and espoused a modernist agenda. It gave considerable support and exposure to photography as an art form when its aesthetic status remained contested. Steichen was a successful photographer, who had worked for *Vanity Fair*, been involved in the famous Armory Show – held successively in New York, Chicago and Boston in 1913 – which is often seen as marking the beginning of modernism in the United States, and had practised as a painter. He had taken celebrity portraits and undertaken advertising photography. To prepare the exhibition, which he regarded as the most important undertaking of his career, he worked in collaboration with many contemporary photographers, including Dorothea Lange, who is discussed later in this essay, and was able to draw upon the huge archives of *Life* magazine, which enjoyed a circulation of 6 million in the 1950s. Steichen wanted 'to have a series of photographs collectively communicate a significant human experience', and to create an exhibition that had 'an element of the universal and an over-all unity'. He believed the exhibition should have an existence of its own; this was viable with photography because of 'the ease with which any given image can be made small or large, the flexibility of placement and juxtaposition …'[6] Thus, despite extensive

32 *Master Tailor*, by August Sander, 1920–5, gelatin silver print, 1993, 18.9 cm high × 26 cm wide, Die Photographische Sammlung / SK Stiftung Kultur, Cologne. The German photographer August Sander pursued a project, formulated in the 1920s, on 'People of the Twentieth Century' for much of his life. He photographed people from many walks of life, including gypsies, the unemployed, artists and the bourgeoisie. He produced more than 600 'typological portraits' of German people, which explored occupation and social position, hence many of the sitters are not individually named. The Nazis disapproved of his project as it did not privilege Aryan types, and materials were confiscated, but he and many of his photographs survived the war. Sander also produced important work on buildings, cities and nature.

collaboration, above all with his assistant Wayne Miller, the photographer most represented in the show, *The Family of Man* bore Steichen's imprint to a marked degree.

This imprint is evident in the involvement of the American writer and poet Carl Sandburg, Steichen's brother-in-law, to whom he was extremely close, and who wrote the book's Prologue. Sandburg conveyed the flavour of the enterprise: 'A camera testament, a drama of the grand canyon of humanity, an epic woven of fun, mystery and holiness – here is the Family of Man!'.[7] The exhibition's name, a phrase from one of Abraham Lincoln's speeches, came from Sandburg's biography of him.[8] Although photographers' names were concealed during the selection process, many photographs would already have been familiar to Steichen – this was certainly the case with Dorothea Lange and other photographers who had worked for the government in the 1930s and with Miller, represented by photographs of his family, including the birth of his son.[9] Thus, complex intimacies were present in a project that aspired to embrace the world. Steichen believed in the power of photography to change attitudes, while recognising that his attempts to use the medium to marshal opposition to the Korean War had failed. Conceding he had been 'negative' in that instance, he offered up *The Family of Man* as a 'positive' counterpoise. Nothing reveals his emotional investment in the project better than his comments about the experience of going to Moscow in 1959, when it was shown there. He observed and photographed visitors and spoke to as many Russians as possible, including the poet Yevgeny Yevtushenko, whom Sandburg admired, concluding that Russians and Americans were essentially alike. This is a striking claim, given the far greater affluence of the United States in the post-war period and the differences between the political systems of the two countries; it points up his profound faith in a universal humanity. Steichen idealised the United Nations, opposed nuclear weapons and quoted Bertrand Russell on the dangers posed by the hydrogen bomb.[10]

The Family of Man was a massive success in numerical terms – as Steichen proclaimed in 1963, it had been seen by 9 million people in sixty-nine countries and was still on display.[11] But it was not well received in all quarters. For example, the Swiss-born photographer Robert Frank, an 'oppositional modernist', was highly critical of it, as was Roland Barthes of the Paris installation.[12] Yet its original location in MoMA indicates not only Steichen's central role in that institution – he was Director of the Department of Photography for many years – but its willingness to embrace both the medium and a populist exhibition. Steichen was not interested in promoting photography as an art on this occasion, rather he concentrated on 'messages', on the democratic potential of photography, and advertised the show as including works by amateurs. He paid no special attention to iconic photographs.[13]

The book

I have been familiar with the book, which is still in print, since childhood. It helped to shape my visual habits, and I can hardly be alone in this respect. It is slightly smaller than A4 in format, with 192 pages. The layout of the pictures varies: some pages contain only one picture, others many. Carefully designed juxtapositions and groupings add to the impact. Quotations are interspersed throughout the volume, as they were in the exhibition, from the Bible and other sacred texts, and from philosophers, writers and poets. The book, reflecting the exhibition, is arranged thematically, although these are not stated explicitly, rather they become clear through the subject matter of each group. Such themes include – and these are my terms – love, work, family groups, weddings, comfort, misery, religion, protest, childhood and so on.[14] For each photograph, the country where it was taken is given, then the name of the photographer and, very occasionally, a place. For the tiny number of nineteenth-century photos, a date is provided. In some cases, the copyright holder is named: *Magnum*, *Life* magazine, *Vogue* or *Picture Post*, for example. Although photographs came from many countries, a significant proportion were taken either in the United States or by an American photographer. The vast majority contain people, with only a few of landscapes or buildings. As is clear from installation shots, the images varied in size – some were quite huge – and were mounted on stands without frames. **33** Thus the book, like the exhibition, plays continually with the effects of juxtaposition and scale.

The Family of Man may be placed in a long line of photography books; from its inception, photography was used in books. By the 1950s, books in which photographs played a central role were common. **34** Their presence in magazines, on hoardings and packaging, as well as in homes had made photographs familiar. Complex relationships existed between text and image, especially in advocacy books. For example, in 1939 Dorothea Lange and her husband, the economist Paul Schuster Taylor, published *An American Exodus*, which received critical acclaim but made little impact upon the general public, whose attention was gripped by war. Lange and Taylor had been working together since 1934, especially on the migrant workers flooding to California. From Taylor, Lange learned to speak to those she photographed, if they were willing, recording their words as close to verbatim as possible. She kept careful notes of her work in the field, and in certain respects operated like an ethnographer. Yet she was never 'neutral', insofar as this is a genuine state of being, seeing herself as an engaged commentator who sought to change policy, to show contemporary life in a way that was implicitly critical of it. Lange and Taylor's book is one example among many publications designed, through photographs and text, to expose the despair of the era.

An American Exodus and *The Family of Man* differ in important respects. In the latter, the images were chosen for their immediate emotional appeal, which is facilitated by quotations. Steichen's project was accessible entertainment, even if it contained 'messages'. By contrast, *An American Exodus* was 'research'. It was republished in an extended version in 1969 after Lange's death by the Oakland Museum in California,

where Taylor had deposited her files. A curator described her work as 'a rare source of American history and art', while the book's implications for social policy were evident. Lange and Taylor explained: 'We use the camera as a tool of research. Upon a tripod of photographs, captions, and text we rest themes evolved out of long observations in the field. We adhere to the standards of documentary photography as we conceived them…' They emphasised that this was not to be treated as an illustrated book, and to the new edition Taylor added 'non-statistical notes from the field'.[15] Thus the relationships between texts and photographs were complicated. The attention Lange and Taylor paid to field notes indicates their sense of specificity – time, place, gender, age, class and economic situation. By contrast, in *The Family of Man*, the photographs are decontextualised, precisely in the style of modernism. When criticising *The Family of Man*, Barthes observed that it 'postulat[ed] a human essence'

33 Installation shot of *The Family of Man*, New York, 1955, by Andreas Feininger, Getty Collection. Installation shots are invaluable for understanding forms of display. This one includes the lighting, for example. It also reveals the scale of the exhibition, since it shows spectators, who provide an immediate sense of how big some photographs were. Steichen used prints of a wide range of sizes. The images are not framed and it was possible in some cases for visitors to stand very close to them.

34 Page from Andreas Feininger, *The Face of New York: The City as It Was and as It Is* (New York, 1955), 22.5 cm wide × 30.4 cm high, Cambridge University Library. Feininger was a versatile and prolific photographer, who also worked for *Life* magazine. He produced this work in collaboration with Susan Lyman, who provided the text. The volume included historical material, but it is primarily a photographer's response to New York around the time of *The Family of Man* exhibition. Feininger, who came from a German-American family, many of whose members were artists and/or architects, also published on photographic technique. Indeed, he provided details of the films, cameras, exposure meters, papers and developers he used to make the photographs of New York. In this plate, the shadow, the onlookers and the displayed pictures all encourage us to think about visual experience.

Sometimes it takes years for a new custom to strike root here, but the Washington Square outdoor art exhibit has been a success ever since its start in 1931. Twice a year, spring and fall, you can wander along and study the pictures displayed by local artists on fences and buildings of the western half of the Square. If your preference runs to books, spend those leisure moments on lower Fourth Avenue between Astor Place and 14th Street where the second-hand book dealers welcome browsers. Or if you want to stroll about, if you want variety, take a look at Fifth Avenue, starting at Washington Square where that world-famous street begins, and follow it north.

and denied 'the determining weight of History'. Steichen had turned phenomena, such as poverty, that could and should be censured, into a form of nature – universal, eternal.[16] While Lange was an enthusiastic collaborator in Steichen's project, her own work was very different, much more in tune with Barthes's ideas. Thus although photography books were ubiquitous by the 1950s, closer inspection reveals divergent agendas.

35 Page 150 in *The Family of Man* (New York, 1955), 28 cm high × 20.7 cm wide. 'Migrant Mother' is one of four smaller photographs on the facing page, including another image by Lange. cf **36** It was not possible to gain permission to use page 151, but the book is widely available. Ben Shahn's thin woman, with her worried face and self-protective posture standing in front of a shack conveys the flavour of many Farm Security Administration photographs.

U.S.A. Ben Shahn. Farm Security Adm.

What region of the earth is not full of our calamities?   Virgil

150

'Migrant Mother'

Open the *Family of Man* book at pages 150 and 151 and you see five photographs, all of which evoke poverty, deprivation and despair. **35** Two of these are by Dorothea Lange and one is particularly well known, so well known that it is frequently made to stand for the American Depression as a whole. It depicts a woman with three children, staring out of the picture past the viewer. The premature wrinkles on her face, the two scruffy children looking away, one resting on each shoulder, and the grubby appearance of her clothes and of the baby's blanket, produce a feeling of hopelessness. Like another picture in this spread, it is credited to the Farm Security Administration (FSA), the US government agency that sought to alleviate and to document the plight of the rural poor, for which Lange worked in the late 1930s. The classical quotation, which presents calamities as global, is worth noting. These pages provide a striking example of the universalising tendency of Steichen's project. In fact, four out of the five photographs were taken in the United States between the wars, while the fifth, depicting a street musician, was taken in England by Robert Frank in 1951.

Lange became interested in documentary photography in the late 1920s and early 1930s, when she started going into the streets to photograph what she saw rather than doing portraits in her studio. Her first show of documentary photographs in 1934 was seen by Paul Taylor, who was then studying migrant labour. They began to collaborate and were married the following year. Later, Lange captured the internment of Japanese Americans following the 1941 attack on Pearl Harbour, another example of her documenting and providing critical commentary upon contemporary suffering.[17] Her own understanding of documentary photography is revealing:

> A documentary photograph is not a factual photograph per se … It is a photograph which carries the full meaning of the episode or the circumstance or the situation that can only be revealed … by this quality … Every photograph really is documentary and belongs in some place, has a place in history – can be fortified by words … I don't like the kind of written material that tells a person what to look for, or that explains the photograph. I like the kind of material that gives more background, that fortifies it without directing the person's mind.[18]

Lange herself saw the affinities with anthropology, and articulated the special kind of visual attention out of which great photographs come.[19] Her 'Migrant Mother' series needs to be seen in this context. One image on page 151 of *The Family of Man* is from this famous suite.

According to Lange's own testimony, she took several shots of the woman in March 1936. On her way home, longing to be back with her family, she turned back despite herself, to follow a sign marked 'Pea-pickers camp', operating on instinct, not reason:

> I saw and approached the hungry and desperate mother, as if drawn by a magnet. I do not know how I explained my presence or my camera to her, but I do remember she asked me no questions … I did not ask her name or her history. She told me her age, that she was thirty-two. She said that they had been living on frozen vegetables from the surrounding fields, and birds that the children killed. She had just sold the tires from her car to buy food. There she sat in that lean-to tent with her children huddled

around her, and seemed to know that my pictures might help her, and
so she helped me. There was a sort of equality about it … I knew I had
recorded the essence of my assignment.[20]

Lange's account invites critical engagement – it expresses a somewhat
romanticised sense of her work. It is nonetheless valuable to know how
she represented a central moment in her professional life.

The woman in the photograph has been called a Madonna, with
'sacred' also being used of the pictures. Certainly many photographs are
best understood in terms of work in other media, to which they may be
said to refer, whether knowingly or not. For example, there is a photograph in *The Family of Man* of a young woman with long hair – her
shoulders are bare, her hair is in motion, with one strand across her
mouth. The print is soft and grainy. It brings to mind Botticelli's *Birth of
Venus*.[21] In Lange's picture, the woman is clearly a mother, but she does
not resemble Mary, mother of Jesus. The migrant is not beautiful and
serene, but worn and lined. She is not engaging with any of her children;
indeed, she is seemingly unaware of them, thoughtful and self-absorbed.
Furthermore, in depictions of the Madonna and Child, the baby is, naturally enough, central. In two of Lange's pictures we can see the face of
one of the older children, but the baby is either asleep or feeding. He
is visible but not prominent. Since the woman became emblematic of
suffering during the Great Depression, idioms were presumably sought
through which to express her special quality, and a mother with children prompted ideas of the Madonna, although this combination – a
woman surrounded by children – is frequently associated with 'Charity'.[22]
Perhaps the term 'Madonna' elevated the woman, gave her additional
dignity. Nonetheless it is misleading – a facile tag that pre-empts careful thought and reflection. 'Migrant Mother' may have become iconic, a
symbol of the Depression, but it is not easy to interpret it or to explain
its appeal. **36**

Interpretation and historiography

Photography has spawned vast literatures, which are diverse in genre,
tone, rigour, approach and implied audience. *The Family of Man*
exhibition has also provoked varied responses, less from historians
than from writers, critics, commentators and those concerned with
the visual arts. This range derives from a number of factors. There is
widespread interest in photography itself, because of its ubiquity and
accessibility. Since photographs are understood to make claims about
the world, they invite direct responses – political, personal, emotional and aesthetic. These come, not from a single constituency, but

from those touched by the medium; other photographers, journalists, photographic experts, politically engaged commentators, media specialists and the general public. Reactions to *The Family of Man* exhibition can be accounted for, at least in part, by the heterogeneity of the issues the exhibition and book touch upon. Historians of photography are an obvious group, and many general histories of the field mention it. More specifically, anyone interested in American photography and in Edward Steichen's role within it cannot ignore a project that was so important to him. Since the exhibition was very much of its time, those concerned with the United States in the 1950s have taken *The Family of Man* as a cultural landmark. Contemporary history and American Studies are distinct fields from the history of photography. Research concerning the histories of institutions, those who lead them and their exhibitions is yet another scholarly domain. For example, there is work on MoMA, on Alfred Barr its founding director, who was interested in and sympathetic to photography, and on shows mounted there. Since *The Family of Man* travelled to many countries, there is also an international dimension to the story. The visit of the show to Moscow was especially important, given the Cold War context, and the significance Steichen himself attached to it.

Many of the photographers represented in the exhibition were major figures, and hence specialist literatures on them exist. In the case of Dorothea Lange many writings and responses exist. Examples range from what are best described as picture books, such as those by Durden and Arrow, where the emphasis is on providing illustrations of a small number of her best-known works, through more extended works, for example by Elizabeth Partridge, that stress her life, to scholarly accounts, some of which set her in broader contexts, such as Karin Ohrn's book on 'the documentary tradition'. Lange worked for the government, and there are also studies of the agencies involved, such as the FSA, and more broadly of the relationships between photography and politics. *The Family of Man* comes up in other contexts. For instance, the writers and photographers Allan Sekula and Victor Burgin have provided sharp critical commentary on Steichen's enterprise. There are many modes of address here for historians to assess and interpret.

Let me note an absence, which is characteristic of writings on photography: many publications on the medium have little or nothing to say on techniques, equipment, and technological change. A few try to integrate context, biography and the visual dimensions of photographs with the technical aspects of the medium, but they are rare.[23] Works on cameras tend to be aimed at collectors or to arise from work on the history of technology. One crucial difference between secondary accounts

is the degree to which they engage with the visual properties of photographs themselves. In the case of *The Family of Man*, it is sometimes
the phenomenon and its ideology that take centre stage: close readings
of the pictures and modes of display are not deemed necessary, while
other writings pay careful attention to both. Works with a biographical
emphasis tend to be more concerned with specific images by the photographer in question. The iconic status of Lange's 'Migrant Mother'
pictures can distract attention from the photographs themselves, rather
than encourage careful looking. Because her work is highly esteemed,
claims concerning her artistry are made. Ironically, Lange was reluctant
to call herself an artist; those who write about her are more willing to
make such a claim.

These diverse literatures deploy a variety of frameworks in relation
to photography in the twentieth century – a situation that prompts
historians to reflect upon the role of theory in relation to visual and
material culture.[24] This becomes an issue when historians engage
with evidence studied by disciplines that are more openly and explicitly theoretical than history itself. The point applies to many aspects
of visual and material culture, and is particularly striking in the case
of photography. We might argue, first, as many scholars have done,
that photography, a technique announced in 1839, was constitutive of
the modern world. It made major contributions to modernity, and to
modernism.[25] Attempts to conceptualise those phenomena, by including photography, have offered frameworks for theorising it. Second, we
may observe that over the twentieth century new theories and ways of
seeing arose that seem especially well suited to (relatively) new media
such as photography and film.[26] Third, photography has been central to mass culture, for example, through photo-journalism. Its role
in politics, generously defined, has been notably complex.[27] Precisely
because photography raises questions about the relationships between
those who take and those who are captured, about the nature of the
self, about propaganda, and about the ethics of photography in situations of conflict, more general discourses have proliferated. Perhaps
this has left historians free to operate in a more empirical mode and to
use photography in an illustrative manner, without getting involved in
debates about its role and status.

Photography: special challenges?

In two important respects *The Family of Man* differs from the subjects
of the other essays in this book. First, the medium, photography, bears
a peculiarly complex relationship with historical practice. Many of the

MIGRANT MOTHER ᴀɴᴅ CHILDREN
CALIFORNIA

PUBLICATIONS WHICH THEY HAVE APPEARED
1935 -'36 -'37 -'38 -'39

36 *Migrant Mother and Children – California*, photographic print on album page, 1936, sheet 58.3 cm high × 48 cm wide, print 23.9 cm high × 18.5 cm wide. Library of Congress Prints and Photographs Division, Washington DC. This is a log sheet used by the Farm Security Administration for which Lange worked. It lists publications in which the picture appeared between 1936 and 1940. The Library of Congress online entry does not give the size of the page, but it provides the original title of the photograph: 'Destitute peapickers in California, a 32 year old mother of seven children'.

photographs I have mentioned were created in a spirit of recording contemporary life for critical purposes and understood by their makers as forms of research. Lange and Taylor saw themselves as cultural historians. Thus there were distinctive types of historical awareness built into the production of some photographs. When historians take photographs and prepare photo-essays, they create new sources, while also offering commentary.[28] It is undeniable that, since the middle of the nineteenth century, photography has played a central role in shaping experience. Thus we have all been constituted, at least in part, through a medium that is one of the richest sources of material for modern historians.

Second, my object of study is a book, one of enduring interest to be sure, but its constituent images are, in fact, elusive. They exist in countless versions and the notion of 'an original' is fragile. Perhaps this is why, in the case of photographs deemed authoritative, forms of authenticity are so desired. Lange changed the negative of one of the 'Migrant Mother' series against the wishes of her FSA boss, Roy Stryker, and his furious reaction is telling.[29] We recognise the one in *The Family of Man* from other publications, but the manner, we might say the 'style', in which it is printed and its size, like the setting in which it appears, shape viewers' responses to it. If there is a stable resting point, it would perhaps be a negative in the Library of Congress in Washington DC. **36**

In both book and exhibition, historians are faced with suites of photographs, rather than with separate images. While a few individual photographs have become iconic, they are atypical and do not necessarily help historians understand photography as a medium and its implications for historical practice. Photographs have impact not in any pure, pristine form, such as a print made and signed by a named photographer – the norm in art photography – but through being constantly reproduced in books, magazines, newspapers, and on advertisements, television and the internet. Repetition and ubiquity are key themes. The single shot may indeed be important, but so are combinations, juxtapositions and sequences, a point that applies to photographic exhibitions too. Thus close attention to forms of display is needed, as well as analytical frameworks that do justice to elaborate assemblages.

The Family of Man project involved distinctive displays, arrived at through processes of selection, printing, mounting and design. Its historical context, for example, the Cold War and the fear of nuclear war, was quite specific, but its universalising claims actively worked to undermine a sense of that specificity, and virtually no information was provided about the settings in which the photographs had been taken. Viewers and readers inferred what they wished. One example is a page showing ruined buildings, clearly the result of bombing, with a boy, the only human figure visible, walking down steps, to or from school perhaps, with a satchel on his back. It is labelled simply, 'Germany. Otto Hagel'.[30] In 1955 the image alone was eloquent, the reference to Germany makes the scene it depicts clearer. Yet its interpretation is underdetermined. Are viewers to feel sympathy for the child, guilt about allied bombing, or victors' pride – in Steichen's terms, what is the 'message'? An instructive comparison is with a famous photograph of soldiers escorting men, women and children along a desolate street. **37** The tiny letters below read 'Warsaw Ghetto. German photographer unknown. *Exhibit at Nürnberg Trial*', and George Sand's forceful words also take the viewer by the hand.[31] By contrast, the spread in *The Family of Man* that included 'Migrant Mother' made no reference to the terrible privations experienced by a significant proportion of the population of the United States between the wars, although many would have recognised Lange's photograph. The specificity Lange valued has been lost, the picture is no longer grounded; it generates, with neighbouring photographs, an undifferentiated sense of hardship.

I began with the idea that photography is both treacherous and seductive. Each image, like every version of a photograph, therefore needs to be interrogated – when, where, who, why, how and so on. The fact that Robert Capa's celebrated 'Death of a Spanish Militiaman', taken on 5 September 1936, still provokes controversy about its authenticity, reveals how troubling these matters are and how vital good faith is, precisely because photography both claims authority and shapes emotional life. According to Jonathan Jones, 'Capa's photograph changed history; it defined the war for everyone who saw it. Spain was the last great romantic war…' If the picture had been staged, that 'would make it a brilliant propaganda image but not the document it claimed to be'.[32] The epistemological and ethical issues photography raises are not adequately met by the claim that all photographs are constructions. This is true enough – all photographs are made things, but this does not do justice to the special faith in photography, which is bound up with its authority and emotional potency.

37 Pages 166 and 167 in
The Family of Man (New York,
1955), individual pages 28 cm
high × 20.7 cm wide.

. . . Humanity is outraged in me and with me.

We must not dissimulate nor try to forget this

NOTES

1   At the time this essay was first drafted, the book was on display at the Victoria
and Albert Museum, London as part of an exhibition entitled 'Libraries of
Light; Photographic Books'. The claim was made on the label. For another estimate of its success, see Eric J. Sandeen, *Picturing an Exhibition: the Family of
Man and 1950s America* (Albuquerque, 1995), Introduction. Sandeen stresses
the art of the exhibition's construction and its modernist aesthetic. The many
versions of both book and exhibition are outlined in Mary Anne Staniszewski,
*The Power of Display: a History of Exhibition Installations at the Museum of
Modern Art* (Cambridge, MA, and London, 1998), pp. 235–59, 334–9, esp. n. 70
on pp. 334–5. The paperback that is currently available is the one most people,

37 (*cont.*)

indignation which is one of the most passionate forms of love.

including myself, mean by 'the book'. Minor changes were made to the cover in 1986 for the thirtieth anniversary edition.

2 Peter Stepan, ed., *Photos that Changed the World: the 20th Century* (Munich and New York, 2000), p. 12. In his introductory essay, Stepan draws attention to the different ways in which historians and art historians use photographs and offers many valuable comments about their interpretation. See pp. 48–9 for his discussion of Lange's 'Migrant Mother', which appears on p. 151 of *The Family of Man* (New York, 1986; first published 1955).

3 *Family* (1986), Introduction by Edward Steichen, p. 3.

4 For example, Victor Burgin, ed., *Thinking Photography* (London, 1982), ch. 4 by Allan Sekula and ch. 5 by John Tagg; and John Tagg, *The Burden of Representation: Essays on Photographies and Histories* (Basingstoke, 1988).

5 Lange's pictures are on pp. 49, 50, 65, 80, 129, 131 and 151; work by members of the Magnum group may be found on p. 11 (by Ernst Haas) and p. 14 (by Werner Bischof); see also *After the War was Over* (London, 1985), with an introduction by Mary Blume, for a useful introduction to Magnum, which still exists. Irving Penn's work had appeared in *Vogue*, see pp. 28 and 30 in *The Family of Man*. Brandt's work is on pp. 41, 138 and 159, and Sander's on pp. 74, 165 and 183. Brandt had been born in Germany but moved to Britain as a young man where he spent the rest of his life.

6 Edward Steichen, *A Life in Photography* (London, 1963), ch. 13, unpaginated.

7 *Family* (1986), p. 5.

8 Steichen, *Life*, ch. 13.

9 F. Jack Hurley, *Portrait of a Decade: Roy Stryker and the Development of Documentary Photography in the Thirties* (Baton Rouge, 1972). Stryker ran the FSA photography programme and both Dorothea Lange and Walker Evans undertook government work.

10 *Family* (1986), pp. 184–5 and 179.

11 Steichen, *Life*, ch. 13. Others give rather different figures, for example William H. Young with Nancy K. Young, *The 1950s* (Westport, CT, 2004), p. 276, who are rather hostile to the exhibition, say that by the *end* of the twentieth century 9 million had either seen the show or bought the book. They argue it used cheap emotion and claim it contained 'snapshots of the human condition'.

12 Roland Barthes, 'The Great Family of Man', in his *Mythologies*, trans. and selected by Annette Lavers (London, 1972; first published 1957), pp. 100–2. Sandeen, *Picturing*, associated Robert Frank with 'oppositional modernism', p. 4. Frank was in fact well represented in *The Family of Man*, see pp. 20, 21, 91, 143, 145 and 155, as well as p. 151 where his photograph of a man with a violin appears next to 'Migrant Mother'.

13 Sandeen, *Picturing*, pp. 1, 2 and 42, and on iconic photos p. 69, where he explains that Dorothea Lange's 'Migrant Mother' 'was relegated to one of the baffles and not given a prominent spot'.

14 Sections of the exhibition were named in the planning and design stages, see Jean Back and Viktoria Schmidt-Linsenhoff, *The Family of Man 1955–2001: Humanism and Postmodernism* (Marburg, 2004), p. 82, for the published 'floorplan and synopsis'. Titles included lovers, disturbed children, fathers and sons, household and office work, folk-singing, learning, thinking, and teaching, death, and faces of war.

15 Dorothea Lange and Paul Schuster Taylor, *An American Exodus: a Record of Human Erosion in the Thirties* (New Haven, 1969; first published 1939), pp. 9, 15 and 136–44. The quotation on p. 15 comes from the original edition.

16 Barthes, *Mythologies*, pp. 100 and 101.

17 Jan Arrow, *Dorothea Lange* (London and Sydney, 1985), unpaginated essay.

18 *Dorothea Lange: Photographs of a Lifetime with an Essay by Robert Coles and Afterword by Therese Heyman* (Millerton, NY, 1982), pp. 108 and 142.

19 Anne Whiston Spirn, *Daring to Look: Dorothea Lange's Photographs and Reports from the Field* (Chicago and London, 2008), see pp. 42–3 for Lange's admiration of the anthropologists Margaret Mead and Gregory Bateson and their photography. On visual attention, see p. 4.

20 Quoted in *Dorothea Lange Text by Jan Arrow* (London, 1985), unpaginated, and also in a longer version in *Dorothea Lange Photographs of a Lifetime*, p. 76. 'Migrant Mother' is mentioned and reproduced so often that it would not be feasible to produce a comprehensive list, but see Spirn, *Daring*, pp. 8 and 9, which provides Lange's original caption and shows a 1998 postage stamp based on it, p. 15 (where she suggests it may be the most reproduced photograph in the world), 29, 51; on p. 323 n. 44 she gives the name of the woman as Florence Thompson, who claimed Lange never asked her permission to take the photograph. See also Stepan, *Photos that Changed the World*, p. 48–9, which describes it as 'Madonna-like' and the mother as 'sad but stalwart' – caption by Barbara L. Michaels.

21 *Family* (1986), p. 162, top left, described as 'USA. Paul Himmel'. Botticelli's painting is in the Uffizi Gallery, Florence and may be viewed on their website.

22 James Hall, *Dictionary of Subjects and Symbols in Art*, rev. edn (London, 1979), p. 64.

23 Ian Jeffrey, *Photography: a Concise History* (London, 1981), deals with all technical matters in a few pages at the end of the book – 'The Development of Photography: a Brief Chronology', pp. 240–5. Michel Frizot, ed., *A New History of Photography* (Cologne, 1998), pp. 755–7, includes a short essay by Anne Cartier-Bresson, 'Methods of Producing Photographic Prints', which describes different processes and then illustrates them so that the visual differences between them are evident. Cameras themselves rarely feature in books on photography, but see Brian Coe, *Kodak Cameras: the First Hundred Years* (Small Dole, West Sussex, 2003; first published 1988), which is for collectors, and Brian Coe, *Cameras from Daguerrotypes to Instant Pictures* (Gothenburg, 1978), a general guide to the history of photographic apparatus illustrated by drawings and diagrams. A distinguished exception is Roger Taylor, *Impressed by Light: British Photographs from Paper Negatives, 1840–1860* (New Haven and London, 2007). An integrative approach to early photography is more common.

24 Introductory works on photography that seek to make explicit the nature and role of theory are Terence Wright, *The Photography Handbook* (London, 1999) (Wright is a photographer, shows examples of his work and discusses practice), and Liz Wells, ed., *Photography: a Critical Introduction*, 2nd edn (London, 2000). This volume aims to offer 'a good, coherent introduction to issues in photography theory', p. xii. It includes a case study of 'Migrant Mother', pp. 35–45.

25 Richard Brettell, *Modern Art 1851–1929: Capitalism and Representation* (Oxford, 1999), is explicit on this point, for example pp. 2 and 3–5.

26 Psychoanalysis would be a case in point. So would critical theory more generally. The link between psychoanalysis and film has been particularly

close. Thus in her *Visual Methodologies*, Gillian Rose uses film to illustrate the potential of psychoanalysis for work on visual materials: *Visual Methodologies: An Introduction to Researching with Visual Materials*, 3rd edn (London, 2012), ch. 7. See also Harry Trosman, *Contemporary Psychoanalysis and Masterworks of Art and Film* (New York and London, 1996); and Maurice Charney and Joseph Reppen, *Psychoanalytic Approaches to Literature and Film* (Rutherford and London, 1987).

27 Eugenics is an excellent example of the political use of photography: Anne Maxwell, *Picture Imperfect: Photography and Eugenics, 1870–1940* (Brighton, 2008).

28 See, for example, Richard Vinen, *History in Fragments: Europe in the Twentieth Century* (London, 2000), which contains 'Clichés: a Photographic Essay'; pp. 260–3 is a short text about photography in the twentieth century; pp. 265–81 are the photographs themselves with fairly substantial captions.

29 She erased a thumb that showed on the negative, and incurred Stryker's wrath as a result. The episode is mentioned, for example, in Hurley, *Roy Stryker*, p. 142. The 'Migrant Mother' series is also discussed on pp. 71, 128 and 143.

30 *Family* (1986), p. 127. Otto Hagel was born in Germany, but became an American citizen and worked for *Life* magazine.

31 *Family* (1986), pp. 166–7.

32 Richard Whelan, *This is War! Robert Capa at Work* (New York, 2007), provides a detailed treatment of this issue. He shows the known shots, attempts to reconstruct their sequence and also shows the use of groups of Capa's photographs in contemporary magazines such as *Vu*, *Regards* and *Match* – see ch. 2 'The Falling Solider 1936'. Jonathan Jones, Caption to the photograph in Stepan, *Photos That Changed the World*, p. 51.

FURTHER READING

The secondary literature on photography and its history is vast. Useful introductions are Ian Jeffrey, *Photography: a Concise History* (London, 1981); Graham Clarke, *The Photograph* (Oxford, 1997); and Mark Haworth-Booth, *Photography: an Independent Art* (London, 1997). Its ubiquity has spawned many attempts to conceptualise the nature of the medium, which also figures in discussions of visual culture studies: Victor Burgin, ed., *Thinking Photography* (London, 1982); L. Wells, ed., *Photography: a Critical Introduction*, 2nd edn (London, 2000); Chris Jenks, ed., *Visual Culture* (London, 1995), esp. ch. 13; and Walter Benjamin, *Illuminations* (London, 1970).

Carol Armstrong, *Scenes in a Library: Reading the Photograph in the Book, 1843–1875* (Cambridge, MA, and London, 1998), is useful on books and early photography.

On documentary photography, see John Raeburn, *A Staggering Revolution: a Cultural History of Thirties Photography* (Urbana, IL, 2006); Lili Corbus

Bezner, *Photography and Politics in America: From the New Deal into the Cold War* (Baltimore and London, 1999), esp. Introduction; Graham Clarke, *The Photograph* (Oxford, 1997), ch. 8; and William Stott, *Documentary Expression and Thirties America* (London, 1976). Graham Clarke, ed., *The Portrait in Photography* (London, 1992), is also useful.

On iconic images, see Peter Stepan, ed., *Photos that Changed the World: the 20th Century* (Munich and New York, 2000), which contains many examples, such as 'Napalm Attack' taken in June 1972 in South Vietnam and published on the cover of *Time* magazine, pp. 134–5.

The following works provide further reading on the principal photographers mentioned in the essay: Theodore Stebbins *et al.*, *Edward Weston: Photography and Modernism* (Boston and London, 1999); Sarah Greenough and Juan Hamilton, eds., *Alfred Stieglitz, Photographs and Drawings* (Washington DC, 1999); for Henry Crabbe Robinson, see Jeffrey, *Photography*, p. 46; Colin Ford, *Julia Margaret Cameron: 19th Century Photographer of Genius* (London, 2003); Nigel Warburton, ed., *Bill Brandt: Selected Texts and Bibliography* (Oxford, 1993); Ian Jeffrey, *Bill Brandt* (London, 2007); Manfred Heitung, ed., *August Sander, 1876–1964* (Cologne and London, 1999); Sarah Greenough *et al.*, *Robert Frank* (Washington and Zurich, 1994); Alex Kershaw, *Blood and Champagne: the Life and Times of Robert Capa* (London, 2002); and Andreas Feininger, *The World Through My Eyes: 30 Years of Photography* (London, 1964).

To pursue the theme of manipulation, compare the various editions of *Let Us Now Praise Famous Men* (Boston, 1941), with text by James Agee and photographs by Walker Evans. They reveal just how different the 'same' photographs look when cropped, printed and placed differently and on different paper. Many versions have been published of this extraordinary book. Compare, for example, the London 1969 edition published by Panther Books with the Penguin one of 2006: the photographs differ with respect to location, size, paper and tones, producing quite distinct viewing-cum-reading experiences.

On emotions and photography, Roland Barthes, *Camera Lucida* (London, 1982; first published in French in 1980), remains one of the most moving, important and widely cited works on photography. It also provides an analytical framework, for example, his distinction between 'punctum' and 'studium'. See also Susan Sontag's influential *On Photography* (London, 1978).

On photography in medicine, see Daniel Fox and Christopher Lawrence, *Photographing Medicine: Images and Power in Britain and America since 1840* (New York and London, 1988), and John Harley Warner and James Edmonson, *Dissection: Photographs of a Rite of Passage in American Medicine, 1880–1930* (New York, 2009). Charles Darwin used photographs in *The Expression of the Emotions in Man and Animals* (London, 1872); see also Chrissie Iles and Russell Roberts, eds., *In Visible Light: Photography and Classification in Art, Science and the Everyday* (Oxford, 1997). Photography has been of fundamental importance for anthropology: for example, Elizabeth Edwards, ed., *Anthropology and Photography, 1860–1920* (New Haven and London, 1992), and Elizabeth Edwards and Janice Hart, eds., *Photographs Objects Histories: On the Materiality of Images* (London, 2004).

Works on Edward Steichen and *The Family of Man* are cited in the endnotes. There is also Ronald J. Gedrim, ed., *Edward Steichen: Selected Texts and Bibliography* (Oxford, 1996), which provides a useful introduction, lists works about Steichen as well as by him, and also the exhibitions he curated at the Museum of Modern Art, New York, between 1947 and 1962.

The Family of Man is mentioned briefly in many books on the history of photography, more sustained analyses are cited in the endnotes. See also Bezner, *Photography and Politics*, ch. 3 'Subtle Subterfuge: the Flawed Nobility of the Edward Steichen's *The Family of Man*'. She provides a good account of the critics of the show. Most discussions emphasise the exhibition rather than the book. On *Life* magazine, see David E. Scherman, ed., *The Best of Life* (New York, 1973), which includes a wide range of photographic materials from the magazine between 1936 and 1972 when it closed, although it includes no more than a tiny selection from its picture collection – claimed to contain more than 18 million images (p. 5).

On MoMA, see Sybil Gordon Kantor, *Alfred H. Barr, Jr., and the Intellectual Origins of the Museum of Modern Art* (Cambridge, MA, and London, 2002), and Mary Anne Staniszewski, *The Power of Display: a History of Exhibition Installations at the Museum of Modern Art* (Cambridge, MA, and London, 1998). Steichen himself acknowledged the importance of Barr's and MoMA's recognition of photography in his *A Life in Photography* (New York, 1963), ch. 13.

J. M. Mancini, *Pre-Modernism: Art-World Change and American Culture from the Civil War to the Armory Show* (Princeton and Oxford, 2005), pays attention to the role of photography in the development of American modernism, see the chapter on *Camera Work* with which Steichen was involved.

There are numerous books on Lange: the 'standard' account is usually taken to be Milton Meltzer, *Dorothea Lange: a Photographer's Life* (New York, 1978). See also Elizabeth Partridge, ed., *Dorothea Lange: a Visual Life* (Washington DC and London, 1994), Partridge was a family friend; Karin Becker Ohrn, *Dorothea Lange and the Documentary Tradition* (Baton Rouge and London, 1980); Jan Arrow, *Dorothea Lange* (London, 1985); Mark Durden, *Dorothea Lange* (London, 2001); and Jan Goggans, *California on the Breadlines: Dorothea Lange, Paul Taylor, and the Making of a New Deal Narrative* (Berkeley and London, 2010), which is a subtle and sensitive study. For an important aspect of Lange's career, see F. Jack Hurley, *Portrait of a Decade: Roy Stryker and the Development of Documentary Photography in the Thirties* (New York, 1972). Books about the Depression have frequently used Lange's work as illustrations; for example, part of one of the 'Migrant Mother' series is on the cover of Anthony J. Badger's, *The New Deal: the Depression Years, 1933–1940* (Basingstoke, 1989), but because it was obtained from a picture library her name is not given, nor is the title and date. Short biographies of Lange appeared in the *Dictionary of American Biography Supplement Seven: 1961–1965*, ed. John Garraty (New York, 1981), pp. 455–7, and *American National Biography*, ed. John Garraty and Mark Carnes, vol. 13 (New York and Oxford, 1999), pp. 145–7.

R. D. Morris is an interesting example of a historian who uses and writes about photographs, including those he has taken himself. See, for example, 'History on the Walls: a photo-essay on Historical Narrative and the Political Wall Murals of Belfast in the Late 1990s', in *Ireland and Scotland: Order and Disorder, 1600–2000*, ed. R. D. Morris and Liam Kennedy (Edinburgh, 2005), pp. 231–44, and R. D. Morris, *Scotland 1907: the Many Scotlands of Valentine and Sons, Photographers* (Edinburgh, 2007).

For the use of non-professional photography in historical accounts, see Gillian Rose, *Doing Family Photography: the Domestic, the Public and the Politics of Sentiment* (Farnham, 2010); Hilda Kean *et al.*, eds., *Seeing History: Public History in Britain Now* (London, 2000), pp. 19–35; Robert Pols, *Family Photographs, 1860–1945* (Richmond, Surrey, 2002); and Julia Hirsch, *Family Photographs: Content, Meaning and Effects* (New York and Oxford, 1981).

Bridge

Photography is indeed evocative: it is significant that it has been an active force in shaping and re-presenting human experience since the middle of the nineteenth century. Historians working on the nineteenth and twentieth centuries cannot afford to ignore the insinuating impact the medium has had. In many respects it is, I have suggested, constitutive of modern life. Photographs are displayed everywhere, making everyone a member of photographic audiences. Its extraordinary and challenging status is thus bound up with audiences and display, the subject of the next chapter.

4 Audiences and display

Audiences fight back

When *The Family of Man* exhibition was taken to Moscow in 1959, a young Nigerian tore down some of the images, explaining, 'African men and women were portrayed either half clothed or naked. I could not stand the sight. It was insulting, undignified and tendentious.'[1] It is a telling story. Images and objects enrage people as well as enchanting, entertaining, moving, challenging and arousing them. In creating the exhibition, Steichen sought as broad an audience as possible. Since it espoused universalist values, affirming the unity of humankind, he presumably did not anticipate fierce negative reactions. His commitments were expressed in the subject matter and every aspect of the display. Objects and images have provoked violence on numerous occasions and such episodes provide historians with opportunities to reflect upon the reactions of audiences to the visual and material worlds on display.

Iconoclasm, that is, the deliberate destruction of religious artefacts, is an obvious example. It is familiar to those working on European religion in the sixteenth and seventeenth centuries, but it is also a feature of contemporary existence. The Taliban's destruction of ancient statues of Buddha in Afghanistan in 2001 is a tragic instance. Famous paintings have been mutilated in recent decades, although not always out of religious motives.[2] In *The Power of Images*, David Freedberg considers topics such as iconoclasm and pornography, setting out 'some of the most dramatic forms of broadly recurrent responses, and [considers] the relations between images and people that are recorded in history and are plain from anthropology as well as folk psychology'. Furthermore, 'certain kinds of imagery provide more than usually direct evidence: for example, wax images, funeral effigies, pornographic illustrations and sculptures, and the whole range of billboards and posters'.[3] By taking behaviour deemed extreme, Freedberg sheds light on the effects some artefacts provoke. In the twenty-first century, we know that artefacts have been destroyed because of intense religious sentiments, and their makers and publishers attacked. Those taking such drastic action are rather particular kinds of 'audience', who remind us that viewers are not passive recipients, but agents whose responses are eloquent. For Freedberg, violence is simply one manifestation of feelings that most people experience.

Concepts and contexts

The theme of audiences and display – these concepts logically entail each other – concerns the relationships between people and objects in particular settings. This subject touches fundamental aspects of human existence, such as belief, sexuality, power, authority, possession, control and intimacy. It surfaces in a range of contexts, including the rejection of commissioned work; the debates that arose from the Salon exhibitions at the Royal Academy in Paris from 1737, making 'public opinion' an important force in the art world; the publication of outspoken criticism; all forms of censorship; and decisions not to put works on public display. 38 For example, the British Museum in London owns Ethiopian religious objects, which are not supposed to be seen, except by a tiny number of priests and hence are not on public view. In such cases, both artefacts and reactions to them have been endowed with potency; they reveal how fundamental questions of audiences and display are for an understanding of visual and material culture. Thus the ability to see things can itself be contentious, and diverse groups have interests in the nature and content of display, who constitutes an audience, where and in what circumstances.

This chapter explores ways of understanding viewers and users, and the forms of display to which they respond. Simply putting an image in a frame constitutes a type of display; the sort of frame selected, along with the image itself, is determined by anticipated audiences and settings, as well as by the framer's preferences, income and judgements. 'Display' refers to many phenomena, including the mounting of artefacts, their containers, labels and location. The *idea* of display is not difficult to grasp. It refers to processes of revelation, to the exhibition of something for inspection. In the context of printed materials, it refers to the arrangement on a page, and in a digital context, to what appears on

Coup d'œil exact de l'arrangement des Peintures au Salon du Louvre, en 1785
Gravé de mémoire, et terminé durant le temps de l'exposition

38 *Coup d'œil exact de l'arrangement des Peintures au Salon du Louvre, en 1785 (A Precise View of the Arrangement of Paintings in the Salon at the Louvre in 1785)*, by Pierre Antoine Martini, etching, Paris 1785, 34.7 cm high × 51.1 cm wide, British Museum. Martini produced a number of views of both the Paris Salon and the Royal Academy exhibitions in London in the 1780s. The hanging of pictures on top of each other is worth noting; Martini shows the audience dwarfed by the array of paintings.

a screen. With the growth of public history, there is increasing interest in the ways the past is put on display. 'Display' can suggest ostentation, especially when it comes to personal possessions and ceremonies. One difficulty with the notion of display is that it simply covers so much.

By contrast, the concept 'audience', which also encompasses many phenomena, is difficult to conceptualise in this context. There is no collective noun for those who see and use artefacts. Etymologically, 'audience' privileges the sense of hearing and suggests performance – plays, music, opera, readings, speeches, lectures and so on. These phenomena have a visual dimension, but the ear plays a central role. Some objects possess performative elements – for example, when they are adjuncts to religious devotion – but 'audience' is not the most obvious word to use. Few books on visual and material culture list the word in their indexes. Since I cannot find a better one, I use 'audience' here. The term suggests a situation where a number of people experience a performance simultaneously. I intend no such implication. Rather I am drawing attention to the fact that artefacts contain ideas about those who will deploy them, even if that only involves visual inspection. I am gathering together those who respond to items of visual and material culture and those whom makers had in mind, with the word 'audience' because, however imperfect it is, it comes the closest to the issues I wish to explore in this chapter.

Three general points about audiences invite attention. First, artefacts elicit a striking range of responses – sometimes, as we have noted, extremely strong ones – and the context and manner of their display shape and shed light on these reactions, and vice versa. It is best to assume, even in the absence of direct evidence, that audiences are active. Second, artefacts typically come under the gaze and touch of many audiences over their lifetimes, sometimes in radically different contexts, as those who study objects produced outside the Western world frequently point out. Some items, now regarded as prized 'art', were not understood either as art or even as commodities in their original settings. They have travelled long distances, and participated in markets, before reaching 'first-world' collections, where their status is, necessarily, radically altered. Take, for example, the small brass African objects that are now on display in a gallery.[4] **39** Their audiences have been strikingly diverse, and forms of display are again crucial. **XXI** Most artefacts have been experienced by multiple, diverse audiences. Ideally, historians attend to as many of the actual audiences as possible, evidence permitting. Third, audiences are implicit in processes of making, even when the item in question is for the producer's own use. Makers do not necessarily explicitly conceptualise their audiences, although some have to, by virtue of the social and economic relationships in which they operate. Those who create, together with their nearest and dearest, are generally the first audiences for things. Working out their implied audiences is integral to analysing artefacts.

A great deal of scholarship on visual and material culture makes assumptions, both general and particular, about what I am calling 'audiences', while a small proportion of it has sought to conceptualise them. We encountered one such attempt in Michael Baxandall's work, although, so far as I am aware, he did not use the term 'audience'. In *Painting and Experience*, Baxandall connected specific types of images with skills that existed in the settings in which they were made both because painters were engaging with their patrons' concerns and wishes, and because the images themselves were designed to be understood in that context. Thus audiences were built into the images he analysed and the interactions he charted. He found further evidence for both actual and implied audiences in records of practices and discourses, which required what we might call audience participation. Similar moves could be made by historians working on other contexts in a bid to explore the themes of audiences and display.

39 Goldweight representing a human couple, maker not known, eighteenth/nineteenth century, brass, 7.5 cm high, Robert and Lisa Sainsbury Collection, University of East Anglia, Norwich, UK, photograph by James Austin. These small objects were used as goldweights in eighteenth- and nineteenth-century Ghana; they are now displayed in a setting that proclaims them as 'art'. They are indeed beautiful and witty in their representation of the human figure. As seen by visitors now, in a building designed by Sir Norman Foster, they are shorn of their originating context, in which they may have been used by a chief. For the Akan-speaking peoples in Ghana and the Ivory Coast, they acted as currency before colonial administrations imposed their own.

40 Two pages of a photograph album compiled in the 1860s, possibly by either Richard Colpoys Haughton or Thomas Felton Faulkner, individual pages 26 cm high × 19.5 cm wide, Cambridge University Library. This album includes pictures of paintings, landscapes, people, horses and buildings. It was assembled by an undergraduate at the university, judging by the inclusion of an image of sportsmen from Christ's College. The compiler acquired photographs of the colleges and university buildings, and mounted them in a splendid album with a motto, monogram and clasp all of metal on the front cover. Making such albums was a common pastime judging by the numbers that survive in libraries and archives. One photograph shows the interior of the Wren Library, Trinity College, with a visitor examining a display case. There are five sides of pictures of Trinity.

Terms and conditions

'Audience' is a convenient umbrella term to convey the idea of being in the presence of something, which is the focus of attention and likely to elicit some response, whether individual or collective. That something need not be an original work or a prized artefact: it could be a reproduction of some kind, items of dress or pottery, a display case and its contents, goods in a shop window, an exhibition, a table set for a meal, playing cards, a spread of pictures in a magazine, an album, treasured personal possessions arrayed on a shelf or a book. **40** These examples of display invite careful analysis of how they function, for whom and in what context: they also imply the existence of one or more agents, who have brought it into being. Displays may be personal, domestic, commercial, occupational, institutional and so on. The precise meanings of 'audience' are context dependent, being shaped by forms of production, the political environment, physical settings, types of technology, taste, fashion and social characteristics, such as income and status. People

41 *L'an 1715. 1er. du regne de Louis XV* (*The Year 1715, 1st of the Reign of Louis XV*), maker unknown, etching and engraving, 1715, 41.9 cm high × 51.9 cm wide, British Museum. Louis XV was born in 1710 and ruled France and Navarre from 1715. This print depicts the boy king sitting on his throne, before an audience of individuals, who are labelled and named. These men were clerics and scholars who had been banished, exiled or imprisoned under the previous regime and were now free. A number of forms of display are operating here. The young king is displayed, as is his magnanimity, so are his grateful subjects, with their elegant gestures. The setting – columns, arches and drapery – presents standard elements of visual display in the period.

from all periods see a wide range of displays in the course of their lives, building up experiences and 'transferable skills' in the process. It is useful for historians to chart that range and what audiences carry from one type of display to another.

One particular use of the term 'audience' – a formal interview with a significant person – is worth noting here. **41** That person, generally someone with palpable power, becomes the focus of attention: that is, they are on display. Two features of such situations are relevant here. First, unequal power relationships are usually involved. Whenever questions of audience and display come up, it is worth probing the types of power that are present. Second, the figure of authority tends to be endowed with some kind of mystique or special powers, which others acknowledge, revere or worship. Such sentiments are also expressed in front of some displayed objects, so what prompts them? And how are forms of display contrived so as to elicit or discourage them?

Evidence of the nature and quality of audience response is rich, if somewhat fragmented, as a result of the disparate situations in which items of visual and material culture are displayed. It is often indirect, at least until recent times when the study of media audiences and the visitor experience has grown exponentially. Situations of innovation and change, like conflicts over the nature of display, tend to bring issues around audiences to the fore. There are historical topics – propaganda, for instance – which lead directly to a consideration of audiences. Some aspects of audiences – listening to music and going to the theatre, for example – have been studied by other disciplines. The themes of audiences and display are thus ripe for interdisciplinary approaches capable of bringing their apparently diverse facets together.

Recently, art historians have been considering the public, public life and public opinion. The concept 'public', whether used as an adjective or noun, is notoriously hard to conceptualise precisely. Its importance in art history derives from the eighteenth-century phenomenon of exhibitions, which more or less anyone could see – the Paris Salons and the Royal Academy exhibitions in London, for example – and which is perceived as a major historical transition in the visual arts. This development is bound up with the growth of specialised institutions for the fine arts, published debates about what was on show, the roles that critics played in public commentary, the growth of public opinion as a cultural force, and patterns of consumption. The notion of the public sphere as articulated by Jürgen Habermas has been influential in directing attention to shifts that took place at the end of the early modern period.[5] Scholars from a number of disciplines and using theoretical frameworks possessing no particular affinity with visual and material culture, have written on these themes. Their current prominence in art history partly arises from a politically engaged social history of art and from the development of museum studies, which is driven by contemporary concerns. Many governments wish to involve 'the public' with cultural matters, and bring more of them to state-funded museums.

Further important changes took place in the nineteenth century, with many more public museums and galleries being opened across the world and an explicit political discourse about the value of bringing working people into them. Whatever the period, however, the concept 'public' remains a slippery term. Sometimes it suggests that entry is free, at others that a display is open to visitors who may be asked to pay, while carrying connotations of state involvement or of the interests of an entire polity. The relatively recent phrase 'public art' is instructive. It refers to art in places, such as streets and squares, to which anyone has access – a phenomenon that is centuries old. Such works have the potential to reach vast audiences, yet precisely because of their location, they are easily ignored. If passers-by do not pay attention, are they still part of the audience? Historians might therefore usefully retain a level of scepticism about the actual impact of items of visual and material culture that are displayed in public.

Anxieties about audiences

We have noted some of the complexities that arise when artefacts are on display and when we seek to conceptualise and explain audience reactions. Those who write about visual and material culture are also types of audience, who are managing their own concerns and relationships with worlds of display, and creating audiences through publication. A first glance at academic analyses of displays and art works suggests that they are concerned with a generalised viewer. That viewer may well be the writer her or himself, although this is rarely avowed. It is a delicate matter whether or not to express strong emotional, personal reactions to artefacts in a scholarly context. One reason is that such sentiments risk being criticised as 'connoisseurial', the implication being that they are personal and appreciative rather than analytical. This pejorative use of 'connoisseurship' treats it with suspicion as elitist, old-fashioned and insufficiently rigorous. There is sensitivity, too, about the status of art history as a discipline that leads some practitioners to emphasise its common ground with philosophy, literature and critical theory, lest it be thought simply a form of art appreciation. This concern is about the audiences for both art and art-historical writings; it betokens a desire to demarcate two audiences – art lovers and those who make their living by analysing art. In practice these audiences overlap. Comparable anxieties do not appear to shape archaeology, which reaches wide audiences in publications, the media and exhibitions. Thus the issues around audiences vary according to the type of artefact displayed. It can be difficult for scholars to detach themselves from contexts in which high art is hyped, and the emotional depth of great works constantly affirmed. Revisionist art history works towards such detachment, while remaining politically and socially engaged. Scholars who write about visual phenomena know how profoundly art can touch the emotions and write,

42 Group of busts, in *Essays on Physiognomy ..., Written by the Rev. John Caspar Lavater* (London, 1797), vol. 1, p. 166, 20 cm high × 12.3 cm wide, Cambridge University Library. This plate comes from an English edition of Lavater's famous work, which was frequently adapted, translated and reprinted in a variety of formats. The interest in interpreting appearance in general, and facial features and expressions in particular, is widespread both temporally and spatially. Thus the human body is a primary site of display, with other people as its audience. As a result, visual skills are constantly being exercised and honed in everyday life, sometimes erupting into artefacts, including books, where the assumptions involved are made more explicit. Physiognomical texts moved between types and individuals, various kinds of works of art, well-known figures and anecdotes.

Group of Busts.

necessarily, out of their own audience reactions. Recognising the point that academic writings about art have to manage these varied pressures is important.

Ways of seeing

Given that reactions to any given artefact are likely to be diverse, the analysis of a single person needs to be seen as such. Experts knowingly school their responses, turn their experiences to good, analytical effect, and cultivate as high levels of awareness as possible. Even so, they cannot speak for all viewers. As a result, direct evidence about audience reaction in the past becomes especially precious. There are many types of ancillary material available through which they can be gauged, some of which have already been mentioned. Texts exist which bear testimony to past modes of viewing. They indicate what audiences brought to any given act of looking, their expectations and skills, what we might call 'the audience's share'. Two examples illustrate the point. For centuries the field of physiognomy, in which human characteristics are inferred from physical, and especially facial, appearance, has existed in learned and popular forms, and been made explicit in publications. **42** It covers a range of changing traditions from ancient times to the present day. That 'knowledge by the visage' – one neat definition of it – is possible, remains a common assumption.[6] Whether transmitted orally or in written form, physiognomy contains ideas about how to interpret what is seen in other human beings, and especially in their faces, and was used extensively by medical practitioners, alert to signs of disease and impending death and interested in how expression functioned. Described by the philosopher

Immanuel Kant as 'the art of detecting someone's interior life by means of certain external signs involuntarily given up', physiognomy provided a shared framework for interpreting what was seen, for example, through resemblances between people and animals.[7] It was available to those making images of people to use in communicating with their audiences, as caricaturists have so often done. The face and body were sites of display to audiences that comprised just about everyone because of widespread anxieties about whether character in general, and trustworthiness in particular, could be reliably detected by looking.

Although perhaps more limited in scope, natural theology provides another example of a field that helps historians understand what audiences brought to their viewing practices. The idea that visual inspection of works of nature provided confirmation of God's existence enjoyed special popularity in the seventeenth and eighteenth centuries, and publications continued to appear and be widely read throughout the nineteenth century. The argument may be heard in our own times on the lips of creationists. Natural theology depended upon an analogy between artefacts and God's work, thus it drew attention to close visual inspection as a way of making inferences about the maker. Natural theologians were certain that God's handiwork was far superior to that of any human being, and took the existence of God to follow logically from visual evidence of natural things having been purposefully designed. Natural theology thus encouraged the development of fine visual skills, which may be understood as 'transferrable', and discussion about the relationships between designed and designer. In natural theological texts we find evidence about attitudes among the literate to human making and assumptions about modes of seeing.

In their original contexts, physiognomy and natural theology were embedded in other practices rooted in visual discrimination, such as hiring servants, admiring scenes, whether natural or man-made, responding to portraits, the collection and display of specimens and so on. Accordingly, it is worth marshalling all the evidence and insights that could possibly bear on ways of looking in the past, paying special attention to places where they were made explicit. Areas such as the theatre, discussions of gesture, and instructions to priests, as well as writings on facial expression and physical comportment, are of great historical interest for their potential to shed light on forms of visual and material culture and audience responses to them. Note how skills and insights shift between ordinary life, artful displays and texts. Recognising this point has implications for our analyses of audiences and display.

When contemplating displays, we may not deploy a fully articulated framework to assess them, although that is desirable in the case of scholars, who, like everyone else, bring an array of skills, experiences and preconceived ideas with them. Since display is integral to so many aspects of human existence, it is helpful to notice how a range of physical considerations affects the experience. Viewers' distance from displayed items, the overall design, the numbers and behaviour of others, and physical comfort, as well as expectations, time of day, the nature and availability of ancillary materials, all play their part. Ways of seeing may take the form of common interpretative traditions, such as physiognomy and natural theology, which are about belief systems and mindsets as well as ordinary daily experience. They are typically composed of many elements precisely because they are integral to social life. Historians will be drawn to areas where issues about audiences and display are particularly well documented, brought up for critical inspection, or become explicit, for example, because of changing ways of making or using artefacts. Thus, there is a growing interest in print culture during the early modern period because of the novelty of the medium and the roles it played in major historical processes.

Prints and markets

Print historians have been particularly attentive to the themes of audiences and display. Very soon after the development of moveable type, prints reached large numbers of people. Students of the Reformation have been effective in pointing out the roles that print culture played in the array of movements that have been gathered together under that name. Similarly, eighteenth-century historians have paid attention to the role prints and book illustrations played in disseminating and commenting upon key ideas and events. Prints could be cheap and numerous. Their subject matter is relevant here in three ways. First, print was a highly responsive medium, able to react quickly to current affairs and trends and pique audience interest. Second, prints frequently depicted audiences and forms of display – the insides of exhibitions, pageants, street theatre, preaching, shops and so on. Third, prints, especially popular and cheap ones, are a form of audience reaction. It is reasonable to assume that when they sell well, their content has touched significant numbers of people. Cartoons depend on just this: the caricaturist's jibe only works when what it represents is readily recognised. **XXII** The genre depends upon audiences identifying the people, events and themes depicted. Sometimes the visual idioms of caricature define the ways in which their targets are thought about for years, even centuries, to come.

Frequently, one image or object acted as a template, spawning innumerable derivative forms, which looked different and cost varying amounts of money. Derivatives both imply and actually reach distinct audiences. In each case, scale, technique and content could be altered without losing a sense of the original. For example, the head could be extracted from a portrait, embellishments added, and a new print created to be used in, say, a magazine. Cf. **50** Furthermore, people also cut up prints, pasted them in albums or on walls, added new borders, and in effect customised them. In the case of print culture, then, modes of production, markets, audiences and forms of display are closely linked.

It was not necessary to buy prints in order to participate in their visual worlds. Prints themselves show displays in print shop windows, with pedestrians looking at them, which suggests that anyone could peer in and enjoy images that were of the moment. Such pictures hint at an awareness on the part of audiences that they were audiences. Artisans, artists and print-makers were necessarily conscious of their audiences and markets, since they were integral to their livelihood. Prints were also made of other kinds of shops and markets and their customers, of exhibitions and their visitors, of street vendors and their clients; these too were displayed in print shop windows. Their ubiquity suggests that the theme of 'audiences and display' was brought into the consciousness of large swathes of the population. The numbers of prints produced, both in terms of the actual images, and of print runs, mean that historians have large bodies of evidence available to them. There is also information on the business side of print-making. Printers were part of the commercial world of skilled artisans – they needed customers. Since the widespread use of printed material in the sixteenth century, multiple markets for images have been exploited. Engravers and printers were crucial intermediaries between, artists, sculptors, designers and architects and their publics. Before photography, prints were the main way of disseminating images of buildings, pictures and three-dimensional objects that viewers were unable to see in person. Drawings reached considerably smaller audiences. Commentators wrote authoritatively about artefacts they had only seen in prints.[8] Printed images enable historians to think about the dissemination of visual materials, actual audiences and implied audiences in conjunction with their social, political and economic dimensions.

Prints took many forms and participated in many markets. 'Market' has two different meanings – one specific, the other abstract. A market is simply a place, generally in a town or city centre, where goods are bought and sold; vendors set out their wares, customers come, look, feel, and perhaps make a purchase. 'Market' also refers to the status of a commodity, with respect to demand, availability and price. It can be as general as 'the art market' or as specific as 'the nineteenth-century market for prints by Rembrandt'. In this second sense, markets give an indication of the cost and desirability of an object, but significant variations occur. For example, provenance can add value when an item has been owned by a famous person. Markets imply institutions – stalls, shops and auction houses – through which artefacts are put on the market, and also consumers. Studies of consumption often emphasise the status-driven acquisition of goods, the desire to possess them, rather than their detailed visual characteristics. Markets operate in specific historical situations, where a range of factors, such as taste, reputation and availability, play a part – they cannot exist without consumers, that is, audiences.

Consider one way in which valued artefacts are sold, by auction, and it is evident that those attending sales constitute an audience, made up of agents, dealers and prospective buyers, and by others who enjoy the spectacle, the company and the objects on offer.[9] Displayed artefacts are integrated into a performance, as they are in the marketplace and by street sellers. In this instance, consumers, customers, clients and audiences cannot easily be separated. Commonly, consumers are taken to be those people who buy mass-produced goods, or at least items that are not unique. 'Consumption' is a major historical phenomenon, taken to be integral to the Industrial Revolution, when making multiples faster and cheaper was made possible by steam-powered machinery. It is worth reflecting briefly on the vocabulary we use in relation to audiences.

Problems of language

The range of terms that can be used to think about audiences and display include patronage, patron and client, which serve to analyse political relationships as well as those around custom-made entities, including buildings. Most work on the history of consumption focuses on items that are made on spec, rather than on bespoke objects, which are frequently considered under the rubric of patronage. This phenomenon presupposes patrons with sufficient resources to *initiate* the production of an artefact, over the appearance of which they normally exercise some control. If they are satisfied, they possess the object in question. Thus patronage is a phenomenon in which social, political and economic elites play a dominant role and complex negotiations with producer(s) may be involved. When patrons commission works, they are simultaneously customers, consumers and clients. 'Patron', however, suggests an individual with more power than either a 'consumer' or 'customer'. When they purchase books or other printed matter, such as newspapers, consumers are also, potentially, readers. It is possible to own reading matter without actually reading it, and to read materials owned by others. Books may be acquired for the purposes of display, for example, to use as interior decoration, a further reminder of the intricate relationships between consumption and display.[10] When people go to institutions specialising in the display of visual and material culture, they are 'visitors'.

Four issues are embedded in these terms: power and control; economic exchange; the nature of property; and the role played by vision. Furthermore, they evoke different kinds of social relationships: some contain direct references to economic transactions, while others privilege the sense of sight. 'Visitor' is economically neutral, although contemporary institutions hope they become customers. Client, customer and consumer all suggest that money changes hands, without implying any particular level of visual engagement with what is purchased. Patron, by contrast, when used in the context of artefacts, conveys both. If texts figure in artefacts, it is reasonable to speak of a reader. Yet images are not 'read' in the same way as words are. Theories of reading have been enormously influential in fields that study visual and material evidence, but they need to be adapted and rethought when applied to objects that do not share fundamental features with texts. Artefacts without texts tend to be non-linear, and those that aspire to verisimilitude involve visual mimesis, which words do not. Those concerned with visual and material culture can draw on rich debates about how to construe 'the reader'. This term may be conceptualised in a number of ways, for example, by those who study the history of the book, who tend have a more empirical orientation to who reads, how much they paid and so on, than the more overtly theoretical approaches that signalled 'the return of the reader'.[11] It is worth observing that 'readership', like congregation, is a collective noun; both bear similarities to 'audience'. 'Spectatorship' is not collective, but refers to the state of being a spectator; 'spectacle' is closely related to 'display'. There is no comparable collective concept for 'viewer' or 'beholder', while 'consumption' refers not to consumers as a group but to the phenomenon of purchasing goods. This discussion of language reminds us of the diverse types of people and processes that a consideration of audiences and display entails. We now turn to possible approaches for getting to grips with them.

Quality and quantity

It is helpful to distinguish between quantity and quality when it comes to studying audiences. How many people saw a given item is certainly useful information. In some cases getting a sense of the volume of a print run and of its likely reach, or of visitor numbers, is relatively straightforward. Toby Clark argued that during the Second World War in the USA, a saturation approach was used; he cites information that suggests the majority of the population was reached by propaganda. What this audience made of the materials in question is hard to say. In such a situation it is likely that different media (radio, TV, film and print) reinforced each other. But it is unwise to assume that government messages were transmitted to mass audiences in an unmediated form. The fact that the US Office of War Information, founded in 1942, produced their main posters in runs of 1.5 million and posted 100,000 messages in subways, streetcars and buses every month, is arresting.[12] But it reveals more about the effort and drive on the part of the government than about responses to their work. It illustrates one of the main difficulties that historians face when they consider print culture – paper has many uses. The late nineteenth-century slang word 'bumf' is derived from the mid-seventeenth-century term for toilet paper, bum fodder.

Whereas those investing a great deal of money in advertising campaigns are likely to engage in tough-minded assessments of their efficacy, the impact of propaganda, especially in authoritarian regimes, is considerably harder to assess. There is no such thing as unmediated transmission, however hard propagandists work to ensure their message is received. Thus the very notion of a 'message' is potentially misleading. There is no doubt that items of visual and material culture are sometimes made with the express intention of conveying something that could be described in this way. But 'message' suggests that clear transmission is possible. The term implies that artefacts are made with specific messages in mind, that it is possible for historians to work out what these were, and that they lack ambiguity. For this reason, direct, qualitative evidence of audience reactions, whether individual or collective, is particularly precious.

The most challenging question remains how the *quality* of people's engagement with what they see and touch may be understood. Quantity, while not necessarily easy to examine in the past, is more straightforward, and the development of market research in recent times provides relevant models.[13] We are now familiar with 'demographic' as a noun, which implies that a group can be meaningfully broken down into its constituent elements for analytical purposes, including marketing. Knowing how many is good, especially where meaningful comparisons can be made, but limited. The attention that has been paid to major acts of patronage is explained not just by the richness of sources, but by their capacity to bear testimony to qualities of feeling and of relationships. In cases where makers, owners and viewers enjoyed direct relationships, and recorded their transactions and thoughts, there are great historical opportunities. In such cases it may be possible to piece together 'audience' reactions, as it is in instances where extensive critical commentary exists.[14]

So far we have noted different types of audience, such as those who only see, those who have purchased and hence both own and see, those who pay for the experience of seeing, and those who originate a work by commissioning it, who then own and see it. Within each type there are significant differences – for example, between collectors who open their work up to the public, and those who keep their possessions private. Since the Industrial Revolution, most people have possessions designed for mass consumption. All of these come into the 'own and see' category, but involve different kinds of audiences and displays, and diverse experiences and relationships between people and objects. Asking about audiences and display helps to open up broad questions about patterns of ownership, the nature of consumption, emulation, taste and relationships between social groups. This works best when the visual and material properties of objects are taken into account, precisely because these bear on the quality of responses.

It is commonly assumed that audiences fragment along certain lines, such as class, race and gender. Where evidence to support such claims is available, this is exceptionally valuable, but it is problematic to simply assume any predictable fragmentation. In *City of Laughter*, for example, Vic Gatrell makes claims about the ways in which women specifically saw prints, yet it is unclear on what basis he does so.[15] We might distinguish, then, between historical claims about the *availability* of given objects and images and those about the *nature* and *quality* of responses to them. For example, works of art and valued artefacts housed in palaces and aristocratic houses were seen daily by servants and retainers, but it is virtually impossible to know how they reacted to them. Similar arguments apply to both the interiors and exteriors of churches, which were familiar to many people in the locality. Yet there is relatively scarce evidence on how worshippers saw and used them except at times of religious conflict.[16] Forms of public display from monuments and statues to triumphal arches and great buildings have a long history. Possibly they have been 'wallpaper' much of the time, not objects of careful attention. Yet their placement and design was undertaken with specific audiences in mind. In some cases, such as royal entries, it is possible to piece together in considerable detail the roles of local constituencies, who were the audiences for displays of power.[17]

Audiences and their disciplines

It is clear from what has been said so far that the study of audiences comes up in a number of disciplines, such as art history, literary studies, market research and museum studies. The number of visits to museums is growing and visitors have increasingly high expectations and more opportunities to voice their reactions. Government-funded museums, in the UK at least, are assigned increasingly exacting and detailed targets. In many countries the goal is to reach a wider range of visitors in terms of age, race and class. Thus audience research has become important for both museums and governments in their negotiations over funding and targets. Developing sound methodologies for assessing reliably the *quality* of visitor experience is challenging.[18] It remains important to seek out sources with which to understand the roles of audiences in the past. Work on contemporary visitor attractions may be indirectly valuable, but it is not easy to extrapolate from it to earlier situations. Nonetheless museology is important for historians because it illuminates current presentations of the past. We may well want to be critical of the ways in which history is brought to diverse audiences, in which case tools for analysing forms of display, including details such as labels, are essential. Museology includes the history of museums, their social roles, buildings, organisation, staffing and funding, the ways in which objects have been acquired, handled (including conservation) and presented. The history of collecting, a related field, has grown markedly in recent decades. The ways in which collections were formed, displayed and visited are matters of general historical interest by revealing prevailing values and interests at a given moment. Collectors are an important group, not least economically. Possessing a grasp of the economics of museums, both past and present, is fundamental for understanding the nature and role of audiences and display practices, as in blockbuster exhibitions.

Other disciplines are also relevant to the study of audiences and display, such as theatre studies, musicology and media studies, while an array of fields now considers publishing and reading practices over long periods of time. The list of disciplines that address the interpretation of visual responses alerts us to four aspects of the importance of interdisciplinarity for the arguments here. First, much of the past could be called a-disciplinary, that is, disciplines in the sense we know them simply did not exist, and where they did, social practices bear little relationship to them. The study of buildings explicitly designed for audiences, such as churches, theatres, ballrooms and arenas, for example, does not fit neatly within contemporary disciplines. Understanding such buildings and the activities that took place in them is necessarily an interdisciplinary enterprise. Second, it is frequently necessary to draw on specialised expertise outside history, as in the case of prints and caricatures. If we want to know about how many prints were produced, the manner in which they were marketed, and where they were seen, it is helpful to collaborate with those from the relevant specialism. This involves not just taking information, and importing it into history, but blending the insights and

The Family of Man

The greatest photographic exhibition of all time—503 pictures from 68 countries—

created by Edward Steichen for The Museum of Modern Art

Prologue by Carl Sandburg

XX

Front cover, *The Family of Man*, New York, 1955, 1986, 21 cm wide × 28 cm high. Slight modifications were made for the 1986 thirtieth anniversary edition, but the basic ideas remain. The design bears the hallmarks of Leo Lionni, well known for his children's books, who was the Art Director of the exhibition. His signature is visible on the cover. The image of the young piper was used in both exhibition and book as a *leitmotiv*.

A panorama of the inside of the Sainsbury Centre for Visual Arts, University of East Anglia, Norwich, UK, designed by Foster + Partners, photographed by Nigel Young, 2006. This is the dramatic setting in which the goldweights are placed. **39** Objects from different periods and cultural settings are displayed close together, creating the possibility for a wide range of visual conversations, which also involve scale and medium. The building has been extended twice, and was initially opened to the public in 1978.

Take care of that Bear, he has set his Mind on Blood, & his voracious appetite will gorge both East, & West, and he is only making you his Tools, to Cut each others Throats that he may devour you all the more easily

You had better not garde a Toi

Pubd by SW Fores 41 Piccadilly London Febn 1823

19 Feb 1823.

A Hasty Sketch at Verona, or the *Prophecies* of *Napoleon unfolding.*

XXII *A Hasty Sketch at Verona, or the Prophecies of Napoleon unfolding*, by J. Lewis Marks, hand-coloured etching, London, 1823, 23.7 cm high × 33.2 cm wide, British Museum. This print satirises European politics, commenting on the positions of Britain, Russia and Austria, whose representatives met at Verona between October and December 1822 to discuss the Tsar's ideas for military invention in Spain or Italy, debated in Parliament the following February. It assumes that its audiences can recognise individual figures, such as Wellington, read and interpret the clues provided, such as the inscription 'Prussia' on the cradle, and grasp the references to Russia as a bear, and to puppet kings, as well as the metaphor implied by the Tsar rocking the cradle with his foot. It displays a perspective on contemporary international relations, capable of being taken in fairly quickly.

Joseph Allen Smith Contemplating Florence across the Arno, by François-Xavier Fabre, 1797, oil on canvas, 70.9 cm high × 90.5 cm wide, Fitzwilliam Museum, Cambridge. Smith was American Consul in Florence; Fabre was a French painter who spent much of his life in Italy. The painting is reminiscent of Tischbein's famous depiction of the writer Goethe in the Roman Campagna of 1787, thus many cultural streams are flowing through it, and it seems reasonable to suppose that contemporary audiences were expected to appreciate a number of such resonances. The city of Florence, or rather parts of it, was laid before viewers, with the capital in the right foreground suggesting past ages. Smith himself is presumably deep in thought, perhaps about history, civilisation and the cultural achievements of the city in question. His refinement and capacity for appreciation, along with his elegant person, are displayed to viewers, who share at least a section of the vista before him.

XXIV Fan, painted by Leonardo Germo, watercolour on kid, with gilt tortoiseshell sticks and tortoiseshell guards, made between 1680 and 1720 in Rome, Victoria and Albert Museum, London. The image shows Venus and Adonis and is based on a painting by Francesco Albani in the Villa Borghese, Rome. The subject was popular at a time when classical themes were ubiquitous. The painter displays his prowess, the owner their taste, while the potential audience for such an item was extensive. This fan was owned by Benjamin West, the American painter who had studied in Italy before settling in London where he became President of the Royal Academy. As part of a collection, the forms of display change, not least because the fan's gendered connotations, heightened by the subject matter, have been lost with a male owner, and by entering a museum.

XXV

The Artist in his Museum, by
Charles Willson Peale, 1822, oil
on canvas, 263.5 cm × 202.9
cm, Pennsylvania Academy of
the Fine Arts, Philadelphia.
In this large painting, Peale
shows himself lifting a curtain
to reveal his museum, peopled
in the distance by two men, a
woman and a child. The woman
is identifiable as a Quaker,
and it has been suggested
that Peale was deliberately
alluding to the diversity of his
audiences. Viewers see a large
room containing both portraits
and curiosities from nature,
with an artist's palette and
natural history specimens in
the foreground. Peale, in dark,
formal costume, looks straight
out, inviting the spectator in.

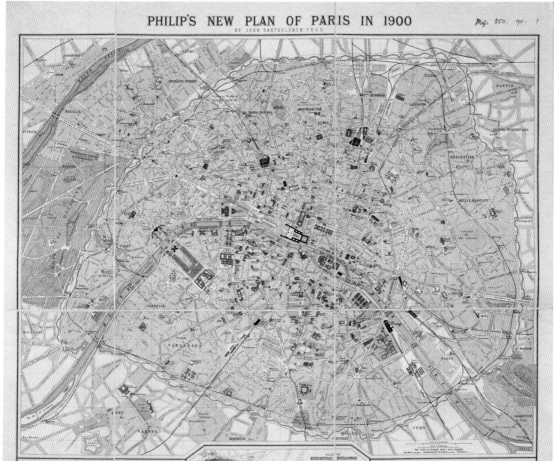

XXVI *Philips New Plan of Paris in 1900*, by John Bartholomew, 1900, 47 cm high × 59.5 cm wide, Cambridge University Library. This map was produced for the Paris Universal Exhibition in 1900. Below the map of the city shown in the plate, three smaller maps represented the environs of the city, the layout of the exhibition buildings, and Versailles. Forty-three countries took part in the World Fair, which was visited by more than 50 million people. It is usual to cite the Great Exhibition of the Works of Industry of all Nations, held in the Crystal Palace, London, in 1851 as the first 'world fair', although the idea of holding fairs to display 'works of industry' goes back to the eighteenth century. These exhibitions prompted many visual responses, which are revealing in terms of audiences and forms of display.

XXVII

Ambroise Vollard, by
Pierre-Auguste Renoir,
1908, oil on canvas, 82 cm
high × 65 cm wide, The
Courtauld Gallery, London.

Ambroise Vollard, by Pablo
Picasso, 1910, oil on canvas, 92
cm high × 65 cm wide, Pushkin
Museum of Fine Art, Moscow.
Picasso was well aware of the
frequency with which Vollard
had been portrayed by 'his'
artists. Picasso depicted him
a number of times, and in a
range of media, including as
part of what is now known as
the *Suite Vollard* (1930–7). This
portrait is a Cubist work; it is an
experiment with an entire way
of seeing and of approaching
the world, which Picasso and
others developed in the years
leading up to the First World
War. Cubism is best seen in the
context of contemporary shifts
in culture, including science.
The fractured planes of the
picture reveal a powerful head
and face. Arguably Renoir's
image, with its emphasis on
the sense of touch, is tender by
comparison.

XXIX

Madame Stora in Algerian Dress, by Pierre-Auguste Renoir, 1870, oil on canvas, 84.5 cm high × 59.6 cm wide, Fine Arts Museum of San Francisco. The sitter, who was nineteen at the time Renoir painted her portrait, was born in Algeria, to parents who made travel goods and were living in Frankfurt by the late 1860s, when she married Nathan Stora, an antiques dealer who specialised in North African goods, in Paris. Renoir painted other pictures with an Algerian theme. Madame Stora wears the formal dress of an Algerian Jewess, which may be found in other depictions, for example, by Delacroix. Although this work elicited mixed feelings on the part of both maker and owners, it came into the possession of Claude Monet in the early twentieth century, when it was exhibited, and appreciated, in a show of French Orientalists.

XXX

Un Amateur (*The Connoisseur*), by Honoré Daumier, *c.*1860–65, pen and ink, wash, watercolour, lithographical crayon and gouache over black chalk, 43.8 cm high × 35.5 cm wide, the Metropolitan Museum of Art, New York. Here a connoisseur sits in a room surrounded by images and objects, and contemplates, with evident pleasure, a version of the Venus de Milo, which was installed in the Louvre in 1821. There is certainly the suggestion that the man is enjoying the depiction of female beauty.

XXXI

Paul Durand-Ruel, by Pierre-Auguste Renoir, 1910, oil on canvas, 65 cm high × 54 cm wide, Durand-Ruel, Paris. Renoir was introduced to Durand-Ruel in the early 1870s by Claude Monet. So began a relationship that only ended with the artist's death in 1919. Durand-Ruel had wide tastes in art. He also commissioned Renoir to paint his children. A conservative man, he was a devout Catholic and a monarchist. This portrait was probably painted at the time of his commemorative exhibition of paintings by Monet, Pissarro, Sisley and Renoir. There is nothing flashy about the work, nor anything to suggest Durand-Ruel's major contributions to the art world and the well-being of the range of artists he supported and promoted. Rather it is a tender evocation of an elderly bourgeois – he was in his late seventies and still working.

Femmes d'Alger dans leur appartement (Women of Algiers in their Quarters), by Eugène Delacroix, 1834, oil on canvas, 180 cm high × 229 cm wide, Musée du Louvre, Paris. Delacroix had visited Morocco and Algeria not long before this picture, exhibited at the 1834 Salon, was painted. Picasso engaged extensively with this work in 1954–5. These elaborate conversations help historians understand the relationships between places and people as mediated by artefacts, and also between generations of makers. Some works provoke strong responses in later commentators, who incorporate past visual worlds into their own.

Opening of an album, compiled by P. B. Porter, 25 May 1906 to 25 March 1907, each page 23 cm high × 18 cm wide, Cambridge University Library. Porter was an officer on RIMS Hardinge, which moved British and Indian troops between Bombay, Rangoon, Madras, Mauritius and elsewhere. The album seems to have been intended for a specific recipient, who is addressed directly in the narrative of his activities. The illustrations are mostly postcards inserted into what look like homemade slots. One of the postcards shown here, 'A Daughter of the Nile', invites an erotic response, although there is nothing in the commentary to indicate anything other than Porter's lively interest in the places he visited and the people he saw. The tone of his writing suggests it may have been addressed to an older relative. Through such albums it is possible to appreciate the range of images that were widely available in the period, especially in postcard format, and to gauge reactions to them.

XXXIV

Mater Dolorosa (*The Virgin of Sorrows*), by José de Mora, *c*.1680–1700, painted pine, 48.5 cm high × 49 cm wide × 29 cm deep, Victoria and Albert Museum, London. Such realistic figures, sometimes with tears on their cheeks, were found in churches and convents in the Iberian Peninsula. The eyes here may be made of glass, and the original colours have faded somewhat. Mary is shown as being young; she invites our identification with her sorrow, and does so all the more insistently for being in three dimensions and lifelike.

XXXV

Jacopo Strada, by Titian (Tiziano Vecellio), 1567, oil on canvas, 125 cm high × 95 cm wide, Kunsthistorisches Museum, Vienna. The term 'dealer' hardly does justice to the range of Strada's interests and activities. He has been described as a polymath, a courtier who was also a collector, painter, architect, goldsmith, inventor, numismatist and linguist. Although the painting implies the presence of another figure, to whom the statuette is being shown or handed, this is neither an intimate nor a tender portrait.

XXXVI

Portret van Reijnier Ottsz Hinlopen (*Portrait of Reijnier Hinlopen*) and *Portret van Trijntje Tijsdr van Nooij* (*Portrait of Trijntje van Nooij*), both by anonymous and Nicolaes Eliasz. Pickenoy, 1631, oil on canvas, 123 cm high × 91 cm wide and 123 cm high × 90 cm wide respectively, Rijksmuseum, Amsterdam. Both portraits give the age of the sitters – they clearly form a pair, by virtue of lighting and pose as well as by style – and date. They have been deemed typical of Dutch marriage portraits of the time, which were shaped by formal conventions. Such pairs of portraits both tie the sitters together visually, as they are figuratively in marriage, and affirm gender differences. These calm, self-contained and poised people represent an established ideal of aristocratic decorum, although neither sitter was noble. The portraits manifest assumptions about appropriate facial expression and bodily demeanour.

approaches of various fields. Third, disciplines possess their own ways
of thinking, sometimes their own theories. Since other fields have been
active in generating models of audiences, it is sensible to engage with
them.

Fourth, many areas of research on audiences and display are not
owned by any single discipline. An excellent example is recent work on
the Grand Tour, and especially on travellers to Italy, which comes from
art history, history and literary studies, as well as women's studies.[19] This
phenomenon reached its peak in the eighteenth century, where being a
self-conscious member of an audience, and responding appropriately to
many forms of display from ancient ruins to artists' studios, theatres and
street life, was central. Written and visual evidence abounds, including
journals, letters, poems and travel books, portraits, topographical scenes,
and sketches by tourists themselves. There was a repertoire of available
responses, including the expectation that antiquities would be admired,
and, if possible, acquired. Portraits of young men on their Grand Tour –
whether sumptuous individual depictions by Batoni, or conversation
pieces, such as that by James Russel of 'British Connoisseurs in Rome' –
did far more than record a visit.[20] They constructed and reconstructed
sitters' experiences, and displayed them to others. **XXIII** Pictures of
landscapes and street scenes, of the insides of museums, and of archaeological sites frequently included visitors, affording historians not a
description of how people actually behaved, but a sense of the comportment expected and thought typical of such situations. Furthermore, the
sought-after Swiss artist, Louis Ducros, went in for 'deceptions of scale,
[he] exaggerated proportions of ancient monuments, [and] condens[ed]
the landscape through a variety of artistic devices, including wide-angle
vision and multiple viewpoints'.[21] Presumably Ducros knew his audience.
In addition to large-scale work, where he added gouache, oil and varnish
to drawings on paper, he produced outline etchings that could be coloured in for the souvenir market. The tradition of recording responses to
Italian art, architecture and archaeology continued into the nineteenth
century, with writers such as Nathaniel Hawthorne and Charles Dickens
publishing on their experiences of going to Italy and seeing for themselves. Such accounts, like the visual and material culture associated with
such travel, helped to construct tourists as an audience. An interdisciplinary response of the part of scholars is manifestly essential.

Arts of persuasion

Some images and objects draw attention both to their audiences and to the
relationships their makers intend to build with those audiences through

them. In all processes of making, audiences are implied: in some cases, such as pornography, propaganda and advertising, target audiences are peculiarly central to these processes. In these examples, issues around audiences and display are particularly crisp. Historians have been keen to use propaganda sources, especially in relation to the twentieth century, wars and totalitarian regimes, while the history of advertising is a field in its own right. Although many histories of advertising concentrate on the nineteenth and twentieth centuries, the phenomenon is far older than that, and newspapers are a particularly rich source. Yet the routine use of sophisticated *visual* materials to sell products is considerably more recent. Advertising relies on forms of display, whether in shops, the media or printed materials. Cf. **8, 43**. So does propaganda, which, like advertising, incorporates an intense sense of its audiences.

Wartime recruitment posters were aimed at young men, certainly, but also at their mothers, sisters, wives and girlfriends, who were targeted as factory workers during the First and Second World Wars.[22] These images generally manifest a certain directness, which is not to say that they were visually simple. Indeed, they had to manage complex, sometimes contradictory, impulses – getting women into factories without threatening conventional images of femininity, which included dependency, for instance. In these posters, words supplement and stabilise the images. The social relationships involved are relatively clear: those working for governments were speaking as persuasively as possible to specific sections of the population. This might be one definition of propaganda – the manipulation of the public, or specific sections of it, by the state.

Target audiences could be in enemy countries. For example, we could see the showing of *The Family of Man* in Moscow in 1959, sponsored by the US government, as a form of propaganda. Furthermore, the CIA secretly funded exhibitions of abstract expressionist art in the late 1940s and 1950s to convey ideas about artistic freedom in a democracy.[23] In these cases the propaganda consisted of funding and organisation, rather than the instigation, design and distribution of persuasive images. Some scholars want to use the term 'propaganda' yet more broadly, to encompass 'the use of art in the service of politics'.[24] A more generous definition helps in extending the chronological range of the history of propaganda. Philip Taylor, for instance, begins his book on the subject with the ancient world. Treating the term flexibly loosens the link between the state and propaganda, enabling historians to track the diverse groups who make propaganda and the audiences towards whom it is aimed. It expands the types of display that might be considered propagandistic, to include, for example, avant-garde installations in galleries, which comment on the nature of 'official' propaganda.[25] In this case the audience is quite restricted, and the displayed items relatively inaccessible compared to, say, posters and postcards issued in wartime.

For Chinese propaganda posters, some direct evidence of audiences and display exists. Anchee Min was intensely aware of them when a girl, and came herself to be the model for one in her teens. She has described her childhood enthusiasm for pictures of Mao, which were ubiquitous. 'My passion for posters began when I was eight years old. One day I brought home from school a poster of Chairman Mao. Although I did not know that the Cultural Revolution had started, my action made me a participant – I removed my mother's "Peace and Happiness" painting with children playing in a lotus pond from the wall and replaced it with the Mao poster.'[26] The fact that her mother was not keen and that Anchee was baffled by her reaction neatly demonstrates the diversity of audience response. Chinese posters tackled diverse subjects – education, leisure, technology, work, political zeal and national development, for example. Yet they shared certain visual features: the use of basic, unsubtle colours; the generally smiling faces, which lend an air of unreality to the images; and the use of flesh tones that are considerably more perky and uniform than those observed in everyday life. While we could view them as blunt ideological tools, it might be worth considering Anchee Min's suggestion: 'the posters are a representation of a generation's fantasy'.[27]

Even with first-hand testimony, propaganda images are challenging to interpret. The relationships between producers and audiences are considerably more mediated than appears at first sight. The images are meant to touch their viewers, while shaping their experiences and expectations. Chinese posters also contained slogans, but it is reasonable to assume that the images themselves made an impact, especially given their ubiquity. It is claimed that 2.2 billion official posters containing portraits of Mao were issued, that is three per person. 'Not only was the man himself made into a divine being; his portrait had to be treated with special care as well, as if it contained the divinity himself. Nothing could be placed above it, and its frame should not have a single blemish'.[28] These comments suggest that posters have a great deal in common with objects of worship and relics, normally associated with rather different contexts, forms of display and types of audience. Hence it might be productive to conceptualise religious artefacts in terms of arts of persuasion.

Shops provide excellent examples of the complex strategies deployed to persuade potential consumers to enter and buy. **43** The architecture of shops, part of street spectacle, their internal use of space, the location and design of windows for display, and features on the outside, all communicate claims about style, status and target audiences to viewers. How goods inside are stored and put on display, given price labels,

43 A window display of shoes, Tylers, Queen Street, Oxford, by Basil Savage, August 1945, 15 cm high × 11.75 cm wide, Oxfordshire County Archive. This arrangement is an artful mix; it combines flowers, columns, shoes, stockings and short texts. The words suggest both practicality and attractiveness. The use of flowers evokes a domestic scene, while the columns provide associations with grandeur. Thus a single commercial display reveals how viewers were expected to transfer visual skills between different settings, what the shop in question anticipated would appeal to their audience, and how elements, in this case from architecture and the home, were brought into the world of shopping.

and shown to customers is revealing. The roles of those who work there, their gender, dress and training also bear on audiences and display. Since these features have undergone significant change, we can make inferences about the values they express and shape, the social assumptions they embody, and the visual trends manifest in them. Shops construct their audiences through forms of display, while seeking to be alert to broad social changes. We can usefully examine the relationships between the presentation of goods for sale and other forms of display, and consider the blending of experiences of display in viewers' minds. A contemporary example is the affinities between museums and galleries and their shops, designed to encourage visitors to spend as much money as possible while 'extending' their museum experience. Such affinities are experienced visually not just in layout and presentation, but in content, where patterns, images and designs are shared.

The culturally dense manner in which modes of persuasion change is evident in advertising. Again we observe complex, shifting relationships between makers and audiences. On the one hand, advertisements draw upon what is generally recognisable and understood by those who will see them – they rely on prevailing assumptions and knowledge. On the other hand, they are designed to influence viewers' behaviour, and in the process seek to be original, even trendsetting – to go beyond what is already there. While it may be tempting to say that advertisements are a kind of index, which enables historians to track what is implicit in the cultures they serve, that is surely too simple. Advertisements do not passively reflect what is 'out there', but are in conversation with their environment in such a way that new images, ideas and desires are generated. Thus advertisers are a type of witness just as other makers of images are; they have a dynamic relationship with their audiences, whom they wish to manipulate economically. Furthermore, the settings of advertisements and their precise forms of display constitute important historical evidence.

Dissecting display

Historians require a flexible template for analysing forms of display, which operate at a number of levels. First we consider presentation – framing and mounting, the role of labels and panels, and the nature of containers. Second, there is the setting: the overall design and architectural elements and the ethos of the organisation or collector. The third level concerns behaviour. How are viewers likely to behave in relation to a given display? Many items of visual and material culture are displayed in domestic settings, implying kinds of intimacy that are quite distinct from the formality expected in most museums. The physical scale involved and the social relationships differ, but whatever the context all three levels need to be addressed. Displays are themselves items of material culture – beholders respond accordingly, with their bodies and not just with eyes and brains. Thus in dissecting display, it is vital to think about somatic reactions to materials, colours, spaces, and the whole scale of things. We can appreciate the point about scale by comparing miniatures, most of which were made for intimate personal use, with grand manner full-length portraits, which require not only walls large enough to take them, but sufficient space in which to view them. Conventions for hanging pictures have changed markedly over time: the preference for plain white walls, single hanging and spaces between pictures is a twentieth-century phenomenon initially associated with modernism. In the present day, labels are sometimes sited several feet away from the object in question. Such practices are dense with assumptions about the status of displayed works and how audiences should comport themselves in their presence. Thus presentation, setting and behaviour all repay careful analysis.

Presentation is important even when artefacts are not on formal display in an institution. Pictures of past interiors help historians understand rhetorics of display, as do pieces of furniture designed for the express purpose of putting artefacts on show. Exploring how, where and why items were displayed in homes is a way of studying changing value systems and patterns of consumption and their meanings. Porcelain is an excellent example of these points; it became a common presence in at least some European homes over the eighteenth century, and was displayed in distinctive ways – on mantelpieces, attached to walls and in special pieces of furniture. Its significance may be inferred from its presence in otherwise rather austere paintings, including being set out on elegant tables for tea. As the name 'china' suggests, the link with the Orient was part of the allure of items whose colours, materials and design were recognisably 'Eastern', even when manufactured in Europe. It was common for pieces to be decorated with oriental figures, flowers, trees and gardens when they had been produced in Liverpool, Delft or Meissen. Porcelain was not made in Europe until the eighteenth century, when it sometimes mimicked styles from China and Japan.

The home provides innumerable modes of display for historians to consider – prints pasted or pinned onto walls, texts and images in albums, wallpaper, table decorations, the presentation of food and drink, framed embroidery and ornaments on a mantelpiece, for example. While naturally the details of these practices varied with period, income and social status, a significant section of the population has for many centuries, undertaken self-aware forms of display at home. Further displays occurred in many other arenas of everyday life from street life to churches, in dress and hairstyles, the arrangement and decoration of pews, the use of statues and relics, sometimes with votive offerings around them, paintings, carvings and inscriptions.

Fans provide an excellent example of these themes – they were ubiquitous for centuries across all social ranks and constituted an important form of gendered display in their own right – both users and fans invited close visual inspection. **XXIV** Frequently given as gifts, fans have long been highly 'collectable'. They are present in painted portraits and photographs. These intricate objects are made up of leaves, sticks and guards with each element contributing to the overall display through their size, materials and manner of decoration. The diverse subject matter of images on fans is revealing, ranging from contemporary events, such as a balloon ascent in the 1780s, to signatures and photographs, paintings of buildings, flowers, neo-classical vignettes, landscapes and other outdoor scenes, flowers and birds. The materials were equally varied, including feathers, lace, jewels and tortoiseshell. Fans conveyed status, personal as well as social, since special mourning fans, for instance, were produced. Fans were deposits of social relationships that involved makers and consumers; hence they may be 'read' in terms of their physical properties and uses – they constituted a common form of display that reached wide audiences.[29]

Numerous other forms of display are available for dissection. I have mentioned shops, but consider, for example, *photographs* of shops, of which there are many thousands, and which reveal how goods were displayed, and in what settings. Sometimes they include both staff and shoppers, indicating something of the behaviour expected inside stores. Goods were on display with the precise visual arrangement varying according to period, the type of commodity, and the target audience of the shop in question. The décor was as important as the items for purchase. Similarly, the appearance and demeanour of staff was on display. Strong associations existed between shops and other institutions, such as the home and the museum. Harrods' new showrooms in London suggest, in a photograph of 1919, a grand home or hotel, with ornate plasterwork ceilings, attractive rugs, plants and flowers, small, yet elegant tables and elaborate light fittings. In the foreground of the picture of the ladies boot and shoe department, six shoes are arranged on a rug, in two groups of three. A provincial butcher's shop around the same time looked entirely different, with a superabundance of animal parts arrayed in tiers. On the top level were animal heads, reminiscent of hunting trophies. Below them were whole carcasses, with joints on the lowest two levels. Such photographs are themselves a form of display.[30] Cf. **43**

We have noted the need to record and describe forms of display as accurately as possible, not least because this helps generate insights into audiences and their possible reactions. For the most part, historical displays no longer exist and we are reliant on the careful interpretation of surviving texts and images. Museums and galleries that had old displays several decades ago have now been refitted or are in the process of being updated. While this is perfectly understandable, there are losses involved. Surviving and re-created rooms are valuable, but inevitably manicured in ways that are not obvious to visitors. Most displayed artefacts have been radically decontextualised. When they are formally presented to the public, labels and panels, which guide visitors' experiences, act as mediators. The display of 'high' art is particularly problematic in this regard, since providing context in labels is given little priority; the emphasis is conventionally on notable features inside the work, occasionally on artists' biographies.

Historians, then, attempt to imagine and interpret past forms of display, assess the levels and types of processing in present-day displays, and critically analyse the textual materials and physical presentation provided, paying attention to the settings of displays and the behaviour associated with them. The goals are to recontextualise both specific items and ensembles, and to integrate findings and insight into written accounts.

Individuals and groups

The conceptualisation of responses in the past that go beyond individuals is particularly challenging. It lurks in the very vocabulary we use, since 'audience' implies more than individual responses. One collective phenomenon has been alluded to in the form of iconoclasm; the history of religion offers historians other cases for thinking about audiences, display, and visual and material culture. Forms of worship, the phenomenon of pilgrimage, the celebration of festivals, the uses of relics, icons and votive offerings are examples where it may be possible to move beyond the experience of individuals. Those present at a church service may be deemed a congregation. Similarly, there are cults of specific

44 Stone statue of St James on the outside of the cathedral, Santiago de Compostela, Spain, exact date of production and maker not known, photograph by Michael Krier, 2006. The statue stands above the Holy Door on the Eastern façade. This door is only opened in Holy Years, such as 2010, when the saint's day falls on a Sunday. There are vast numbers of representations of St James, who typically wears a characteristic hat and pouch, carries a staff and displays scallop shells (see 2), frequently on his hat. The display of these attributes does far more than aid recognition, it builds a sense of common commitment among pilgrims, who sport similar signs, and who are thus a special category of audience.

relics and icons, even if 'worshippers' is a simple plural. Confraternities, like guilds, are groups for historians to consider, for example, when they commissioned art, worshipped in dedicated chapels, and constructed their identity around imagery. We can also turn to the history of specific religious orders and study their use of patron saints, relics and places of worship. The sites to which pilgrims have flocked over extended periods of time provide insights into audiences and display. Typically, worshippers want to see the special object, perhaps to kiss or touch it, and to retain something that evokes it. Much, naturally, depends on the form that object takes. Freedberg claims that we transfer respect for a king to that king's image, although that phenomenon is surely highly context-dependent. Certainly attacks on idolatry are premised on the fear that the unwary confuse the idol with the original. It is undeniable that cultures build up around a few, specific super-charged items of visual and material culture, which many people want to see for themselves – a description that applies as much to, say, the Mona Lisa at the Louvre in Paris, as it does to pilgrimage sites, such as Lourdes in France, Santiago in Spain, and Knock in Ireland. Thus collective cultures develop around special places as well as objects; what drives people to visit them may be as much being in the presence of the object with other like-minded souls as looking at it intently and in detail; in such cases the precise forms of display have to serve the highly distinctive needs of audiences. 44 Near Bologna, for example, lies the eighteenth-century shrine of the Santuario della Madonna di San Luca, reached by the world's longest portico. This Madonna is regarded by locals as 'their celestial guardian'.[31] Visitors enter the church at the top of the hill, where they queue to file past the icon, and have a chance to kiss it. The kind of prolonged, thoughtful visual contemplation expected before great works of art is neither possible nor expected.

The need to understand groups – corporations, orders, political parties, factions, pressure groups and so on – lies at the heart of historical practice. Classes are groups, and so are crowds, yet they are quite different types of collectivities, as are guilds, sports teams, those who are linked by kinship, religious affiliation and friendship. Such groupings are frequently implied by forms of display, and depicted inside images – as art historians sometimes put it, 'thematised' in works of art. This suggests that articles of visual and material culture can themselves provide evidence for the nature and display of group identity. Thus, group portraits, whether of seventeenth-century Dutch worthies or of nineteenth-century artists, are valuable sources for understanding audiences and display.

Susan Siegfried's account of the French painter Louis-Léopold Boilly, who was active in the late eighteenth and early nineteenth centuries, provides a particularly elegant and compelling account of how 'audiences and display' work in his imagery. Like Sébastien Mercier, who wrote about Parisian life in the 1780s, Boilly offers a *commentary* upon contemporary life – he did not *record* Parisian life, he *recast* it in pictorial form. Boilly consistently tackled subjects related to the themes of this chapter: spectators viewing paintings, magic lantern displays, the street shows that were common on the boulevards with crowds around them, and people assembled for leisure activities, watching each other and, sometimes, visibly aware of themselves as part of the display. Siegfried observes how often the artist placed himself in the picture looking out at the viewer, mediating between the depicted scene and audiences, perhaps challenging viewers to consider what they are seeing. Boilly explored the relationships between painted scenes that proclaim their verisimilitude and the lived experience of beholders, both collective and individual.[32]

Visual powers

So far I have explored the subject of audiences and display and sketched in their historical importance, while noting the challenges, both conceptual and empirical, they present. I have drawn attention to the rich *visual* materials that are available for thinking about these themes. A self-portrait by the American artist, entrepreneur, inventor, collector and naturalist Charles Willson Peale exemplifies the point. **XXV** His 1822 canvas, *The Artist in his Museum*, which is a many-layered act of display, has become a standard reference point for those interested in collecting.[33] Audiences in a number of forms are central to the picture: punters for his museum, both those pictured and anticipated ones in the future; clients for the artist whose tools of the trade are prominent; and those spectators who gaze upon him, his painted work and his institution.[34] Theatrically, Peale addresses and displays his audiences. The canvas is, in effect, a piece of advertising, an assertion of his position and achievements.

Peale's diverse output contained pictures that are considerably more 'private' – for example, a portrait of his first wife Rachel weeping over their dead child. Pictures that are peculiarly intimate remind us of discussions about what should *not* be displayed, about audiences that can never be. There are many reasons for refusing display and aborting audiences. In *Camera Lucida*, Roland Barthes does not reproduce the picture of his beloved mother when young, although his search for her photograph lies at the heart of the book. He deemed it irrelevant to his readers, although it meant so much to him. To include it would have pandered to curiosity and distracted from his main points. The story of Courbet's 1866 painting *L'Origine du Monde*, probably a portrait of a particular woman's belly, genitals and open thighs, raises rather different questions about limiting audiences. Now in the Musée d'Orsay in Paris, it was acquired in lieu of tax after the death of the psychoanalyst Jacques Lacan, in whose possession it was for close to thirty years. Originally commissioned by a Turkish diplomat for his personal collection of erotic pictures, Courbet probably anticipated limited audiences for this work. In fact, the image has been taken up by writers and film directors, and subjected to art-historical scrutiny. The painting is deeply arresting, even shocking, and I have chosen not to reproduce it here. Within the last twenty years, its use on the cover of a book drew the attention of police. Possibly the abiding force of the image is connected with the fact that it is an oil painting, and not a photograph, the medium of much current pornography. Thus, *L'Origine du Monde* prompts us to consider its own origins – the woman on display and the first audience of the picture, Courbet himself. These issues around audiences and display are predicated on the potent power of sight.

Censorship, in its quest to limit audiences and display, sheds light on this power. Does censorship punish those who create works because it prevents them from gaining access to audiences? It evidently speaks to questions of display, since it attempts to prevent images, texts and objects entering the public domain. Censorship is certainly directed against consumers, precisely and only because they are deemed visually susceptible. The power of what is seen is thereby affirmed. Visual potency takes many different forms – artefacts may offend 'decency', be sacrilegious, incite violence, or sexually arouse onlookers. As David Freedberg suggests, when such responses are acted out, we can learn from the testimonies of those who do so. What is censored or proposed for censorship illuminates audiences, display and artefacts as these are understood at a given time and place. Images that are parodic of, or hostile to, religious figures and themes are especially vulnerable to demands that they be removed from public view. Such demands imply that artefacts undermine beliefs and institutions and that audiences are impressionable, likely to behave differently as a result of their visual experiences. Current attempts to control images of children, including those made by their own families, neatly reveal the power of visual culture, the imagined consequences if it is not subject to strict laws, and the historical specificity of claims about what should, and should not, be seen.

NOTES

1 Eric Sandeen, *Picturing an Exhibition: the Family of Man and 1950s America* (Albuquerque, 1995), p. 155. He is quoting from a clipping in the Steichen Archives at MoMA. In chapter 4 he analyses the Moscow American National Exhibition of which the *Family of Man* was a part.

2 David Freedberg, *Iconoclasts and their Motives* (Maarssen and Montclair, NJ, 1985).

3 David Freedberg, *The Power of Images: Studies in the History and Theory of Response* (Chicago and London, 1989), pp. xx–xxi.

4 Steven Hooper, ed., *Robert and Lisa Sainsbury Collection. Volume II: Pacific, African and Native North American Art* (New Haven, London and Norwich, 1997), p. 136. Similar goldweights are on p. 137.

5 Jürgen Habermas, *The Structural Transformation of the Public Sphere: an Inquiry into a Category of Bourgeois Society* (Cambridge, 1989; first published 1962); Craig Calhoun, ed., *Habermas and the Public Sphere* (Cambridge, MA, and London, 1992); Anthony La Vopa, 'Conceiving a Public: Ideas and Society in Eighteenth-century Europe', *Journal of Modern History*, 64 (1992), pp. 79–116. Cf. Thomas Crow, *Painters and Public Life in Eighteenth-century Paris* (New Haven and London, 1985), and David Solkin, *Painting for Money: the Visual Arts and the Public Sphere in Eighteenth-century England* (New Haven, 1993).

6 Martin Porter, *Windows of the Soul: the Art of Physiognomy in European Culture, 1470–1780* (Oxford, 2005), p. 320, where he attributes the phrase to Edmund Cootes, *The English School-maister*, first published 1596.

7 *Ibid.*, p. 321, which quotes from *Anthropology from a Pragmatic Point of View* (The Hague, 1974), p. 120.

8 The famous Laocoon statue in the Vatican Museum, much discussed in the eighteenth century, is a good example: see Gotthold Lessing, *Laocoon: An Essay Upon the Limits of Painting and Poetry* (London, 1874); Richard Brilliant, *My Laocoön: Alternative Claims in the Interpretation of Art Works* (Berkeley and London, 2000); Alex Potts, *Flesh and the Ideal: Winckelmann and the Origins of Art History* (New Haven and London, 1994).

9 See, for example, Frank Hermann, *Sotheby's: a Portrait of an Auction House* (London, 1980). See also John Michael Montias, *Art at Auction in 17th-century Amsterdam* (Amsterdam, 2002), for the kind of work that can be done when the records of auction houses survive.

10 Simon Eliot and Jonathan Rose, eds., *A Companion to the History of the Book* (Malden, MA, Oxford and Carlton, Victoria, 2007), ch. 35, 'Some Non-Textual Uses of Books' by Rowan Watson, and other chapters on how to study actual readers.

11 Elizabeth Freund, *The Return of the Reader* (London, 1987), is designed as an accessible introduction to these matters. See also Robert Holob, *Reception Theory* (London, 1984), for an account that stresses German thinking during the late 1960s. He defines 'reception theory' as 'a general shift in concern from the author and the work to the text and the reader' (p. xii).

12 Toby Clark, *Art and Propaganda in the Twentieth Century: the Political Image in the Age of Mass Culture* (London, 1997), p. 111.

13 Paul Hague, *Market Research: a Guide to Planning, Methodology & Evaluation*, 3rd edn (London, 2002); John Downham, *BMRB International: The First Sixty Years, 1930–1993* (London, 1993), on the British Marketing Research Board.

14 The essays in David Solkin, ed., *Art on the Line: the Royal Academy Exhibitions at Somerset House 1780–1836* (New Haven and London, 2001), use such commentary effectively and have much to say about audiences.

15 Vic Gatrell, *City of Laughter: Sex and Satire in Eighteenth-century London* (London, 2006), and Jordanova, 'Image Matters', pp. 786–8.

16 For example, Eamonn Duffy, *The Stripping of the Altars: Traditional Religion in England c.1400–1580*, 2nd edn (New Haven and London, 2005); Kenneth Fincham and Nicholas Tyacke, *Altars Restored: the Changing Face of English Religious Worship 1547–c.1700* (Oxford, 2007); and Mia Mochizuki, *The Netherlandish Image after Iconoclasm, 1566–1672* (Aldershot, 2008).

17 A compelling example is Margit Thøfner, *A Common Art: Urban Ceremonial in Antwerp and Brussels During and After the Dutch Revolt* (Zwolle, 2007); her epilogue is particularly explicit on the matter.

18 Beverly Serrell, *Judging Exhibitions: a Framework of Assessing Excellence* (Walnut Creek, CA, 2006); Sara Selwood, *Investigating Audiences: Audience Surveys in the Visual Arts: a Resource Pack for Administrators* (London, 1991).

19 For example, A. Wilton and I. Bignamini, eds., *The Lure of Italy in the Eighteenth Century* (London, 1996); Clare Hornby, ed., *The Impact of Italy: the Grand Tour and Beyond* (London, 1993), contains contributions from scholars from a range of disciplines and perspectives; Bruce Redford, *Venice and the Grand Tour* (New Haven and London, 1996).

20 On grand tour portraits, see Edgar Bowron, ed., *Pompeo Batoni: Prince of Painters in Eighteenth-century Rome* (New Haven and London, 2008). See Wilton and Bignamini, *Lure*, p. 88, on Russel's picture, which is described as 'the quintessential representation of the Grand Tour in Rome'.

21 *Images of the Grand Tour: Louis Ducros 1748–1810* (Geneva, 1985), p. 7.

22 See, for example, the posters on pp. 105–9 of Clark, *Art and Propaganda*.

23 *Ibid.*, pp. 8–9.

24 *Ibid.*, p. 9.

25 *Ibid.*, pp. 155–6.

26 Anchee Min, *Chinese Propaganda Posters* (Cologne and London, 2003), p. 5.

27 *Ibid.*, p. 5.

28 *Ibid.*, p. 16.

29 I have taken these examples from *Unfolding Pictures: Fans in the Royal Collection* (London, 2005). Cheap fans, for example, with printed decoration on the leaves, were widespread. There is to my knowledge one fan museum in the world: www.fan-museum.org.

30 For photographs of shops, see Kathryn Morrison, *English Shops and Shopping: an Architectural History* (New Haven and London, 2003), pp. 166 and 88, for Harrods and the butcher's shop respectively; Alexandra Artley, ed., *The Golden Age of Shop Design: European Shop Interiors 1880–1939* (London, 1975).

31 *Italy*, Nagel Travel Guide Series, 4th edn (Geneva, Paris, New York and Karlsruhe, 1956), p. 398.

32 Susan Siegfried, *The Art of Louis-Léopold Boilly: Modern Life in Napoleonic France* (New Haven and London, 1995).

33 In her edited collection, *Acts of Possession: Collecting in America* (New Brunswick, NJ, and London, 2003), Leah Dilworth remarks, 'it is a truth universally acknowledged that no book about collecting can fail to include a reproduction of Charles Willson Peale's 1822 self-portrait, *The Artist in His Museum*' (p. 3).

34 David Brigham, *Public Culture in the Early Republic: Peale's Museum and its Audience* (Washington DC and London, 1995).

FURTHER READING

Audiences have been very much the preserve of media studies, for example: Roger Dickinson *et al.*, eds., *Approaches to Audiences: a Reader* (London, 1998); Barrie Gunter and David Machin, eds., *Media Audiences*, 4 vols. (London, 2009); and Ien Ang, *Desperately Seeking the Audience* (London, 1991). See also Asa Briggs and Peter Burke, *A Social History of the Media: From Gutenberg to the Internet* (Cambridge, 2002). There is interesting work on the history of musical audiences, such as James Johnson, *Listening in Paris: a Cultural History* (Berkeley and London, 1995); see also Jennifer Hall-Witt, *Fashionable Acts: Opera and Elite Culture in London, 1780–1800* (Durham, NH, 2007); and John Rice, *Mozart on the Stage* (Cambridge, 2009). For theatre history, see, for instance, W. H. Bruford, *Theatre, Drama and Audience in Goethe's Germany* (London, 1950); John McGrath, *A Good Night Out: Popular Theatre: Audience, Class and Form*, 2nd edn (London, 1996); Jim Davis and Victor Emeljanow, *Reflecting the Audience: London Theatregoing, 1840–1880* (Iowa City, 2001); and David Wiles, *Theatre and Citizenship: the History of a Practice* (Cambridge, 2011). Historians may also be interested in the architecture of theatres and in visual depictions of performances and performers that depend on wide 'audience' interest in particular roles: Louise Pelletier, *Architecture in Words: Theatre, Language and the Sensuous Space of Architectures* (London, 2006); Oscar Brockett *et al.*, *Making the Scene: a History of Stage Design and Technology in Europe and the United States* (San Antonio, TX, 2010); and Gillian Perry, *Spectacular Flirtations: Viewing the Actress in British Art and Theatre* (New Haven and London, 2007).

Display refers to a vast range of phenomena; a good place to start is work on museums and exhibitions, such as Ivan Karp and Steven Lavine, eds., *Exhibiting Cultures: the Poetics and Politics of Museum Display* (Washington DC and London, 1991); David Carrier, *Museum Skepticism: a History of the Display of Art in Public Galleries* (Durham, NC, 2006); Franco Borsi, *Paris 1900* (London, 1978) includes material on shops and their displays; Robert Lumley, *The Museum Time-Machine: Putting Cultures on Display* (London, 1988); Reesa Greenberg et al., eds., *Thinking about Exhibitions* (London and New York, 1996); Paul Greenhalgh, *Ephemeral Vistas: Great Exhibitions and World's Fairs, 1851–1939* (Manchester, 1988); Lara Kriegel, *Grand Designs: Labor, Empire, and the Museum in Victorian Culture* (Durham, NC, and London, 2007); Alexander Geppert, *Fleeting Cities: Imperial Expositions in Fin-de-Siècle Europe* (Basingstoke, 2010); and Philippe Jullian, *The Triumph of Art Nouveau: Paris Exhibition, 1900* (London, 1974), see ch. 10, 'The Public'. Eileen Hooper-Greenhill, *Museums and their Visitors* (London, 1994) is designed to help museums address their target audiences.

For one historian's take on public opinion, see Arlette Farge, *Subversive Words: Public Opinion in Eighteenth-century France* (Cambridge, 1994), who specifically focuses on popular public opinion. Other works are cited in note 5. See also W. J. T. Mitchell, ed., *Art and the Public Sphere* (Chicago, 1992).

On gesture there is Jean-Claude Schmitt, *Gestures* (London, 1984); Jan Bremmer and Herman Roodenburg, *A Cultural History of Gesture: From Antiquity to the Present Day* (Cambridge, 1991); and Michael J. Braddick, *The Politics of Gesture: Historical Perspectives* (Oxford and New York, 2009).

For a recent introduction to natural theology, see Peter Harrison, ed., *The Cambridge Companion to Science and Religion* (Cambridge, 2010). For an example of how it touches the themes of this book, one could turn to the Scottish surgeon Charles Bell, who was an artist and taught artists as well as being a natural theologian: Charles Bell, *Essays on the Anatomy of Expression* (London, 1806), and *The Hand: its Mechanism and Vital Endowments as Evincing Design* (London, 1833).

M. Dorothy George was a pioneer historian, who used satirical prints, for instance, *Hogarth to Cruikshank: Social Change in Graphic Satire* (London, 1967); see also Mark Hallett, *The Spectacle of Difference: Graphic Satire in the Age of Hogarth* (New Haven and London, 1999). Ronald Paulson made interesting comments about Hogarth in relation to audiences in *Popular and Polite Art in the Age of Hogarth and Fielding* (Notre Dame, IN, 1979). For a nuanced and visually acute account of eighteenth-century caricature, see Diana Donald, *The Age of Caricature: Satirical Prints in the Reign of George III* (New Haven and London, 1996).

There is an extensive literature on consumption, for example: John Brewer and Roy Porter, eds., *Consumption and the World of Goods* (London, 1992); Robert Fox and Anthony Turner, eds., *Luxury Trades and Consumerism in Ancien Régime Paris: Studies in the History of the Skilled Workforce* (Aldershot, 1998); Maxine Berg and Helen Clifford, eds., *Consumers and Luxury: Consumer Culture in Europe* (Manchester, 1999); Daniel Roche, *A History of Everyday Things: the*

Birth of Consumption in France, 1600–1800 (Cambridge, 2000); Clive Edwards, *Turning Houses into Homes: a History of the Retailing and Consumption of Furnishings* (Aldershot, 2005); and Roberta Sassatelli, *Consumer Culture: History, Theory and Politics* (Los Angeles and London, 2007). Amanda Vickery, *Behind Closed Doors: at Home in Georgian England* (New Haven and London, 2009), is a historical work that engages specifically with interiors.

On shops and shopping, in addition to many works on specific localities, there is Kathryn Morrison, *English Shops and Shopping: an Architectural History* (New Haven and London, 2003); Dorothy Davis, *A History of Shopping* (London, 1966); Lindy Woodhead, *Shopping, Seduction & Mr Selfridge* (London, 2007); and Rachel Bowlby, *Carried Away: the Invention of Modern Shopping* (London, 2000).

Philip Taylor, *Munitions of the Mind: a History of Propaganda from the Ancient World to the Present Era*, new edn (Manchester, 1995), provides a panorama of the subject; for a variety of approaches to visual materials, see James Aulich, *War Posters: Weapons of Mass Communication* (London, 2007); Stefan Landsberger, *Chinese Propaganda Posters: From Revolution to Modernization* (Armonk, NY, 1995); Roland Belgrave *et al.*, eds., *Prints as Propaganda: the German Reformation* (London, 1999); Nicholas Cull *et al.*, *Propaganda and Mass Persuasion: a Historical Encyclopedia, 1500 to the Present* (Santa Barbara, 2003); Evonne Levy, *Propaganda and the Jesuit Baroque* (Berkeley and London, 2004); James Thompson, '"Pictorial Lies" – Posters and Politics in Britain c. 1880–1914', *Past and Present*, 197 (2007), pp. 177–210; Cora Goldstein, *Capturing the German Eye: American Visual Propaganda in Occupied Germany* (Chicago and London, 2009); and Pearl James, ed., *Picture This: World War I Posters and Visual Culture* (Lincoln, NE, 2009).

Other works relevant to the themes of Chapter 4 and not already cited in the endnotes are in alphabetical order by author: Alain Besançon, *The Forbidden Image: an Intellectual History of Iconoclasm* (Chicago and London, 2000); Melissa Calaresu, 'From the Street to Stereotype: Urban Space, Travel and the Picturesque in Late Eighteenth-Century Naples', *Italian Studies*, 62 (2007), pp. 189–203, and 'Looking for Virgil's Tomb: the End of the Grand Tour and the Cosmopolitan Ideal in Europe', in *Voyages and Visions: Towards a Cultural History of Travel*, ed. Jás Elsner and Joan-Pau Rubiés (London, 1999), pp. 138–61 and 302–10; Alden Cavanagh and Michael Yonan, eds., *The Cultural Aesthetics of Eighteenth-century Porcelain* (Farnham, 2010); Victoria de Grazia, ed., *The Sex of Things: Gender and Consumption in Historical Perspective* (Berkeley and London, 1996), esp. ch. 4; John Elsner and Roger Cardinal, eds., *The Cultures of Collecting* (London, 1994); Norman Foster and Kenneth Powell, *Sainsbury Centre for Visual Arts: Foster + Partners* (Munich and London, 2010); Leonard Freedman, *The Offensive Art: Political Satire and its Censorship around the World from Beerbohm to Borat* (Westport, CT, 2009); Dario Gamboni, *The Destruction of Art* (London, 1997); Ellen Gruber Garvey, 'Dreaming in Commerce: Advertising Trade Card Scrapbooks', in *Acts of Possession: Collecting in America*, ed. Leah Dillworth (New Brunswick, NJ, 2003), pp. 66–88; Ruth Harris, *Lourdes: Body and Spirit in the Secular Age* (London, 1999); Lucy Hartley, *Physiognomy and the Meaning of Expression in Nineteenth-century Culture* (Cambridge, 2001); Lynn Hunt, ed., *Eroticism and the Body Politic* (Baltimore, 1991); Lynn Hunt, ed., *The Invention of Pornography: Obscenity and the Origins of Modernity, 1500–1800* (New York, 1993); Derek Jones, ed., *Censorship: a World Encyclopedia*, 4 vols. (London, 2001); Jytte Klausen, *The Cartoons that Shook the World* (New Haven and London, 2009); Marie-José Mondzain, 'Can Images Kill?', *Critical Inquiry*, 36 (2009), pp. 20–51; Melissa Percival, *The Appearance of Character: Physiognomy and Facial Expression in Eighteenth-century France* (Leeds, 1999); John Potvin and Alla Myzelev, eds., *Material Cultures, 1740–1920: the Meanings and Pleasures of Collecting* (Burlington, VT, 2008); George Roeder, *The Censored War: American Visual Experience during World War Two* (New Haven and London, 1993); Ulinka Rublack, *Dressing Up: Cultural Identity in Renaissance Europe* (Oxford, 2010); Frances Saunders, *Who Paid the Piper? The CIA and the Cultural Cold War* (London, 1999); Katie Scott, *The Rococo Interior: Decoration and Social Spaces in Early Eighteenth Century Paris* (New Haven and London, 1995); Ellis Shookman, ed., *Faces of Physiognomy: Interdisciplinary Approaches to Johann Caspar Lavater* (Columbia, SC, 1993); John Styles and Amanda Vickery, eds., *Gender, Taste, and Material Culture in Britain and North America, 1700–1830* (New Haven and London, 2006); and Peter Vergo, ed., *The New Museology* (London, 1989) and *We are the People: Postcards from the Collection of Tom Phillips* (London, 2004).

See also *Journal of Advertising History* (1977 onwards) and *Journal of the History of Collections* (1989 onwards).

Bridge

Why should historians think about audiences at all? This is a somewhat neglected area, especially for items produced before the era of mass culture. Media studies as a field has been notably attentive to audiences. One huge advantage of research on modern media has been not only the possibility of asking people what they think and feel, but the existence of advertising and market research. We noted that advertising is a rich historical field for earlier periods as well. Items made by human beings inevitably imply audiences of some kind, making them integral to work on artefacts. The need to distinguish between implied and actual audiences has also been affirmed. It is impossible to think about consumption, now a major historical topic, without considering audiences and display. Audiences change; visual and material culture both expresses and shapes these shifts. Admittedly, 'audience' is an imperfect term, but the complexities it implies are to be embraced given the capacity of artefacts to touch people so profoundly. The very term 'audience' implies some kind of display, and without 'display' there is no audience. Furthermore, 'display' implies people, who select artefacts and design settings for them, as well as organisations, including homes, and ideologies, that enable such settings.

Detailed case studies, especially those examining the personal relationships between makers and users of artefacts, are an effective way of opening up the layers implied by the subject 'audiences and display'. The last essay discusses Renoir's 1908 portrait of his dealer Ambroise Vollard. The painting displays the pleasures to be found in objects and the relationships they engender with their audiences. **XXVI**

Coda

Before moving on to Renoir's work, let us consider *The Look of the Past* in the light of this chapter. In order to write it, I had to imagine the audiences I want to, and might realistically, reach. The result was a conversation between myself as author, and a range of people, both real and imagined. Some of the real ones read the book in draft. I had to ask myself what I most wanted to say to them, and how my audiences, both implied and actual, would respond, what level of detail they would expect, which terms should be explained, how they would react to the examples I chose and so on. The material result, this book, may be understood as a collaboratively produced display, to be analysed by readers as such. Such an analysis would consider the choice of page size – a bit wider than usual to accommodate illustrations in both portrait and landscape format – and of illustrations, which was governed by many practical considerations. The size of each illustration had to be selected and decisions made about whether to use colour or black and white. Then images have to be placed, which is an integral part of the design process. Similarly the captions, which vary considerably in length, are central to the final form of the display. All these factors shape readers' experiences. Seen in this way, the book, itself a piece of visual and material culture, embodies the key concepts it interrogates.

ESSAY

Deposits of friendship: Renoir's 1908 portrait of Ambroise Vollard

The painting

XXVII Here is a complex display: a canvas depicts a man sitting at a table holding a statuette. Other beautiful objects are on the surface, which is covered with patterned cloth. He is shown absorbed; his pleasure and appreciation are palpable. The man's face and body are rounded, his dress unobtrusive, his age indeterminate, perhaps early middle age. This painted portrait, executed in 1908 and given to the sitter, shows someone finding joy in the material world. It is currently hung near windows and a fireplace in a high-ceilinged eighteenth-century room, available to be seen by anyone paying the gallery's entrance fee. It depicts a named man; the broad circumstances in which the canvas came into being are known. In front of portraits, viewers are accustomed to search for particularity; they focus on the sitter, as if the image generates privileged insights about them.

The painting, set in a carved and gilded wooden frame, depicts Ambroise Vollard, 'celebrity, art merchant, socialite, publisher and writer', according to the blurb on one of his books, *Recollections of a Picture Dealer*.[1] The artist, Pierre-Auguste Renoir, 'a leader of the Impressionist movement who soon repudiated its aims', is probably one of the best-known and most popular painters in the world.[2] Vollard kept the picture for nearly twenty years. It now hangs in the Courtauld Gallery, London, having been sold by him to Samuel Courtauld in June 1927 for 800,000 francs. Vollard, it seems, loved having his picture done: he was depicted by Bonnard, Cézanne, Rouault and Picasso, amongst others. He and Renoir knew each other well; Vollard was one of the dealers who sold Renoir's works, and he recorded his conversations with the artist who, by the end of his life, was highly fêted. Vollard's published accounts of Renoir, whom he probably met in 1894, may also be said to be portraits. This picture is one of five portraits that Renoir did of a man 'who became a familiar of the household' and it has been said to be the most affectionate.[3]

Here is another description of the picture:

> Vollard is shown seated with his elbows on the table, caressing the original plaster of Maillol's *Crouching Woman* in his large, fine hands … Vollard

now appears the prosperous bourgeois, whose collar is a little tight, and whose short-cropped hair has started to turn grey … So mesmerized is he by Maillol's statuette that Vollard is oblivious to any untidiness in his appearance. His concentration and the massiveness of his presence are relieved only by the gaily patterned table cloth…[4]

This account, from an exhibition catalogue, treats the painting as if it opened out onto a real scene, which it then describes. It also introduces new elements: Vollard's hands are evaluated ('fine'), his mood is specified ('mesmerized') and his class position alluded to ('prosperous bourgeois'). Of course, the displayed scene is a painting, a construction by the artist that arose out of long-standing dynamics between the two men. It is one deposit of their relationship. It was Renoir, not Vollard, who created for spectators the sense of obliviousness, of mesmerisation, through marks of paint on a canvas.

Visitors to the room where it hangs experience the painting in a setting composed of architecture, furniture, other works displayed, and the labels. **45** The long room contains many of the Courtauld's best known paintings, including Manet's *Bar at the Follies bergères*. Renoir, who had significant links with Manet, Monet, Sisley, Bazille and Pissarro, is thus surrounded by works that formed part of his immediate context. Vollard's image is framed by the wood around it, the label, other nearby works, the room itself and the gallery. Speaking figuratively, it is 'framed' by what visitors bring with them, including notions about portraiture, the artist, maybe the sitter, and about the environment they find themselves in.

At the time I drafted this chapter the label read:

Ambroise Vollard (1867–1939) was the foremost Parisian art dealer of the early 20th century. He gave Cézanne, Picasso and the sculptor Aristide Maillol their first one-man shows, became Renoir's principal dealer after 1900 and supported several leading members of the Fauve group. Here, Renoir shows him as a traditional connoisseur, examining a statuette of a crouching woman by Maillol, while an oriental figurine and bowl lie nearby.

Vollard's image was captured by Cézanne, Picasso, Bonnard, Rouault and numerous other artists. Picasso once noted how 'the most beautiful woman who ever lived never had her portrait painted, drawn or engraved more often than Vollard'.

Labels explicitly frame a work; they guide visitors' responses. In this case, we are encouraged to think of Vollard as the champion of innovative art. Like most labels accompanying portraits, this one focuses on the sitter. It alludes to the connections between artist and subject, while placing the canvas within certain traditions of portraiture. There is a brief

45 The room in which Renoir's portrait of Vollard is currently hung, photographed by the author, 2011. It is near another painting by Renoir, *Woman Tying her Shoe* (*c*.1918), some small female figurines by Degas, and a Monet scene, *Antibes*, 1888.

description of the picture itself, but the emphasis remains on Vollard, who, by virtue of Picasso's words, is presented as unusually vain for a man. This text ensures that the portrait is seen in terms of three main protagonists: Renoir, Vollard and Maillol. A label can hardly do justice to the multiple relationships between these men. For example, both Renoir and Vollard owned works by Maillol, who made a portrait head of Renoir in 1907. Vollard encouraged both men in significant ways. He urged Renoir to take up sculpture, although his hands were so crippled that he had to use an assistant, Richard Guino, who had previously worked with Maillol; he suggested to Maillol that he cast his terracotta and wood figures in bronze. Thus the label only lightly evokes these intricate artistic and personal networks. It does so in a lively way, although it does not locate them temporally. Then there is 1908 – what kind of specificity does a consideration of the date introduce? How long had these protagonists known each other and can we get a sense of the quality of their relationships?

Such questions arise when portraits are executed from life: whether they can be answered depends on the available evidence, but they should still be raised precisely to remind us that portraits are deposits of specific social relationships. In the case of artistic communities, the relationships are, literally, more visible, and when famous participants are involved, more extensively documented. Renoir portrayed other dealers he worked with, his patrons, as well as their families. He depicted other artists, such as Bazille, Monet and Sisley, and on occasion their families. Sometimes this was because he did not have to pay for them to act as models. But this hardly accounts for his five portraits of Vollard, and neither do claims concerning Vollard's exceptional vanity. Renoir's 1908 image of Vollard may be grounded by locating it within the genre of portraiture, as well as by setting it within Renoir and Vollard's lives and relationships.

The genre

Portraiture as a genre claims to show viewers and commentators something particular – nameable human being(s) – at a specific moment in time. **II, X, XXIII, XXV, 15, 16, 24, 28, 31, 32, 50** It asserts the reality of the sitter in a variety of ways. This alleged reality does not in fact depend upon the artist adopting a naturalistic style. The point is neatly demonstrated by the story that a child immediately recognised Vollard in Picasso's Cubist rendering of him from 1909–10; for the child, the picture still evoked a man he knew.[5] **XXVIII** This story may well be apocryphal, but it nonetheless speaks to the idea that portraits take many visual forms while remaining accounts of specific people. Picasso's Cubist portraits depend to a significant degree on the name of the sitter being provided. Viewers can tell that a human being is being represented, but, children notwithstanding, not necessarily which one. Thus Cubist portraits stretched the genre to its limits, as other artists and approaches have done. In such cases, viewers' attention is drawn to them as works of art. Nonetheless, viewers generally see through portraits to their subject matter. In the Renoir–Vollard example, however, the artist's fame preempts automatic assumptions about the precedence of the sitter, while the multi-faceted relationship between the two men invites an approach that respects psychological, emotional and economic complexities.

The specificity involved makes portraits appear more 'historical' than some other genres. Spectators expect to see in them actual people, known to have lived and died, which risks marginalising the makers, who mediated and transformed their sitters. In many contexts sitters are given priority over artists: in some places where portraits are displayed, the artist is known but not named. Portraits done from life are necessarily collaborations, and not just between artist and sitter. The sitter is not always the patron, which can be an institution, another person or group. It is precisely because portraits come up in so many contexts that they are rich historical sources. However, historians tend to use them as illustrations, to reveal to readers what someone in the past looked like. Sometimes seen as a lowly form of art, portraiture as a genre is more complex than it appears, and certainly does not simply present sitters as they really were. Although there has been a marked revival of interest in portraits among art historians in recent decades, their full potential for historical analysis has yet to be realised.

'Portrait' and 'portraiture' are tricky to define. For me, a portrait is a representation, in any medium, of a named or nameable person, designed to evoke in viewers some sense of their actual appearance. Hence we might ask whether someone with appropriate knowledge would recognise that person. Naturally enough, some artists have sought to explore and push the boundaries of the genre as the Cubists did. Picasso's works, for example, are portraits, arising from his direct encounter with particular individuals. Ideally the process of making a portrait involves the main protagonists spending time together, but a posthumous portrait, which used photographs, or a portrait made during the lifetime of the subject without face-to-face sittings, could certainly count.

When so-called 'great artists' undertake portraits, more attention is generally paid to their aesthetic properties. One account of Renoir's 1908 portrait of Vollard states: 'The warm tonality of this portrait is characteristic of Renoir's so-called "red period", as is the concern with rounded curves'. Notice two features of this sentence. It is concerned with formal features (tonality, rounded curves) and it places the picture in the context of the artist's creative development. It continues, 'Renoir captures Vollard's interest in and enjoyment of the statuette by Maillol that he is examining'.[6] While this way of putting it is not 'wrong', it posits Vollard's interest and enjoyment as prior to and independent of Renoir, who then 'captures' and fixes it as a naturalist would a specimen. Such language misses some fundamental features of portrait painting, especially what could be termed its psycho-dynamic aspects, which are best understood biographically through an analysis of relationships and networks. Thus the nature of Renoir and Vollard's dealings with each other is central to an understanding of the picture, which is ideally placed in the context of the genre and the ways Renoir practised it.

Renoir was not primarily a portraitist, although he was active and successful in the genre throughout his life, and relied upon it financially at some stages. From the beginning he painted family and friends, and most of his popular works involve the human figure. Renoir's nudes and scenes of contemporary life, for example, attracted considerable attention, and continue to be his most loved paintings. Since he used models extensively, the boundaries between these genres were fluid: they all explored the human body and its representation. 'Renoir loved women', begins one popular book about him, 'this simple fact is the most important thing to know about his personality and his art'.[7] It is true that Renoir was a self-consciously sensual painter, who talked about his pleasure in women's flesh, his delight in skin that caught the light. The sentence I quoted is, however, reductive in the ways it treats the relationships between biography and work, and contains no hint of a historical approach to the production of images, which would, for example, consider Renoir's treatment of male figures.

Based on the available evidence, we can locate portraiture at the centre of Renoir's artistic practice, even when the name of the model – he frequently used his servants – is not recorded in the title of the work. Portraits in a stricter sense formed a central element within his oeuvre, and, like the genre scenes, these include men as well as women. It is misleading to move from Renoir's overt sensuousness to the assumption that his relationships with, and representations of, men were marginal to his life and work. His 1908 portrait of Vollard is, like the images he made of many men who were important to him, as warmly engaged with their masculinity as the images of women were with their femininity. Since Vollard is shown holding a female form, the portrait foregrounds his masculine appreciation of feminine bodies, an appreciation that chimes with Renoir's own. Renoir further explored Vollard's masculinity in a portrait of 1917, where he is dressed as a toreador. In 1912 Renoir painted Vollard's Creole mistress, Madeleine de Galéa, in Nice, using a semi-recumbent pose reminiscent of David's portrait of Mme Récamier. Renoir was indeed engaging with both masculinity and femininity.

Renoir came to his career as an 'artist' from an artisanal background – his father was a tailor. His first job was painting on porcelain, including portraits of Marie-Antoinette. Then he decorated blinds and fans, and painted murals. Renoir started visiting the Louvre when young and remained a devotee of old master traditions, especially of Venetian art and of French eighteenth-century painters. He was well aware of portrait traditions and of his own place within them. Yet Renoir, who had an intense sense of history, had no interest in academic approaches. I put 'artist' in inverted commas because his son reported him to have been hostile to the term: 'Renoir went so far as to eliminate the word "artist" from his vocabulary. He thought of himself as a "workman-painter".'[8] The phrase suggests someone proud to work with their hands, a part of the body in which Renoir manifested great interest. As his remarks about Cennino Cennini's *The Craftsman's Handbook* suggest, Renoir valued

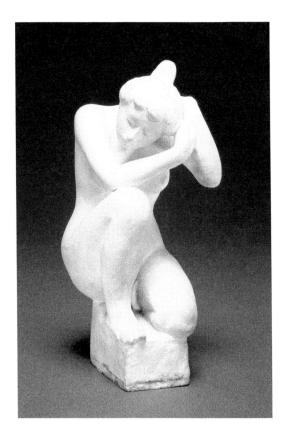

46 *Petite Baigneuse Accroupie* (*Little Bather Squatting*), by Aristide Maillol, 1900, off-white terracotta, 8.6 cm wide × 9.7 cm deep × 23 cm high, Fitzwilliam Museum, Cambridge. In Renoir's portrait, Vollard is holding what appears to be a pinkish terracotta version of the figure. Other versions of this statuette exist in which the woman seems to be adjusting her hair. Women grooming themselves have had wide appeal as a subject that is full of potential for depicting the naked body and for evoking a sense of intimacy.

good artisanship, and the skilled labour of individuals.[9] We therefore have good reason to note the way he represents Vollard handling the plaster figure, and reflect upon his respect for manual activity. Commentators differ markedly in the way they see Vollard's hands. Colin Bailey commented that they were large and fine, that they were caressing Maillol's *Crouching Woman*. By contrast, John House claimed, 'the painting evokes the dealer's power over the sensuous image of a woman that he holds in his hands and in his gaze; his pudgy fingers are startlingly similar to the limbs of the statuette'.[10] Vollard made his money out of the hands of others, and hands are an important element within portraiture, given the long-standing interest in their expressive power. It is implausible that Renoir would be careless in their representation.

Renoir's own pleasure in the physical act of painting continued to his death, even though his hands were deformed and he had to have his brushes strapped on. If we take Renoir to be wedded to the identity of a workman, it renders his portrait of Vollard particularly interesting. Here was an upwardly mobile man who marketed Renoir's handiwork. Using his own manual skills, Renoir showed Vollard holding and admiring another piece of handiwork, made by someone they both admired, and out of whom the dealer also made money. 46 On this account the portrait speaks about the ways in which art work is made, circulated and creates pleasure.

However much the role and status of portraiture were in flux in Renoir's time, it was, and had been for several centuries, a recognised way of making money for artists. Renoir painted those who were dear to him, those who were in his circles, and he generated income from commissioned portraits. In this case, the artist gave the portrait to the sitter, who kept it until it was sold. That same year, 1927, Samuel Courtauld paid more for a Degas, a van Gogh and a Cézanne, but spent considerably less on the other seven works that he purchased.[11] Vollard was notorious for being a wily man; he was extremely successful financially, manipulative with his clients, and kept a careful eye on his own status. He believed that his portrait would go eventually to the National Gallery in London, which apparently pleased him. Thus Renoir's portrait of Vollard can be used as a springboard into questions about the status of handmade things, including paintings, the manner in which they were bought, marketed and sold, the ways in which artistic labour was valued, the representation of looking, appreciating and owning objects, and negotiations around the status of art-workers.

Portraits are not just surrounded by, but are embedded in, texts of various kinds through which they reach a range of audiences. It is principally through verbal accounts rather than from objects and images that we know about Vollard's relationship with Renoir. Texts and portraits mediate each other; portraits mediate relationships. Artefacts never tell their own stories, and portraits are peculiarly interwoven with texts by virtue of their links with biography, because of their common use as frontispieces and illustrations in books, and because they prompt conversations that may be recorded in some way as Vollard, and others who knew Renoir, did. Portraits are commonly used to embellish historical publications from the scholarly to the popular. Visitors and readers are likely to be highly dependent on labels or captions for portraits, unless the sitter is exceptionally famous. In the case of well-known sitters and artists, many texts, including from newspapers and magazines, form part of what we could call a textual penumbra, an array of writings in which any given portrait is embedded, where the writings are likely to be connected to each other, and to objects, in myriad ways.

The textual penumbra

Let us consider some of the texts alluded to so far. I have mentioned Vollard's *Recollections*, which is an autobiography, and his reminiscences of Renoir, which some have called a biography. He also published, during Renoir's lifetime and with his approval, a catalogue of the work containing small illustrations of hundreds of items. Then there was an entry on Renoir in a dictionary intended for non-specialist audiences, an exhibition catalogue of Renoir portraits, and general works on Renoir. In addition I mentioned labels and the ways in which portraits are presented to gallery audiences. Here are seven different genres – biography, autobiography, reference works, exhibition catalogues, overviews of an oeuvre, books for non-specialists and labels for works on public display. In some cases, the genre is notably fluid – a huge range of writings could be called 'biographical', for example. There are many further kinds of relevant writing, such as letters, diaries and monographs, newspapers and learned journals. Here I consider briefly just two categories of publication, first those produced by the Courtauld Institute, and then Vollard's writings on Renoir.

The Courtauld Institute, named after its main benefactor, came into being in 1932. Its foundation 'was presided over by a triumvirate of collectors, brought together by a common wish to improve the understanding of the visual arts' in Britain.[12] The activities of Samuel Courtauld may be understood in terms of the history of collecting, which is currently enjoying prominence. The field sheds light on taste, fashion, mentalities, markets, travel and institutions. Thus, we might investigate, for example, the ways in which Courtauld collected and the impulses behind his activities in the art world. Two works do precisely this.

The Courtauld Gallery at Somerset House provides an introduction to the collections housed there, and offers brief discussions and illustrations of some of the principal works, including Renoir's portrait of Vollard. Readers learn about the Courtauld family, about Samuel's life and values, and the biographical circumstances that led him to set up a museum in his home following the death of his wife in 1931. Samuel and Elizabeth Courtauld were active philanthropists, who were especially interested in the 'spiritual and aesthetic advancement of mankind'. Furthermore, Samuel believed that 'the formal and emotional qualities of the Old Master tradition were alive and well in the "modern" French school, especially in Manet, Renoir and Degas'. His purchase of the portrait in question should be located within this broad cultural setting. The book contains a reproduction of Renoir's painting with commentary by the art historian John House.[13] In form it closely resembles an entry in an exhibition catalogue in being a brief essay on the work and its immediate context of production. The first paragraph outlines Vollard's life and work and his meeting with Renoir. The second discusses the portrait itself, evaluates it and comments on other depictions of the sitter. The third extends the account of the canvas, evaluating it further, largely in style terms. The fourth and final paragraph continues the formal approach and pays particular attention to Renoir's use of colour.

In House's comments we find five main kinds of statements: biographical, contextual, descriptive, stylistic and evaluative. Sometimes it is perfectly clear which category a sentence falls into: 'Renoir met the young dealer Vollard around 1895' is biographical. When House mentions Maillol executing a portrait bust of Renoir, he is providing context. 'Vollard is shown holding a statuette of Artistide Maillol' is descriptive. The phrase 'monumental classicism' presents a stylistic claim. When we read that 'Renoir's is one of the least acute' portraits of Vollard, the reader is in no doubt that an evaluation has been made, even if its basis is unclear. But what about phrases that mention Vollard's 'pudgy fingers', his 'ugly, bulldog features' and 'his cunning, quirky personality', which appear to describe the painting, while in fact are passing judgement upon both it and the sitter? This example reveals some of the challenges of writing about paintings and especially about portraiture, a genre that seems to invite personal comments, although readers may be unaware of the supporting evidence. Nesting remarks about specific works within a publication outlining the history of an institution and its benefactors is useful because it shows them as being attached to a range of historical processes, such as collecting and philanthropy.

A more scholarly publication covers similar ground. *Impressionism for England: Samuel Courtauld as Patron and Collector* accompanied an exhibition exploring the taste for French art in the context of modernism. This project implies three types of contextualisation: first, the location of collectors with respect to 'taste'; second, English responses to another nation's culture; and third, the role and importance of an aesthetic movement – modernism. Two further contexts are examined in the book: the Courtauld family and their financial situation, and the art market. A checklist of Courtauld's acquisitions of modern French paintings provides the date a work was acquired, the price paid and the name of the vendor. I drew on that information when I compared the amount spent on Renoir's portrait of Vollard with the cost of other works. Thus, in studies of collectors, taste and money are natural bedfellows. Courtauld's values may usefully be seen in the context of his social position, personal development and the broader context in which he functioned. Markets create and shape value both in the sense of price and in the sense of what is esteemed and desired. Courtauld was dedicated to bringing what he saw as the riches of modern French painting to British audiences. He was especially drawn to Renoir, who 'was naturally enough one of Courtauld's favourites among nineteenth-century painters'. More specifically, he found in some of Renoir's works 'a particular attitude towards humanity, and an incredible visual beauty which brought the art very close in spirit to the Renaissance masters whom Courtauld admired'.[14]

The prices Renoir commanded, who was buying his work and from whom, are not narrow economic matters, but bear on broad questions about reputation, the public role of art, fashion, and the parts played by intermediaries such as dealers, who acquired fresh prominence in the second half of the nineteenth century. Publications from the Courtauld Institute thus enable historians to set Renoir's portrait in multiple settings. In one account of the painting, however, we noted a tangle of claims about which it was necessary to be sceptical. Lively accounts of artefacts help readers engage with them, but the assumptions and value judgements they contain can distort that engagement, especially when their basis is unstated. Portraiture, precisely because it concerns other human bodies with which viewers are likely to experience elaborate forms of identification, needs to be treated with particular care.

In turning to Vollard's textual 'portraits' of Renoir, we move from secondary accounts to primary ones, to the testimony of a participant who made no pretence at detachment. The two were friends, although it is noteworthy how complex the concept and the practices of friendship are. Vollard felt free to comment on any aspect of Renoir's life, such as the behaviour of servants and children, the food, the organisation of the household and his impressions of others who interacted with the artist. Accordingly he evoked the multiple dimensions of artistic life in Renoir's time. Renoir himself was the natural centrepiece, and Vollard invests the painter's opinions with a certain reverence, and seems to relish their strength, presumably because they gave colour and immediacy to Renoir's personality, which comes across as strong, even domineering. Vollard's writings are mainly anecdotal, moving from one vignette to another, without regard for chronology. At first sight this mixture of stories and impressions is frustrating, because it is unsystematic and ill-suited to historical understanding. Vollard's main publications on Renoir followed the latter's death, and are sometimes treated as unreliable and distinctly lightweight. Yet if we are concerned with the textual penumbra around Renoir and his art works, they need to be given careful consideration, not least because they continue to be cited in some quarters as a major source on the artist.

Anecdotal accounts of artists were hardly a new phenomenon; they meet a curiosity that is frequently elicited by the lives of those with uncommon talent.[15] Vollard helped to meet that curiosity, as did Jean Renoir – the artist's son and a renowned film director. By about 1900 Renoir was world famous, and Vollard made a substantial contribution to his reputation. He also wrote about Degas and Cézanne as well as about himself, and there is much of interest in texts by one of the most powerful men in the art world. It is possible to interpret his books as ways of generating publicity for 'his' artists. But this does not account for their detailed properties, for the tones he adopts or the precise selection of topics.

Three features of Vollard's portraits of Renoir are particularly eloquent from a historical point of view. The first is the prominent role Vollard gives to money. It should come as no surprise that the subject loomed large in the early life of a painter, or that continuing success with sales was taken as one indicator of artistic achievement. Vollard is notably specific on such matters, including relations with patrons and collectors. Thus Renoir's strategies and ways of dealing with purchasers are presented as integral to his life, as indeed they were. The politics and economics of the visual arts sit in Vollard's account quite happily next to the second feature, namely his concern with what Renoir actually did when he painted. Given Renoir's complex relationship with Impressionism, his views about how to paint, and especially his approach to colour and working in the open air, are of some interest. He was so severely crippled with arthritis that his ability to carry on painting until the end of his life was noteworthy, and Vollard describes exactly how this was achieved. The emphasis on technique possesses further forms of significance, and fits well with Renoir's emphasis on the hands. In describing how Renoir worked, Vollard was able to construct an artistic persona with strategic advantages. It endowed him with a special type of heroism that William Gaunt gave voice to: 'The struggle of the crippled man is one of the heroic legends of art. Not only would he not give in, he contemplated fresh triumphs, was able to achieve them.'[16]

In the chapter of *Renoir: an Intimate Record* entitled 'Renoir Paints my Portrait', Vollard observed: 'Renoir always attacked his canvas without the slightest apparent plan. Patches would appear first, then more patches, then, suddenly, a few strokes of the brush, and the subject "came out". Even with his stiffened fingers, he could do a head in one sitting as easily as when he was young.'[17] This chimes with Renoir's impatience with theories, and Impressionist theories in particular: 'the truth is that in painting, as in the other arts, there's not a single process, no matter how insignificant, which can reasonably be made into a formula'.[18] Renoir's seeming spontaneity encourages readers to appreciate his natural talent, his genius. Vollard records Renoir's interest in the Old Masters, and the ways in which he was shaped by their study, so he is not presenting Renoir as naïve or uneducated, but as a painter in whom exceptional ability and immediate visual responses dominate.

The third noteworthy feature of Vollard's account is the way in which he sets Renoir within the wider culture, attributing to him views on music and literature, for example. In his youth, Renoir was a proficient singer; he was taught by the famous composer Charles Gounod, hence his views on music are of some interest. According to Vollard, his portrait of Wagner was painted in twenty-five minutes. 'I used to like Wagner very much. I was quite carried away by the kind of passionate fluidity that there seemed to be in his music; but a friend took me once to Bayreuth, and I need hardly tell you that I was frightfully bored.'[19] Sometimes Vollard's text is set out like a play. It seems implausible that he remembered whole passages with perfect accuracy; thus his 'biography' of a man he clearly felt affection for is an elaboration, a kind of strategic fiction. The influence of Vollard's publications has been considerable, so that Renoir lives, as it were, through these texts as well as through his works.

Since I characterised Vollard's writings as anecdotal, we should consider briefly the status of anecdotes in this context. In his *Recollections*, there is a short chapter just over four pages long, entitled simply 'My Portraits', which recounts a series of little stories about his encounters with Renoir, Cézanne, Bonnard, Raphael Schwartz and Picasso. These vignettes are designed to illustrate something amusing or significant about the artist in question. His Renoir story concerns the genesis of the 1917 portrait of him as a toreador. There are many different accounts of this picture, so clearly the anecdote cannot be taken as gospel. In Vollard's account he arrived at the studio already wearing the costume he had brought back from Spain at Renoir's request. "'I have always wanted to paint a *torero*", he said. "One of my models is about your size, so do try and bring me back a *torero*'s costume that fits you.'" Vollard was wearing it only because the customs officer found 'the swagger costume', and, when Vollard claimed these were his working clothes, challenged him to put them on. Because a crowd was collecting, he jumped in a taxi and went straight to Renoir's where the reaction was gratifying. "'Bravo!" cried the painter as soon as he set eyes on me; "I shall make *you* sit for my picture'". Vollard, with what degree of self-awareness is unclear, actually reveals much of himself in this anecdote, especially when he confesses, 'I felt magnificent in the gold-embroidered jacket and equally gorgeous breeches'.[20] But what does it say about Renoir?

In giving the idea of painting a toreador to him, it speaks to the nature of his visual imagination, to his interest in the 'exotic'. This is clear from Renoir's enthusiasm for Delacroix, for example, and manifests itself in an early portrait of a Jewess in Algerian dress. **XXIX** Renoir had visited Spain: his trip is the subject of a chapter in Vollard's *Intimate Record*. The vignette presents Renoir, once again, as a spontaneous artist, one who reacted with immediacy to sensual experience. These themes are central to the Renoir that Vollard created: an artist who worked fast, whose reactions to the world were characterised by joy, pleasure and the power of his senses. Anecdotes can be exceptionally effective in constructing a personality. They deploy just the qualities Vollard imputes to Renoir – humour, immediacy, fun, quick reactions. They are effective vehicles for myth-making, and hence valuable resources for analysing the forging of reputation, personality and genius.

I now move from the tissue of texts within which Renoir's 1908 portrait of Vollard is embedded, to its visual penumbra. This separation between verbal and visual is purely for the sake of convenience: these two orders of representation are intricately entwined.

The visual penumbra

This canvas is as densely surrounded by images and objects as it is by texts. Its contents – the sitter, the objects, the tablecloth – all lead the spectator on to other representations. Three types of visual associations have already been mentioned: Renoir's other portraits of Vollard, portraits of Vollard by other artists, and portraits of Renoir himself. From portraits of Renoir, we can move on to his self-portraits: he was not a particularly assiduous self-portraitist, although several are known, including a 1915 drawing inscribed 'à Vollard, mon raseur sympathique, Renoir'.[21] **47** In addition there are photographs of both men. Furthermore, the picture depicts several objects: the Maillol statuette of 1900 has already been mentioned. It leads the viewer on to both other works by the same artist and other works of sculpture, especially female nudes. Colin Bailey refers to 'the gaily patterned tablecloth, with its bounding animals' and 'the blue and white Oriental figurine and pot that have just been unwrapped'.[22] Vollard was interested in blue porcelain, and commissioned ceramics from artists in his circle. It is worth remembering here Renoir's own history as a painter of porcelain in his youth. Pieces of china and depictions of china thus surround the portrait. The tablecloth is somewhat gnomic, since it is unclear precisely what kind of animal is depicted. The prancing beasts suggest a hunt, and perhaps tapestries in which they were commonly represented.

The items mentioned so far possess a direct connection with the painting itself. There is also a less direct visual penumbra, such as the thematic one of collectors or connoisseurs examining objects of special interest to them. Portraits of collectors and connoisseurs are not uncommon, although they rarely show someone so absorbed in handling and inspecting a work that they are not looking at the viewer or displaying their possessions. These motifs are more common in caricature, where the myopic, sometimes desiccated, connoisseur is a recognisable figure. Indeed, there is just such a drawing in the Courtauld Collections, showing a man with an animal-like face looking through a glass. **48**

Renoir's world contained examples in the work of Honoré Daumier, whom he, like Vollard, admired. Daumier was a frequent and sharp

47 Renoir self-portrait, 1915, lithograph, 62.5 cm high × 47 cm wide, private collection, inscribed to Vollard. This image was used as the frontispiece to Vollard's book on Renoir, published in 1920, the year after his death, where it is described as a reduced facsimile of an engraving from an 'édition de luxe'. There are a number of self-portraits by Renoir from youth to old age. This one depicts a figure familiar from photographs, of a gaunt and aged man, attired in what is recognisably artist's garb: a soft hat, the suggestion of a cloak and loose ties around the neck.

48 *Caricature of a Connoisseur*, by George Howland Beaumont, not dated, graphite on paper, 9.9 cm high × 8.3 cm wide, the Courtauld Gallery, London. The connoisseur is holding up a magnifying glass, which implies close visual scrutiny. Dressed in what appears to be gentleman's clothing, his face turns into an animal's snout. Beaumont was an amateur artist, who exhibited at the Royal Academy, a collector and patron of art, thus he was himself a connoisseur. He was noted for his strong, and to some eyes, conservative views about the visual arts. The Courtauld Gallery contains other works by Beaumont; the main collection of paintings he owned is now in the National Gallery, London, the foundation of which he supported.

commentator on the art world of his day. In the 1860s, Daumier produced a number of works around the theme of collectors and art-lovers, including *The Connoisseur*, which shows an unnamed seated man, hands in lap, admiring a small, partially clothed Venus. **XXX** This work was sold at least three times during Renoir's lifetime, at one point passing through the hands of Paul Durand-Ruel, one of Renoir's dealers, so it is possible that he knew it. **XXXI** Yet its look is entirely different from Renoir's canvas, with its intense focus on one man and the item he holds, and the lack of a worked-up setting. Daumier, by contrast, shows the man in a room full of pictures, folders and other objects. He was acute on the nature of looking, whether on the part of specialists or members of the public.[23] The ways in which dealers, collectors and connoisseurs are represented is of great historical interest. What visual languages existed for presenting those with marked visual interests? How are acts of looking and touching portrayed? Such questions lead from one particular portrait into a number of artistic traditions, of which depictions of collectors and connoisseurs are just one.

The visual penumbra exists at a number of analytical levels. The first one is literal, such as the Maillol figurine – an independent object that is depicted on the canvas. The second could be called filiative – works that are directly related, showing the same sitter or by the same artist of related subjects, other dealers in his life, for example. The third is contextual and includes such items as photographs of Renoir and Vollard taken around the time the painting was made. The fourth is thematic, and includes works on similar and related subjects: whether or not Renoir knew these at first hand, they are of historical interest. A final type of visual penumbra consists of Renoir's own visual reference points: decorating porcelain in his youth, for example. He carried this experience with him – it constituted a resource that was available to him as he worked. A full historical account, evidence permitting, contains as many of these levels as possible. Making such connections work in an argument can involve an element of supposition that is best avowed. I have *assumed* that Renoir's early working experiences, like his visits to the Louvre and his travels, shaped his visual world in appreciable ways – an assumption that is generally plausible and is to be modified by whatever specific evidence is available. This approach gives weight to a range of visual experience; it uses biographical and contextual materials in the service of a historical account that is as rounded as possible.

NOTES

1 The measurements given vary – I have taken these from the file in the Courtauld Institute. Colin Bailey, *Renoir Portraits: Impressions of an Age* (New Haven and Ottawa, 1997), p. 238, gives them as 81.6 × 65.2 cms. It is not known whether this is the original frame. The first edition of Vollard's book was the English one of 1936.

2 Erica Langmuir and Norbert Lynton, *The Yale Dictionary of Art and Artists* (New Haven, 2000), p. 586.

3 William Gaunt, *Renoir* (London, 1994; first published 1962), p. 21; Bailey, *Renoir Portraits*, p. 238.

4 Bailey, *Renoir Portraits*, p. 238.

5 Ambroise Vollard, *Recollections of a Picture Dealer* (London, 1936), p. 224.

6 Gaunt, *Renoir*, p. 118.

7 Patrick Bade, *Auguste Renoir* (New York, 2003), p. 3.

8 Jean Renoir, *Renoir: My Father* (London, 1988; first published in English, 1962), p. 34.

9 Renoir's comments on Cennini are mentioned by his son in *Renoir: My Father*, pp. 387–90. Renoir *père* was hostile to the division of labour, and thought the ideal was an article 'made, from its inception to its completion, by the same workman' (p. 390).

10 John House, *Impressionism for England: Samuel Courtauld as Patron and Collector* (London, 1994), p. 140.

11 *Ibid.*, p. 223.

12 From 'A Short History of the Courtauld' on the website.

13 *The Courtauld Gallery at Somerset House* (London, 1998), p. 7. See p. 95 for the entry on Renoir's portrait of Vollard, the text is the same as in *Impressionism for England*.

14 Douglas Cooper, *The Courtauld Collection: a Catalogue and Introduction* (London, 1954), p. 7.

15 The notion of writing artists' lives is usually associated with Vasari, whose first publication on the subject appeared in 1550. There are numerous biographies and biographical dictionaries. For its currency, see Edward Lucie-Smith, *Lives of the Great Modern Artists*, rev. and expanded edn (London, 2009), and Nigel Cawthorne, *Sex Lives of the Great Artists* (London, 1998). Cf. Sue Roe, *The Private Lives of the Impressionists* (London, 2006), and Bernard Denvir, *The Chronicle of Impressionism: an Intimate Diary of the Lives and World of the Great Artists* (London, 2000; first published 1993).

16 Gaunt, *Renoir*, p. 23.

17 Ambroise Vollard, *Renoir: an Intimate Record* (New York, 1990; first published in English, 1925), ch. 23, p. 96.

18 *Ibid.*, p. 55.
19 *Ibid.*, pp. 48–9 and 96, quotation from pp. 49–50.
20 Vollard, *Recollections*, p. 221, emphasis in original.
21 *Ibid.*, facing p. 268. Note that if consulting the Dover reprint of 1978, where the illustrations are in slightly different places, it is facing p. 283. It is also the frontispiece to Ambroise Vollard, *Auguste Renoir (1841–1919)* (Paris, 1920).
22 Bailey, *Renoir*, p. 238.
23 See also the sketch *The Connoisseur (un Amateur)*, which is reproduced on p. 402 of Douglas Campbell and Usher Caplan, eds., *Daumier, 1808–1879* (Ottawa, 1999), pp. 394–411, concerns 'Collectors and Art-Lovers (1860s)'.

FURTHER READING

There is a huge number of accessible works on Renoir, of which the one by Paul Joannides is particularly thoughtful: *Renoir: Life and Works* (London, 2000). On his portraiture, the exhibition catalogue by Colin Bailey is essential: *Renoir's Portraits: Impressions of an Age* (Ottawa, 1997). The biography by Lawrence Hanson is not an academic work, but it provides (pp. 249–50) a useful list of works about the artist by his contemporaries: *Renoir: the Man, the Painter and his World* (London, 1970). Vollard was by no means the only person to record his conversations with Renoir and other artists; see, for example, Michel Georges-Michel, *From Renoir to Picasso: Artists I have Known* (London, 1957). Like Vollard he makes a virtue of an anecdotal approach. The film-maker Jean Renoir's book on his father may fruitfully be compared with Vollard's writings: *Renoir: My Father* (London, 1988; first published in French in 1958 and in English in 1962). He mentions Maillol. Renoir's relationship with Impressionism was complex; for an introduction to that phenomenon, see Belinda Thomson, *Impressionism: Origins, Practice, Representation* (London, 2000). On Renoir's broad artistic context, Richard Brettell, *Modern Art 1851–1929: Capitalism and Representation* (Oxford, 1999), is useful. On Renoir, see also John House, *The Genius of Renoir: Paintings from the Clark* (New Haven and London, 2010), and *Renoir* (London, 1985). Anthea Callen discusses Renoir in *Techniques of the Impressionists* (London, 1982), pp. 50–3, 76–9 and 118–21, and in *The Art of Impressionism: Painting Technique and the Making of Modernity* (New Haven and London, 2000).

Vollard's own writings, cited in the endnotes as appropriate, are worth sampling. In English, these are *Renoir: an Intimate Record* (New York, 1990), taken from the 1925 English edition, and *Recollections of a Picture Dealer* (New York, 1978), taken from the 1936 English edition. See p. 204 of *Recollections* for Renoir on Maillol. Both Vollard's books are illustrated. More information on Vollard's publications is presented in the list in Jean-Paul Morel, *C'était Ambroise Vollard* (Paris, 2007), pp. 573–97. For a more analytical approach to Vollard, see Rebecca

Rabinow, ed., *Cézanne to Picasso: Ambroise Vollard, Patron of the Avant Garde* (New York and New Haven, 2006), and esp. pp. 143–9 on Vollard and Renoir by Anne Distel. This exhibition catalogue allows comparisons to be made between the relationships he enjoyed with his artists, including Maillol. On Maillol's life and work, see Bertrand Lorquin, *Aristide Maillol* (London, 1995), where the head of Renoir faces p. 96, and Waldemar George, *Aristide Maillol* (London, 1965), which shows it from two angles, pp. 147 and 149.

The Courtauld Institute published a volume about its genesis and some of the highlights of the collection, including the portrait that is the subject of this chapter: *The Courtauld Gallery at Somerset House* (London, 1998). The scholarly study by John House and others, *Impressionism for England: Samuel Courtauld as Patron and Collector* (New Haven and London, 1994), gives a sense of how Courtauld's acquisition of Vollard's portrait fits into broader patterns of collecting. 'A Short History of the Courtauld' on their website, which also offers a virtual tour, is illuminating. On the history of collecting generally, see Neils von Holst, *Creators, Collectors and Connoisseurs: the Anatomy of Artistic Taste from Antiquity to the Present Day* (London, 1967; first published in German in 1960), in which the 1908 portrait features (facing p. 279), and *Journal of the History of Collections* (1989 onwards). Philipp Blom, *To Have and to Hold: an Intimate History of Collectors and Collecting* (London, 2002), is highly accessible.

On portraiture in general, there is Richard Brilliant, *Portraiture* (London, 1991); Joanna Woodall, ed., *Portraiture: Facing the Subject* (Manchester, 1997); and Shearer West, *Portraiture* (Oxford, 2004) – these books arise out of predominantly art-historical concerns. It is worth looking at the websites of the major portrait galleries, for example, in London, Edinburgh, Washington DC and Canberra. Historians are still in the early stages of developing projects that use portraiture systematically. Some historically orientated art historians, however, have produced work that is inspirational. For example, two pieces on Picasso's 1910 portrait of Daniel-Henri Kahnweiler (1884–1976), who was also a dealer, publisher and writer with close associations with his artists: Michael Baxandall, *Patterns of Intention: On the Historical Explanation of Pictures* (New Haven and London, 1985), ch. II; Marcia Pointon, 'Kahnweiler's Picasso; Picasso's Kahnweiler', in Woodall, *Portraiture*, ch. 9. See also William Rubin, ed., *Picasso and Portraiture: Representation and Transformation* (New York and London, 1996), and Natasha Staller, *A Sum of Destructions: Picasso's Cultures and the Creation of Cubism* (New Haven and London, 2001). On Cubism, John Golding, *Cubism: a History and an Analysis 1907–1914*, 3rd edn (London, 1988), remains a good introduction.

On caricatures of connoisseurs there is Harry Mount, 'The Monkey with the Magnifying Glass: Constructions of the Connoisseur in Eighteenth-Century Britain', *Oxford Art Journal*, 29 (2006), pp. 167–83. On Daumier, see Douglas Campbell and Usher Caplan, eds., *Daumier, 1808–1979* (Ottawa, 1999), which reveals Daumier's interest in depicting collectors, artists and audiences.

Bridge

This essay has only begun to probe the complex relationship between Renoir and Vollard and one of its numerous deposits. For example, I have not explored the tensions between them, nor mentioned the many stories that suggest Renoir's ambivalence, even hostility, towards his great fan. Vollard had been born and raised in La Réunion, and was vulnerable to jokes about his colonial origins. Renoir's ambivalence was hinted at in the 1915 inscription – 'raseur' means 'bore', although the intent may well have been humorous. Nor have I tracked their business dealings with one another, which began in 1894, it seems, with Renoir making a purchase from the young dealer. Renoir's portraits of Vollard were just one manifestation of a friendship that lasted more than twenty years. They are a material presence, available to be displayed and reproduced without limit. I have argued, however, that while portraiture provides many opportunities for historical work, it needs to be approached with caution. Its claims to reveal the sitter to the spectator cannot be taken at face value. The seductions of portraiture, which are genuine enough since portraits mobilise a profound curiosity about other human beings, can be kept in check by a comparative approach, which is central to visual analysis. The last chapter explores the nature of comparative analysis.

5   Comparative analysis

Similarity and difference

Many portraits of the art dealer Ambroise Vollard exist, including several by Renoir. **XXVII** and **XXVIII** Each artist who depicted him executed other portraits. **XXIX** From these two statements we can draw out several types of comparison using four variables: artist, medium, date, sitter. In those involving the same sitter and medium, but different artists, or the same sitter at a similar date in different media, some elements are the same, while others are varied. Each act of comparison draws the scholar's attention as sharply as possible to the element of difference. This move is accomplished most effectively by having as many points of similarity as possible. Thus, if we want to understand Renoir as a portraitist, we look at his other portraits to compare them with those of Vollard. Renoir's portrait oeuvre is extensive. In order to focus the comparison, we might select those of adult men, and then further restrict ourselves to pictures of those he knew well, who were in the art world, and painted at about the same time. Portraits of other dealers he worked with are of special relevance. For example, in 1910, he painted Paul Durand-Ruel, a dealer closely associated with the Impressionists, who sold works by Renoir. It shows him seated, as sober and elderly, a conventional man, and neatly reveals the artist's very different relationship with the two men.[1] **XXXI**

Such procedures allow us to consider the relationships between Renoir's treatment of Vollard and of other comparable men, and between his representations of art dealers and those of the same occupational group by other artists, such as Picasso. What was distinctive, it is then possible to ask, about Renoir's treatment of Vollard? How do his images compare with those of other artists dealing with similar subject matter? Clearly what counts as 'similar subject matter' is a crucial step in comparative analysis. These questions about Renoir and Vollard illustrate the ways in which visual analysis can be made precise through comparison. The precision comes from the constant assessment and scrutiny of both difference and similarity.

Comparison and disciplines

The approach I have just sketched is used in many fields, and made an explicit feature of a few, such as comparative linguistics and comparative anatomy. In the second case, visual analysis is central; in the first it is not. Comparative approaches are not inherently tied to work on visual sources, although they possess special roles within it. The method of constant adjudication between similarities and differences underlies much work in the sciences, social sciences and humanities, and in history in particular, even when it is not signalled as 'comparative'. The phrase 'comparative approaches' covers a number of distinct procedures, and is the expression of a wide range of impulses, as commentators on comparative history have made clear. Much historical research is based on the examination of a single country. For patterns in politics, society, culture or the economy to be meaningful, some sense of the differences and similarities between comparable countries is essential, even when researchers do not think of themselves as working comparatively. As Stefan Berger put it, 'Historians compare. They cannot avoid it, unless they restrict themselves to listing dates and events.'[2]

Accounts based on a single nation are *implicitly* comparative, and assumptions about the special path a country's history has followed, sometimes called exceptionalism, reveal the point. In such cases, it is differences that are at issue, even if they are taken for granted. By contrast, comparative history as a field *explicitly* addresses more than one zone, using geographical areas as foils for each other, or, more rarely, considers more than one period. Debates about the nature of industrialisation reveal the comparative elements within historical practice.[3] Insights derived from the study of the world's first industrial nation – Britain – can be considered when charting the move to large-scale factory production in others, and vice versa. It is possible to pull out key variables, such as the types of energy available, the nature of markets and the profile of the labour force, and explore their explanatory potential. These factors in turn can be examined in any geographical area or political unit. Here the unit of comparison is a region or a nation, the type of analysis applied to it is fairly abstract, and does not demand close attention

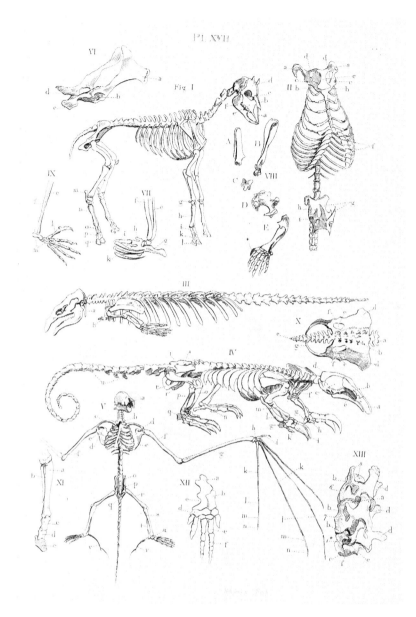

49 Plate XVII, from *Twenty Plates with Explanatory References, Illustrative of an Introduction to Comparative Anatomy*, by C. G. Carus, London, 1827, 19.5 cm wide × 26.3 cm high, Cambridge University Library. The only information given on the plate is 'Hobson sc Bath'. This plate was accompanied by an explanation, to which the letters and numbers refer. Note the variety of scales on a single page. Carus, who worked in Dresden, was himself an artist as well as being medically trained and an influential thinker. Comparative anatomy was of particular importance in the later eighteenth and nineteenth centuries. This image is not to be interpreted in evolutionary terms, but as part of a sustained exploration of the relationships between organic forms, which required sophisticated visual skills, and, when dissection was performed, manual ones.

to visual phenomena. But many fields do involve just this – archaeology and comparative anatomy, for example. **49**

Before considering the nature of comparative *visual* analysis specifically, it is necessary to explore comparative approaches more generally. While their origins are, arguably, ancient, they were self-consciously espoused in the eighteenth and nineteenth centuries, and in some fields, such as evolutionary biology and taxonomy, they remain central. The same is true of linguistics, where precise comparisons between specific features of languages, whether living or dead, lie at the heart of the subject. Note that these are all *historical* fields in that they concern change over long periods of time. The alterations they seek to document and explain are of a rather specific type. In historical linguistics, for example, the goal is to chart the development of particular languages: to show as convincingly as possible how one thing led to another. My use of the word 'thing' is, of course, figurative (and playful). Linguists are concerned with direct, documentable relationships between and within languages over time – relationships that can be conceptualised in terms such as descent, lineage and development. These notions are found in biology too, where it is material relationships – common ancestry, for example – that are at issue. The forms of comparative analysis I explore here rarely involve such relationships; rather they are tools, which focus and refine visual responses and prompt further research. Despite these differences, it is worth considering the kinds of reasoning involved in disciplines based on comparison in order to be clear about their forms. To proceed in this way, is, after all, to be comparative.

I have mentioned a range of phenomena that can serve as units of comparison. I started with portraits, a genre, and then considered sub-categories: portraits of Vollard; portraits by Renoir; portraits of dealers and so on. The object of *visual* analysis was specific portraits, which could be categorised in a variety of ways, such as by gender, occupation, identity of sitter and medium. When I mentioned comparative history, I noted that both countries and complex phenomena, such as the Industrial Revolution, were units of comparison, and suggested specific factors, such as the supply of energy and labour, through which the analysis could be pursued. Nations are commonly taken as key variables when it comes to explaining patterns of change. 'Industrialisation' refers to many features of a society and economy, hence a multi-factorial analysis is required. In practice, such phenomena may be more effectively studied in terms of geographical and economic regions rather than nations. Thus the nature and level of comparisons chosen shape the ensuing analysis. In the case of linguistics, languages and their component parts, principally understood in terms of grammar, vocabulary and pronunciation, are compared over time and space; in biology, it is species and varieties, as well as specific organs and anatomical parts.

These apparently diverse types of comparative analysis influence each other, partly because taxonomy is a common factor. When we speak of French or Spanish art, or the Northern or Italian Renaissance, the value of either nation-based or broad regional comparison is implied, even when the countries did not exist at the time the works were produced. Many museums and galleries organise their holdings in similar ways. For historians, physical space, and especially the nation state, is the dominant unit of comparison, and it is helpful to ask why it exercises such a strong hold in so many fields. Thus it is worth thinking critically about forms of comparison, the basic units selected and the types of analysis involved.

Comparison and context

We are concerned here with the value of a type of visual analysis that begins with a specific object, or group of objects, and seeks comparatives that are appropriate for historical approaches. Historians' use of visual and material culture is shaped by the priority given within the discipline of history to context. Assessing similarities and differences is in fact integral to processes of contextualisation. Finding the right context to put an artefact in depends upon a prior assessment of which other artefacts it is like or unlike and in what respects. These are historical judgements. Our sense of context is built up through the search for patterns, that is, for similarities and differences. Comparison is thus fundamental for a distinctively historical interest in items of visual and material culture. Here I propose giving analytical priority to images and objects, and moving from them, by a series of carefully considered steps, to broader phenomena. This procedure necessarily involves suites of comparisons, the precise nature of which is determined by the starting point chosen and by the questions leading the enquiry.

In order to sharpen our sense of comparative approaches in relation to visual and material culture, I will operate comparatively and consider three areas where comparative thinking is undertaken, which are relevant to visual analysis: connoisseurship, comparative literature and general history.

Connoisseurship

The term 'connoisseurship' came into use in the seventeenth century to suggest a refined kind of knowledge of valued items based on first-hand experience. Such expertise was based on the ability to make fine visual discriminations. It was intended to produce accurate attributions and judgements about quality and date. Connoisseurship implies comparative visual skills, which help viewers distinguish one maker, workshop, school or period from another, a fake from the genuine article, and to appreciate techniques and levels of craftsmanship. Already in the eighteenth century, connoisseurship polarised opinion, as the caricatures of connoisseurs as dry, ridiculous or pretentious reveal. **48** cf. **XXX** In some circles it continues to have a bad press as elitist and precious.

Connoisseurship can, however, be presented quite differently in terms of a range of visual skills that are cultivated with a high level of self-awareness. Frequently these are put to commercial ends, which does not render the skills themselves any less valuable. Because connoisseurship is fundamentally comparative, it provides a possible model for historians who seek to develop their ability to make precise discriminations based on close visual inspection. As Carlo Ginzburg pointed out, there are affinities between the development of scientific connoisseurship in the nineteenth century, psychoanalysis – which searches for signs that will assist in the interpretation of mental conditions – and the ways in which Sherlock Holmes was presented by his medical creator as solving crimes.[4] All are based on finding clues, frequently small ones, which demanded refined sensory acuity. The comparative analysis that underpins connoisseurship, then, is related to similar approaches found in other fields, a point that becomes apparent when its history is considered. One seminal figure, Giovanni Morelli, was medically trained, and saw close analogies between the natural sciences and art history. As a systematic field, with scientific aspirations, connoisseurship is associated with the second half of the nineteenth century, indeed with the beginnings of art history as a formal scholarly domain. The skills required for fine and precise visual distinctions to be made are now associated less with formal academic art-historical instruction and more with the training given within auction houses and commercial galleries. The financial implications of poor visual judgement – misattribution, for instance – are so serious that training it becomes a high priority; such honing is about the constant exercise of comparative visual analysis.

Comparative literature

The contrast with comparative literature could not be greater, yet it is pertinent to our concerns here. The idea of comparative literature goes back to the early nineteenth century, when it was suffused, unsurprisingly, with an interest in the character of national cultures. Comparisons between countries with respect to their literary productions could, it was claimed, generate an understanding of what was distinctive about each one. This now seems a dated approach; it assumes both that nations are unproblematic units of comparison and that their cultures reveal their defining features, but it is worth considering briefly. It is customary to speak of artefacts in terms of the region in which they were made, and it can be productive to do so since there may be genuine similarities to be discerned in the process. Historians are interested in how such regional similarities are explained. Likewise, in the case of literature, scholars sometimes speak of 'the English novel' or 'the Russian novel', which implies comparisons, although in practice these are articulated to varying degrees. The custom of studying the literature of a country along with its language, as many degree courses attest, reinforces both the idea that nations are natural units and the need to work comparatively when a broader perspective is sought. What underpins assumptions about national literary characteristics and the value of approaching writing comparatively, and what is their relevance for the study of artefacts? To answer such questions, it is necessary to have ways of conceptualising what is common to works produced in a given area, whether these are texts or items of visual and material culture. Reflexive modes of comparative analysis probe just these issues.

Two main routes can be taken to achieve such conceptualisation; one is more 'internal', the other more 'external', and they may be seen as complementary. An examination of traditions within the areas in question, where the search is for ideas and approaches that are transmitted across time and space, is an example of the former route. Traditions might be communicated through shared training, workshops and studios, as well as by more diffuse ways of doing things, if we are thinking of artefacts. In literary contexts it might be common educational patterns, reading practices, and the nature of the language itself. Certainly, 'tradition' is a complex notion. What counts as a tradition? How is it to be defined, and what evidence is required to substantiate it? Is direct contact, whether between persons, or between readers/viewers and specific works, necessary, for example? Are there less tangible forces to be considered – the sort of thing that is suggested by the terms 'worldview' or *Zeitgeist*? The concept 'tradition' is particularly challenging to use in a historical context, since it can also mean custom and practice, what is done unthinkingly in everyday life – not the meaning I am invoking here. Rather, I am drawing attention to a sense of shared frameworks and values, passed between individuals and groups who generate and consume cultural products, and evident in them.

Another related phenomenon, intertextuality, which implies meticulous comparative analysis, is important in literary studies. This, too, is an 'internal' matter in that texts themselves are the focus of attention. Intertextuality explores the relationships between texts, which take many forms, from explicit reworkings of myths, motifs and stories, through direct quotation, to allusion. Parody is a prime example. Authors speak to and are in conversation, literally or figuratively, with other authors. The phenomenon is widely recognised by those who study visual and material culture, who sometimes speak of 'quotation' and even 'intermediality'. 'Intervisuality' is little used, however, and I have never seen the word 'intermateriality'. Students of artefacts, such as furniture, coins and so on, are generally more comfortable speaking about influence, imitation and contact. Trade is a major topic here: for all of human history it has been a mechanism for innovation and change, for different cultures to transfer skills as well as goods, to compare themselves, rub up against each other and blend their ways of doing things. As post-colonial scholars have pointed out, unravelling these situations is complex, important and politically charged – and some sort of comparative approach is helpful. Comparative literature has played a crucial role in opening up these questions in relation to areas that were colonised by European powers. It has done so using a range of methods and approaches; attending to the complex phenomena that 'intertextuality' evokes have been central to these endeavours.[5]

When considering how to conceptualise what is common to works produced within a given area, it is possible to think in terms of influence, and to find ways of substantiating the direct impact of one writer upon another. Close textual analysis is required, as well as contextual evidence that such influence could plausibly have been exercised. The routes I have just outlined could all be described as 'internal' in giving priority to texts. Similar manoeuvres can be used in relation to objects, although there is no equivalent to comparative literature in the fields that specialise in visual and material culture, with the possible exception of world art studies.[6]

The second broad approach to regional similarities is to consider the contexts within which writing occurs – this is more 'external' and historical. The subject matter of much nineteenth-century Russian literature, such as the tedium of life on distant country estates, the role of the aristocracy especially in relation to peasants, and the threat of modern ideas, are hardly echoed in North American writings of the same period, which have their own master themes, such as the relationships between the Old World and the New.[7] Understanding Russian culture involves, naturally enough, paying attention to the historical contexts in which it came into being, i.e. some kind of comparative analysis, however implicit. It is precisely because literary modes travel and become transformed in the process that a comparative approach is attractive. Given the current interest in 'world literature', thinking carefully about the range of settings in which writing takes place is worthwhile. Many literary critics, whether they label themselves 'comparativists' or not, are sensitive to the precise historical conditions in which texts are made and received. One example is the recent attention paid to writing by women, and to the historical conditions within which female writers operated, which builds on the comparative nature of gender.

It is well worth historians who are interested in deploying artefacts in their work engaging with comparative literature and with literary fields more generally. These are mature areas of study, where there has been considered reflection upon a wide range of theoretical perspectives. Lively debates have ensued about methodological issues that are relevant to other fields; for example, the analysis of reception, reading practices, and the ways in which texts construct relationships with audiences. Comparative literature has cast its net particularly wide and, like literary studies in general, increasingly uses images and objects alongside texts. Comparative literature gives itself permission to range widely between cultures and approaches, examining translation practices in the process.

Translation is an evocative metaphor as commentators on comparative literature have noted, one that is useful when working with visual and material evidence. Designers commonly translate (mental) ideas into (two-dimensional) lines on paper, before (three-dimensional) models and products are made. Indeed, by seeking out shifts from one medium to another, historians gain a better understanding of processes of making and of implied audiences. In the case of languages, it is now recognised that translation is a creative act in its own right, rather than a technical exercise. This recognition is pertinent to the study of visual and material culture. It means, for example, that the work of print-makers in generating derivative prints can viewed as similarly creative. These are processes of reimagining – they are forms of mediation. Careful comparative work is worthwhile here, as it is in the case of making copies and replicas of paintings – a common practice especially in the early modern period. Think of the myriad ways in which Gilbert Stuart's depictions of George Washington have been disseminated.[8] **50** 'Translations' also occur between periods, giving rise to rich materials for comparison when those in a later period engage with the visual idioms of an earlier one. The phenomena gathered together under the term 'classicism' are an obvious example.

The idea of comparison, especially in the capacious form it takes in comparative literature, highlights a theme that runs through this book: the role of historical consciousness in the making of cultural products. Makers draw on the past of their craft as they work, doing so with varying degrees of awareness. Any training is bound to be a conduit for

50 *George Washington*, after Gilbert Stuart, after 1796, lithograph, 47 cm high × 32.4 cm wide, National Portrait Gallery, London. The American portrait painter Gilbert Stuart worked on both sides of the Atlantic and depicted many of the most notable figures of the Federal period in the United States. He painted Washington many times and numerous derivative prints exist. Washington enjoyed an elevated reputation as both a military and a political leader who led a successful revolution against a colonial power. The result has been ubiquitous images of him. An infinite range of adaptations from templates was possible in the medium of print. Sometimes, as in this case, additional scenes were added.

inheritance, while those who travel, forge collaborations, read books and collect are, in every moment, bringing the past into the present. Makers act comparatively. We, in tracing what may be called affinities, are also seeing and reasoning comparatively.

Comparative history

Comparative history has been shaped by sociological concerns. Big issues such as the nature of revolution, class formation and labour movements have attracted particular attention from historical sociology, and for such themes a comparative approach is especially apt. It has been suggested that there was a significant coincidence between the profession-alisation of history writing and the rise of nation states that has bound them together. The aptness of this level of human organisation for historical analysis is frequently taken as read. When combined with a sociological approach, the result can be comparative histories concerned with abstract ideas, such as gender, the state, welfare and social structures.

Stephen Smith's *Revolution and the People in Russia and China: a Comparative History* grapples with large questions about major transformations in the identity of working people, without becoming an exercise in sociological theorising or losing sight of historical texture. 'This book', he says, 'is an exploration of how the social identities of peasants who left their villages to work and settle in St Petersburg, 1880s–1917, and Shanghai, 1900s–1940s, were transformed under the impact of capitalist modernity'.[9] Smith examines four specific forms of identity: native-place, individuality, gender and identification with the nation state. Here it is possible to see how studies of material and visual culture could contribute to comparative history, especially when it discusses a number of analytical levels as Smith's does. Each of his types of identity has manifested itself in images and objects, although these are not his primary concern. But we can appreciate how historians of different kinds, in this case, those using comparative approaches and those concerned with visual and material culture, might learn from each other's work, and blend their methods.

Comparative historical work may be pursued at a number of levels, including the full range of geographical ones: regions, villages, cities, *quartiers*, countries, empires and continents. The history of *ideas* of nationhood is relevant here, since it encourages critical attention to be paid to the fact that so much material in museums and galleries is organised and displayed along national lines.[10] How did this come about and how does it shape responses to artefacts? Thus historians of visual and material culture can probe concepts such as 'nation', while making common cause with comparative history.

There is a further opportunity within comparative history, given the current interest in processes of globalisation and the growth of world history.[11] Sometimes the focus is on studies of cultural transfer. Since these relationships were brought about and mediated by commodities, many of which held specifically visual appeal, the links with visual and material culture are close and the opportunities for comparative analysis correspondingly great. Thus we can compare not only specific items and genres of commodities, but markets, empires and trade routes. Anthropology and archaeology, which employ comparative approaches, from the close examination of artefacts to assessing whole cultures, form a significant element of the intellectual context within which comparative history is practised. They are accustomed to using images and objects in a sophisticated and integrated way, and have built up elaborate visual methodologies. Comparative history could learn, for example, from the anthropology of art, which has paid careful attention to artefacts that travel long distances and reach a range of audiences, as well as to tourist art.[12]

Comparative history, then, embraces a range of approaches and topics, many of which offer opportunities for the analysis of visual and material culture. A final point about comparative history: it may be only a minority of historians who deploy explicitly comparative approaches, but all historians rely on implicit comparisons between countries, periods, social groups and so on. The advantage of making comparison explicit is that it then sharpens historical understanding by refusing to take any phenomena as natural or unexceptional. Comparative historical analysis helps in testing explanations, generating new questions and by making 'history a less provincial undertaking'.[13]

Looking comparatively

So how does comparative thinking help historians working on visual and material culture? Just as Stefan Berger suggests that all history involves comparison, all looking involves comparative analysis, even if scholars make the fact explicit to varying degrees. We might present comparative visual analysis in terms of discrimination and discernment, to use Marcia Pointon's terms.[14] Most forms of reasoning contain comparative elements: my purpose here is to make those elements as clear as possible to enable them to be used more precisely and effectively. I have suggested that it helps, for example, to reflect upon units of comparison and the variables chosen. We have noted a number of possibilities – artists, makers, sitters, subject matter, medium, occupation and gender, for instance, but there are many more. Comparisons can be temporal; for example, representations of a single building or statue from different periods. Such a comparison is *relatively* straightforward in that the building or statue remains *relatively* constant, while time, as it were, provides the difference. Variations on a theme, subject or social group could be treated in a similar manner: the family, elderly people, the nude male, death, for instance. In such cases many variables are likely to change with time, including fundamental categories of thought and experience such as kinship, ageing and the body.

Comparisons involving specific themes, subjects and symbols lie at the heart of visual analysis, as we know from scholarly traditions of iconography. The accessible *Dictionary of Subjects and Symbols in Art* contains hundreds of examples of ideas, figures, objects and events that are available for comparative treatment: victory, Flora, the Italian goddess of flowers, halos, and the Annunciation, for instance.[15] Some fields of history offer particularly fertile ground for comparative visual analysis. It is possible to compare the various forms, genres and media of religious expression at a given time and place or between periods. Statues, altars and their decorations, murals, prints, artefacts such as votive offerings, icons and other imagery, can be considered together along with the architecture of temples, shrines and churches, and systematically compared, not just for the sake of their themes and subjects, but between eras, regions and denominations as well. This approach involves paying careful attention to the differences between forms, genres and media, and between various manifestations of the religion in question. Writings on the Virgin Mary provide an instance of comparative analysis that holds the central subject matter constant, while exploring other variables.[16]

A brilliant example of a thematic approach is *Manifestations of Venus* (2000), a collection of essays on the representation of the Goddess of Love from the Renaissance to the present day, in five countries and in a range of media and materials, including stone, metal, paint, print, drawing and photography. **XXIV** Although the editors do not present their volume as a comparative project, it draws upon scholarly traditions in iconography, which are themselves comparative, and puts them to new uses in the theoretically informed way it explores themes such as eroticism, power and gender. The authors stress juxtapositions and common themes that emerge when the Venus motif is explored in a variety of contexts.[17] Similarly, when scholars consider the ways in which symbols, such as the tree of liberty or the Phrygian cap, are used, their practice is comparative. Visual symbols, such as the trident, the crown, eyes and triangles, provide ways into large themes such as the representation of

power and the Christian Trinity. Such evidence may be found in jewellery, clothing, furniture, tableware and so on, as well as in art more
conventionally defined.

Another form of comparison has become particularly fashionable
since scholars started to think more critically about relations, both direct and imaginative, between different parts of the world, and especially
to track them through visual and material culture. I have already alluded
to the links between comparative approaches and a rich sense of changing relationships across the world, which have recently been explored
by historians of economics and consumption using commodities as evidence, especially of luxury trades. Since the publication of Edward Said's
influential book in 1978, 'Orientalism' has been a dominating concept for
thinking about the imaginative and intellectual links between Europeans
and Eastern cultures.[18] Although not primarily a work about visual and
material culture – his intellectual concerns were predominantly literary –
Said certainly drew on such sources, and his legacy has encouraged
sustained engagement with the complex relationships between colonis-
ers and colonised, including with respect to art broadly defined. Some
compelling and subtle work has been undertaken in this area. Timothy
Barringer's *Men at Work*, for instance, explores what he calls 'colonial
gothic', 'the critique of industrial society and aesthetics … [which] was
based on the comparison of modern life and labour with the supposedly
idyllic worlds both of medieval England and of village India'.[19] In the
English-speaking world, writings on trade, colonialism and global relationships have tended to focus on themes and geographical regions
with which Britain and the United States have been directly associated.
Since other European powers participated in globalising trends, there
are further opportunities for comparative perspectives. French colonialism had a particularly painful, poignant and long-lasting impact in
Algeria, a country that provoked significant visual responses, including
from Renoir, an example that illustrates some key points about looking
comparatively.

Renoir was interested in the Old Masters, thinking about his own
work in the context of what had gone before. In this respect he undertook comparative visual analysis. There is strong evidence for these
activities, their significance in his life and their impact upon others. For
example, he was particularly drawn to the work of Eugène Delacroix
and the enthusiasm is manifest in his painting, inviting comparisons
between the two men. Renoir once said of Delacroix's *Women of Algiers*
that there was no more beautiful picture in the world.[20] **XXXII** In 1875,
Renoir made a commissioned copy of Delacroix's *The Jewish Wedding
in Morocco* (1837–41). It is a faithful full-scale work, but is by no means

202 Alger – Rue Kléber

51 '202 Alger – Rue Kléber', date and photographer unknown, 13.7 cm high × 8.8 wide, Cambridge University Library. This is an example of the postcards available in Renoir's time, depicting what would likely be taken by purchasers to be a typical street scene. The fully covered female figure contrasts not only with the 'Daughter of the Nile' in **XXXIII**, but with the more sumptuously dressed women shown at ease in the privacy of their apartments in the painting in **XXXII**. The number, suggesting this was one of a series, reinforces the point that postcards were ubiquitous, diverse and highly collectable.

identical, especially in the palette and level of detail.[21] Such interpretative copying was not uncommon, and it helps us to focus on the differences between painters, where one of them felt a special affinity for, and paid homage to, the other. Furthermore, Delacroix's *Women of Algiers in their Apartment* of 1834 and Renoir's *Parisian Women in Algerian Costume (The Harem)* 1872 are closely related. Renoir did not visit Algeria until 1881 and 1882, when it had been in French hands for more than half a century. As we have noted, in 1870 he painted a portrait of a young Algerian woman living in Paris with her husband, who sold North African objects. Wearing a costume that was typical of her social position, Madame Stora glows with loose brushstrokes of ivory, golds and blue – she is 'exotic'. **XXIX** The subject of other, considerably more conventional portraits that she herself preferred, Clémentine Stora represents one of Renoir's early encounters with Algeria, encounters that were shaped by his love of Delacroix. When he finally visited Algiers, he produced scenes that conform to types that were already established in photographic practice, as we know from careful comparisons between different media. These scenes represent a particular vantage point – that of the European visitor to an exciting, foreign land.[22] **XXXIII** and **51**

We could call Renoir an 'orientalist': he viewed North Africa through the lens provided for him by nineteenth-century French culture, but he also brought his own preferences, skills and attitudes to the process. These are brought out through comparisons with other 'orientalist' painters and photographers, especially with contemporaries who visited Algeria and worked there. Ideally, we would compare European visions with those produced by people living permanently in Algeria, whether they were indigenous or French settlers. Renoir needs to be put into the context of other artists who visited North Africa, and Algeria specifically. While it is useful to know about those who preceded him, it is just as important to recognise how significant he became for later painters, such as Henri Matisse. These affinities are registered in the subject matter of works, and in their composition, palette and manner of making. Paintings, sketches and drawings are usefully seen in relation to photographs. The relationships between France and Algeria changed markedly between 1830, when Algiers was captured, and the early twentieth century, when Matisse engaged with North Africa. France possessed other colonies, and it would also be possible to compare the visual culture of French colonialism with that of other powers. What, if anything, was distinctive about the ways in which Algeria and Morocco were mediated in visual and material culture? Are there significant differences between, for example, British and French forms of 'Orientalism'? These questions could usefully put pressure on the very concept of Orientalism, all too often treated as a blunt, moralising instrument. Such modes of enquiry engage with traditions of image-making within colonised territories, and examine their transformations in and through colonial encounters. Similar approaches have been explored in a number of fields and are increasingly the domain of historians.

A wide-ranging comparative approach can be applied to any artefact, for example, through an examination of materials, scale and the relationships between two- and three-dimensional representations. A recent study of the relationships between Spanish painting and polychrome sculpture in the seventeenth century reveals the fruitfulness of comparing two- and three-dimensional works. Realism in both cases was designed to give 'the faithful a sense of direct access to the scene depicted'. The result was works, sanctioned by the Catholic Church, which shocked the senses and stirred the soul. **XXXIV** Arguably, careful comparisons between two- and three-dimensional representations shed new light not just on Spanish art, but on the nature of religious experience in the period. Contemporary commentators themselves made the comparison, especially when paintings provided the illusion of depth.[23] Other visual phenomena can be explored using this approach. For example, articles of clothing existed in three dimensions, but frequently survive in the form of designs, drawings, paintings and photographs, offering the chance to develop an understanding of how fabrics and clothes were imagined and re-presented.

Looking comparatively rests on the ability to make and interpret fine visual discriminations, based on precise, detailed and accurate observations. We could think of 'spot the difference' puzzles in newspapers and magazines, where two apparently identical images are printed side by side. Finding the tiny respects in which they differ requires focused visual attention. Looking comparatively involves far more than this, however. Appropriate comparatives have to be found. Deciding what is 'comparable' involves the full range of historical skills, including judgements about the contexts into which the artefacts are best set. Training in close visual inspection and in expressing what is seen in words are indispensable steps. The field of art history is built around the issues that 'comparative analysis' implies; art-historical publications reveal the

52 *Ambroise Vollard*, by Pierre-Auguste Renoir, 1908, oil on canvas, 82 cm high × 65 cm wide, the Courtauld Gallery, London. See **XXVII**.

nature of comparative thinking by the images they contain, images that are called 'comparatives'. They serve to clarify the reader's sense of which works are like (or unlike) each other, and the significance that can be attributed to this. Making such judgements is not straightforward; hence it is prudent to attend to the difficulties involved through a particular example, in which we return one last time to Renoir's 1908 portrait of Vollard.

Pitfalls and problems

When slide projectors were used, it was customary to deploy two or more in art-historical teaching and to encourage students to speak to the similarities and contrasts presented by juxtaposed images. This practice had deep roots in the history of the discipline. In a pedagogic setting, comparison refines perception and inculcates healthy visual habits of precise and skilled observation. If such an approach is to be used effectively by historians, there needs to be a sense of its limitations as well as of its advantages. Here I consider the limitations through an example, which illustrates the importance of the ways in which comparatives are selected, and the need to subject those chosen to rigorous scrutiny.

The portrait of Vollard by Renoir depicts a man holding a sculpted female figure in an appreciative manner. **52** The sculptor in question was admired by Renoir and closely associated with the sitter, who was a collector as well as a dealer. Furthermore, his pleasure as depicted by Renoir, marks him as a 'connoisseur', which suggests a well-informed and visually discerning appreciation of artefacts. This work has been presented as 'an image of an archetypal connoisseur … very much in the tradition of such collector portraits of the Italian Renaissance'.[24] John House is here comparing the 1908 depiction with portraits undertaken in another country centuries earlier. Similarly, Colin Bailey suggests: 'in keeping with a long-established tradition in Western portraiture, it is as a voracious art lover that Renoir has chosen to portray his dealer, updating Titian's portrait of Jacopo Strada, antiquary and supplier of works of art to the Hapsburgs'.[25] He suggests that by comparing the portraits by Titian and Renoir, it is possible to detect a shift, namely, 'updating', which implies significant affinities between two works across more than three centuries. A glance at Titian's work, which is somewhat larger than Renoir's, reveals how problematic the comparison is. **XXXV**

Strada is opulently dressed and standing; he holds a nude female statue in both hands as if displaying it to an unseen figure. He is not looking at the viewer, but out of the picture, to his left. On a table in front of him lie other objects, such as coins and a folded piece of paper. There is also a cupboard with books on the top, and an inscription hanging on the wall, apparently added later and not by Titian himself. The rich red sleeves of his costume, the fur, a sword and a large chain around the neck proclaim him to be a man of considerable status. There are three points of similarity between the two portraits: both men are dealers, who had close relationships with their portraitists; they are holding a female figure; and there is a table with objects on it in the picture. The differences, however, are striking: the overall composition, the pose of the figure, and its relationship with the viewer. Strada is depicted as if showing an object to someone, perhaps a client, and we catch him doing so, mid-movement. Most of his face is visible. It would be possible to describe this as an outward-looking work. Renoir's work is different. He shows Vollard, who is unremarkably dressed, totally absorbed by what he holds, looking at it intently, and unaware of being overlooked. This is an inward-looking work. The Maillol figurine may be a commodity, but it was made by someone for whom artist and sitter felt a significant affinity.

It has been said that Titian's portrait was 'intended to impress'. The sculpture is a Roman copy of a figure by Praxiteles, and there is an antique torso as well as fine coins or medals on the table: 'coins were particularly valued in the Renaissance both as immediate and tangible manifestations of the ancient world and for their information about ancient art'.[26] Thus in addition to the display of wealth, learning and expertise, Titian's portrait invokes the authority of the ancient world. Strada was a scholar who had published on coins. Commentators, including contemporaries, remarked appreciatively on the portrait's vitality: Strada's 'enthusiasm, energy and dynamic nature are projected by Titian in the vivid action of his pose and in the driving determination of his glance'.[27] By contrast, Renoir's picture is not designed to impress in these ways. The main artefact depicted is contemporary, while Vollard's wealth and power is not on display. The sitter is still, contemplative, and shown in an intense, direct relationship – visual and tactile – with the figurine, not theatrically displaying an object. Furthermore, although Vollard was indeed a significant force in the art world of his time, his social status was, at least initially, somewhat insecure. We noted that he came from La Réunion, the French island off the coast of Madagascar, and although 'white', suffered from the stigma of being a 'colonial', as anecdotes involving Renoir and his family reveal.[28] He abandoned the law to become an art dealer, a path that was hardly easy.

These points of similarity and difference are of two kinds – visual and biographical. The differences are sufficiently strong that they outweigh any useful similarities, I suggest. It is known that Renoir admired Titian, although there is no evidence that he saw this particular work. Thus there is unlikely to have been a direct relationship between the two portraits. Scholars seem to have scouted around for a work to compare the Vollard with, and this was what they found. The need for such a search is partly a result of the claim that there was a 'tradition of such collector portraits'.[29] What might be meant by a 'tradition' in this context? My immediate point concerns the need to be clear about the relationships implied by comparative analysis, since any historical claims rest upon them.

Types of affinity

The core of comparative analysis is the search for meaningful associations between two or more entities, using an adjudication of similarities and differences in order to probe significant relationships between them and eliminate spurious ones. When it is claimed that one item is 'comparable' to another, what is involved? There are many kinds of comparability – biographical, thematic, contextual and material, for instance. These are palpable affinities. I use the term 'affinity' to suggest a connection of some kind: it can express the idea that the link has an emotional or aesthetic component, as was the case with Renoir's admiration for Delacroix, and Matisse's for Renoir.

All the following words, if in different ways, evoke aspects of the relationships that comparative analysis probes: contact, allusion, evocation, worldview, training, collaboration, tradition, travel, trade, template, update, analogy, parallel, imitation and derivative. There are many more. The keywords used to speak of relationships have implications for the historical explanations that follow. Some of these terms are about direct contact, such as training and template. When those working together in a studio or workshop produce artefacts that manifest marked similarities to each other, but not found elsewhere, the likely explanation lies in their actual social contact, of which 'training' is one form. It should be possible to be specific about the shared characteristics of items made by those working together, by those in the same region, country and so on. Templates are sometimes acknowledged, for instance, in prints when the name of the original artist is provided, again rendering the relationship quite specific and palpable. Other terms posit considerably looser affinities – evocation and analogy, for instance. In these cases similarities are noted, they may be interesting and suggestive, but no direct contact is implied, and any historical claims need to reflect that. The burden remains on us to show why and how one artefact being reminiscent of another is worthy of comment. One way is through detailed, meticulous comparative analysis, making explicit the resulting conclusions. When Scott and Arscott presented the essays on Venus in terms of 'juxtapositions and common themes', they implied the importance of suggestive comparisons and continuities rather than asserting other, more direct links between the various 'manifestations of Venus'.[30]

Comparison in practice

I have indicated some of the comparisons that scholars interested in visual and material culture can undertake and pointed out the operations and sources that they entail. Being aware of the relationships specific comparisons reveal, of the units and key variables involved and the motives for making comparative moves in the first place, is vital. Comparison is a fundamental part of visual skill: it prompts specific reactions. What characteristics does artefact A possess and how are these different from or similar to those of B, C, D and so on? How is this historically significant? The characteristics that are analysed are to be found initially in artefacts themselves, followed by features of their contexts; for example, the lives of those who made, commissioned and owned them, their location and forms of display. Thus the visual skills of close 'reading' are integral to the historical skills of understanding the range of settings in which artefacts live, move and have their being.

Some of the concepts we have considered in this book are more comparative than others. For example, I discussed the notion of style, which is precisely a comparative concept. In using any single style term, comparison with other styles and periods is implied. Such terms are best deployed with an awareness of their underlying assumptions. Gender is another comparative term, since the very notion implies an exploration of masculinity and femininity and the dynamics between them. In a pair of celebrated articles, Carol Duncan analysed the representation of motherhood and fatherhood in eighteenth-century France.[31] Although she pursued these themes in separate articles, the comparative intention was evident – gender and its associated social roles invite comparison. The wealth of material on representations of femininity and masculinity shows how rewarding this specific form of comparison can be.[32] Duncan's articles focused on states that are also phases of life and evocative ideas; there are rich, potent and pervasive metaphors involved. Comparisons can readily be made in terms of age, social, occupational

53 Photograph of a Gallery in the *Entartete Kunst* (Degenerate Art) Exhibition, Munich, 1937. The exhibition of so-called Degenerate Art opened in Munich in July 1937. It had been hastily put together and the whole display was designed to denigrate not only the artists, but also members of the art world, such as curators, dealers and museum directors, who had paid money for allegedly corrupting items. The quotations from defenders and detractors of modern art that are visible on the walls served to support the emotionally charged rhetoric of the entire display, which likened the 'degenerate' pieces to works by the mentally ill.

and marital status. **XXXVI** Since fundamental forms of social difference are mediated through items of visual and material culture, this form of comparison is full of historical potential.

In order to further extend the sense of how comparative analysis works, I return briefly here to items, themes and ideas that have been mentioned earlier in the book to make more explicit how some of the examples readers have already encountered may be viewed comparatively. In the four essays, I hinted at the insights a comparative dimension can provide. In some instances the comparisons have already generated considerable scholarly interest. My aim is to indicate some further ways in which comparative analysis can be generative.

Consider the work of Ernst Barlach, branded a 'degenerate artist' in Germany during the 1930s. **53** and **10** The label itself implies a morally charged comparison between healthy and unhealthy forms of visual culture. Barlach was one of many artists who suffered in this way, not just by seeing their work removed from public display, but by being vilified and knowing that their creations were being destroyed. What range of reactions did this situation prompt? Did the artists who were so branded have significant features in common? What sort of a category was 'degenerate'? What kind of historical account does the label, and the practices it spawned, invite? How did 'degenerate' artists differ from those who were approved of by the regime? In what other historical situations have similar processes occurred? These are comparative issues, which range from those amenable to detailed visual analysis, to broader ones requiring comparisons between political situations.

54 The interior of the Codrington Library, All Souls' College, Oxford, from the south-east, by Thomas Malton, aquatint, 1802, page size 22.5 cm high × 30.5 cm wide, Bodleian Library, Oxford. Malton depicts the library at a very particular moment in its history, since changes were made in 1804 to remove decorative plasterwork added in 1750. It is presented both as a place of scholarship – a man with mortarboard and gown is reading on the right – and as a venue for polite leisure activities – note, for example, the woman and child on the left. Many busts are shown; these were a common element of library decoration. Malton was an architectural draughtsman, who depicted many scenes in Oxford, Cambridge and London.

Similar questions are prompted by the work of any maker. Christopher Wren has been compared with other architects of his time, just as his buildings are compared with one another, with those of other architects, and contemporary reactions assessed. The Wren Library at Trinity College, Cambridge, may be compared with other libraries, for example with the Codrington at All Souls' College, Oxford, built by Nicholas Hawksmoor between 1716 and 1720. 54 and VIII, IX Hawksmoor, a generation younger than Wren, had worked with him, making comparisons between their buildings historically plausible. College libraries are a sufficiently specific building type that an analysis of the similarities and differences between these two buildings is valuable in revealing the ways in which the two men, and their patrons, approached the challenge. This example raises the question of style. I have noted the difficulties of using 'classicism' and 'baroque', especially in relation to Bernini and Wren, who have been associated with both styles. However slippery and elusive 'style' is, it acts as shorthand in discussions of differences and similarities between artefacts. Style terms are particularly eloquent when they are used by historical actors, who were making comparisons that were meaningful to them.

The case of Bernini suggests two further forms of comparison. He worked in many materials, being an architect and painter as well as a writer and theatre designer. Hence there is the possibility of comparing his achievements across media. He made portraits in paint, chalk, metal and stone, a situation ripe for comparative analysis. We can also think comparatively about Bernini's working processes. When he made terracotta *bozzetti* – three-dimensional 'sketches' – that were preparatory to larger works, it is possible to watch his thinking evolving and to compare its stages. **23** and **25** Comparisons between plans and final works, like the stages of print-making, are revealing. Photography affords similar opportunities for considering processes of making, including the effects of cropping, digital manipulation, printing and retouching. With the growth of photo-journalism, many photographers work in the same geographical area and strive to capture similar subjects. How do their approaches differ and what has made a relatively small number of photographs iconic on a global scale?[33] In the case of the *Family of Man* exhibition, three principal forms of comparison spring to mind: between it and other photographic exhibitions; between the various places to which it toured, especially with respect to the reception it received; and between the pictures as they appeared in the exhibition, and their appearance in other contexts. **XX, 33,35,36,37**

Historical problems and artefacts have the capacity to generate numerous forms of comparison. Knowingly attending to comparative analysis brings a productive self-awareness. Such analysis rests on carefully honed visual skills and on the ability to deploy them in a historical manner. By thinking of comparative analysis as a step-by-step process, holding as much constant as possible, while changing one element at a time, it is possible to approach the role of visual experience in historical thinking both imaginatively and methodically.

Analysis?

I used the word 'analysis' in the title of this chapter to suggest a meticulous, systematic approach. The verb to 'analyse' means to 'examine minutely the constitution of … ascertain the elements of … find, show, the essence of…'.[34] While I do not believe that there is an essence to be found, scrutinising the elements of things, and then putting the examination to good historical effect, is a way of proceeding that underlies the project of this book. So, does this make comparative analysis a method, an approach, even a theory? Sometimes these words are used more or less interchangeably. The term 'theory' should be reserved for general accounts of a range of phenomena that aspire to explain them and treat them coherently. Marxism and psychoanalysis are theories. The role of theory in historical practice is a significant and controversial issue.[35] This book touches on and is informed by many theories, but it is not about theory. It is, however, about approaches, about ways of looking, thinking and writing in the discipline of history. It concerns our orientation to certain kinds of evidence, and the frameworks they invite. Approaches are looser than theories, and the term is well suited to the eclectic manner in which most historians practise. 'Approaches' suggests an overall orientation towards one's subject, composed of diverse elements, including the personality and preferences of the researcher. 'Method' refers to something more limited and structured, a definable manner of undertaking a task. I take comparative analysis to involve both approaches and methods, and to be drawing on ideas from many disciplines, but without a single theory underlying it, merely the conviction that comparison is a powerful form of reasoning that can be used to guide thinking with the eyes. By conceptualising the activity of looking in comparative terms, we assist in the task of further refining and developing visual analysis as an integral part of historical practice.

NOTES

1 Colin Bailey, *Renoir Portraits: Impressions of an Age* (New Haven and Ottawa, 1997), pp. 249–51.

2 Stefan Berger *et al.*, eds., *Writing History: Theory and Practice* (London, 2003), p. 161.

3 See 'Further Reading' for Chapter 3.

4 Carlo Ginzburg, *Clues, Myths, and the Historical Method* (Baltimore and London, 1989; first published 1986), and 'Morelli, Freud and Sherlock Holmes: Clues and Scientific Method', *History Workshop Journal*, 9 (1980), pp. 5–36.

5 Peter Hulme's work is especially useful: *Colonial Encounters: Europe and the Native Caribbean* (London, 1986); Peter Hulme and William Sherman, *'The Tempest' and its Travels* (London, 2000). See also Francis Barker *et al.*, eds., *Colonial Discourse/Postcolonial Theory* (Manchester, 1994), and Rochona Majumdar, *Writing Postcolonial History* (London, 2010).

6 Hugh Honour and John Fleming, *A World History of Art*, 7th edn (London, 2009), which takes an entirely different approach from John Onians, *Art, Culture and Nature: From Art History to World Art Studies* (London, 2006). Yet another mode of address may be found in Thomas DaCosta Kaufmann and Elizabeth Pilliod, eds., *Time and Place: the Geohistory of Art* (Aldershot, 2005). The fact remains there is nothing like comparative literature with respect to art.

7 Henry James's novels, for example, *Roderick Hudson*, first published in 1875, exemplify this distinctive preoccupation with comparing American and European culture, especially with respect to the visual arts.

8 Wendy Wick, *George Washington, an American Icon: the Eighteenth-century Graphic Portraits* (Washington DC, 1982).

9 S. A. Smith, *Revolution and the People in Russia and China: a Comparative History* (Cambridge, 2008), p. 1.

10 Benedict Anderson, *Imagined Communities: Reflections on the Origin and Spread of Nationalism* (London, 2006; first published 1983), esp. ch. 10, 'Census, Map, Museum'.

11 The terminology used to express these trends is complex, and the notion of 'globalisation' a veritable minefield. But see the *Journal of Global History* (2006 onwards); Bruce Mazlish and Ralph Buultjens, *Conceptualizing Global History* (Boulder, 1993); A. G. Hopkins, ed., *Globalization in World History* (London, 2002); and Manfred Steger, *Globalization*, new edn (Oxford, 2009).

12 Howard Morphy and Morgan Perkins, eds., *The Anthropology of Art: a Reader* (Malden, MA, and Oxford, 2006); Jeremy Coote and Anthony Shelton, eds., *Anthropology, Art and Aesthetics* (Oxford, 1992); Marcus Banks and Howard Morphy, eds., *Rethinking Visual Anthropology* (New Haven and London, 1997); Christopher Steiner, *African Art in Transit* (Cambridge and New York, 1994).

13 Berger *et al.*, eds., *Writing History*, p. 165.

14 Marcia Pointon, *History of Art: a Student's Handbook*, 4th edn (London and New York, 1997), p. 6.

15 James Hall, *Dictionary of Subjects and Symbols in Art*, rev. edn (London, 1984).

16 Compare Marina Warner, *Alone of all her Sex: the Myth and the Cult of the Virgin Mary* (London, 1976), and Miri Rubin, *Mother of God: a History of the Virgin Mary* (London, 2009), for different approaches.

17 Caroline Arscott and Katie Scott, eds., *Manifestations of Venus: Art and Sexuality* (Manchester, 2000).

18 Edward Said, *Orientalism* (London, 1995); Conor McCarthy, *The Cambridge Introduction to Edward Said* (Cambridge, 2010); and John Mackenzie, *Orientalism: History, Theory and the Arts* (Manchester and New York, 1995).

19 Timothy Barringer, *Men at Work: Art and Labour in Victorian Britain* (New Haven and London, 2005), p. 16.

20 Ambroise Vollard, *En écoutant Cézanne, Degas, Renoir*, 6th edn (Paris, 1938), p. 276. Renoir's comments, as reported by Vollard, are couched in the language of Orientalism. See also *De Delacroix à Renoir: L'Algérie des peintres* (Paris, 2003). The title of more than one painting by Delacroix starts with 'femmes d'Alger', so it is difficult to know exactly which one Renoir meant.

21 Roger Benjamin, *Renoir and Algeria* (New Haven and London, 2003), pp. 30–7.

22 On Mme Stora, see Bailey, *Renoir Portraits*, pp. 108–9. Benjamin, *Renoir*, examines his time in Algeria.

23 Xavier Bray, *The Sacred Made Real: Spanish Painting and Sculpture, 1600–1700* (London, 2009), p. 15.

24 John House, *Impressionism for England: Samuel Courtauld as Patron and Collector* (London, 1994), p. 140.

25 Bailey, *Renoir Portraits*, p. 238.

26 David Jaffé, ed., *Titian* (London, 2003), p. 168.

27 Harold E. Wethey, *The Paintings of Titian*, 3 vols. (London, 1969–75), vol. 2, p. 49.

28 For example, Jean Renoir, *Renoir: My Father* (1962), p. 287.

29 House, *Impressionism*, p. 140.

30 Arscott and Scott, *Manifestations*, p. 2.

31 Reprinted in Carol Duncan, *The Aesthetics of Power: Essays in Critical Art History* (Cambridge, 1993), chs. 1 ('Happy Mothers') and 2 ('Fallen Fathers'), first published in 1973 and 1981 respectively.

32 For example, Gill Perry and Michael Rossington, *Femininity and Masculinity in Eighteenth-century Art and Culture* (Manchester, 1994); and Gill Perry, ed., *Gender and Art* (New Haven and London, 1999).

33 Michael Koetzle, *Photo Icons: the Story Behind the Pictures*, 2 vols. (Cologne, 2002).

34 H. W. Fowler and F. G. Fowler, eds., *The Concise Oxford Dictionary of Current English*, 5th edn (Oxford, 1964), p. 41.

35 See the journal *History and Theory* (1960 onwards); Mary Fulbrook, *Historical Theory* (London, 2002); and Ludmilla Jordanova, 'What's in a Name? Historians and Theory', *English Historical Review*, 126 (2011), pp. 1456–77.

FURTHER READING

The following works provide a sense of a range of comparative disciplines: Susan Bassnett, *Comparative Literature: a Critical Introduction* (Oxford, 1993); Stefan Berger *et al.*, eds., *Writing History, Theory and Practice* (London, 2003), see ch. 9, 'Comparative History'; Charles Bernheimer, *Comparative Literature in the Age of Multiculturalism* (Baltimore and London, 1995); Anne Cova, ed., *Comparative Women's History: New Approaches* (Boulder, 2006); Philip Curtin, *Cross-cultural Trade in World History* (Cambridge, 1984); Iain Hampsher-Monk *et al.*, eds., *History of Concepts: Comparative Perspectives* (Amsterdam, 1998); Peter Hulme, *Colonial Encounters: Europe and the Native Caribbean, 1492–1797* (London, 1986); Kenneth V. Kardong, *Vertebrates: Comparative Anatomy, Function, Evolution*, 2nd edn (Boston, 1998); Ray Kiely, *Industrialization and Development: a Comparative Analysis* (London, 1998); Thomas Munck, *The Enlightenment: a Comparative Social History, 1721–1794* (London, 2000); Haun Saussy, ed., *Comparative Literature in an Age of Globalization* (Baltimore, 2006); Stephen Shennan, ed., *Pattern and Process in Cultural Evolution* (Berkeley CA and London, 2009); Charles Tilly, *Big Structures, Large Processes, Huge Comparisons* (New York, 1984); Robert L. Trask, *Dictionary of Historical and Comparative Linguistics* (Edinburgh, 2002) (Preface and entries on comparative method, external history, social history); and Aram Yengoyan, ed., *Modes of Comparison: Theory and Practice* (Ann Arbor, 2006) (esp. the Introduction, and the essays by Grew).

For the comparative issues raised by Renoir, see Colin Bailey, *Renoir's Portraits: Impressions of an Age* (Ottawa, 1997); Roger Benjamin, *Renoir and Algeria* (New Haven and London, 2003); Roger Benjamin, *Orientalist Aesthetics: Art, Colonialism and French North Africa, 1880–1930* (Berkeley CA, and London, 2003); Jack Cowart and Pierre Schneider, *Matisse in Morocco: the Paintings and Drawings, 1912–1913* (Washington DC and London, 1990); and William Rubin, ed., *Picasso and Portraiture: Representation and Transformation* (London, 1996). See also Beth Wright, ed., *The Cambridge Companion to Delacroix* (Cambridge, 2001), esp. ch. 5.

The following could provide starting works for following up comparative themes in relation to visual and material culture: Dawn Ades, *Art and Power: Europe under the Dictators, 1930–45* (London, 1995); Norman Bryson, *Tradition and Desire from David to Delacroix* (Cambridge, 1984); Stefan Berger *et al.*, eds., *Narrating the Nation: Representations in History, Media, and the Arts* (New York and Oxford, 2008), esp. ch. 11; Eric Fernie, ed., *Art History and its Methods: a Critical Anthology* (London, 1995), esp. chs. 8 and 10; John Gage, *Colour and Culture: Practice and Meaning from Antiquity to Abstraction* (London, 1993); Iris Hahner-Herzog *et al.*, *African Masks: from the Barbier-Mueller Collection, Geneva* (Munich and London, 2002); Michael Hatt and Charlotte Klonk, *Art History: a Critical Introduction to its Methods* (Manchester and New York, 2006), esp. chs. 1, 2, 4, 5 and 6; Steven Hooper, ed., *Robert and Lisa Sainsbury Collection: Catalogue in Three Volumes* (New Haven, London and Norwich, 1997); Robert Nelson and Richard Shiff, eds., *Critical Terms for Art History*, 2nd edn (Chicago and London, 2003); John Onians, ed., *The Art Atlas* (London, 2008; published as *Atlas of World Art* in 2004); and Robert Ross, *Clothing: a Global History Or, the Imperialist's New Clothes* (Cambridge, 2008).

Also relevant to the themes of this chapter are Benedict Anderson, *Imagined Communities: Reflections on the Origin and Spread of Nationalism* (London, 2006); Carlo Ginzburg, *Clues, Myths and the Historical Method* (Baltimore and

London, 1989), esp. pp. 96–125; Sarah Hyde, *Exhibiting Gender* (Manchester, 1997); James McDougall, *History and the Culture of Nationalism in Algeria* (Cambridge, 2006); Benjamin Stora, *Algeria 1830–2000: a Short History* (Ithaca, 2001); and Raymond Williams, *Keywords: a Vocabulary of Culture and Society*, rev. edn (London, 1983), see entries 'nation', 'tradition'.

REFERENCE WORKS

This short list of reference works related to the themes of this book covers a range of subjects and fields. I have, however, excluded biographical dictionaries.

Abrams, M. H., *Glossary of Literary Terms*, 8th edn (Boston, 2005; first published 1971).

Banham, Joanna, ed., *Encyclopedia of Interior Design*, 2 vols. (London and Chicago, 1997).

Bennett, Tony *et al.*, *New Keywords: a Revised Vocabulary of Culture and Society* (Malden, MA, Oxford and Carlton, Victoria, 2005).

Biedermann, Hans, *Dictionary of Symbolism* (New York and Oxford, 1992).

Boger, Louise Ade, *The Dictionary of World Pottery and Porcelain* (London, 1971).

Byars, Mel, *The Design Encyclopedia* (London and New York, 2004; first published 1994).

Calloway, Stephen, ed., *The Elements of Style: an Encyclopedia of Domestic Architectural Detail*, new edn (London, 2005; first published 1951).

Chilvers, Ian, and Harold Osborne, eds., *The Oxford Dictionary of Art*, 2nd edn (Oxford, 2001; first published 1997).

Cumming, Valerie *et al.*, *The Dictionary of Fashion History* (Oxford, 2010).

Curl, James Stevens, *A Dictionary of Architecture and Landscape Architecture*, 2nd edn (Oxford, 2006; first published 1999).

Edgar, Andrew, and Peter Sedgwick, *Cultural Theory: the Key Concepts*, 2nd edn (London, 2008; first published 1999).

Ehresmann, Donald, *The Fine Arts: a Bibliographic Guide to Basic Reference Works, Histories, and Handbooks* (Littleton, CO, 1975).

Ehresmann, Donald, *Applied and Decorative Arts: a Bibliographic Guide to Basic Reference Works, Histories and Handbooks* (Littleton, CO, 1977).

Hall, James, *Dictionary of Subjects and Symbols in Art*, rev. edn (London, 1984; first published 1974).

Harris, Cyril M., ed., *Dictionary of Architecture and Construction*, 2nd edn (New York and London, 1993; first published 1976).

Harris, Jonathan, *Art History: the Key Concepts* (London, 2006).

Hartley, John, *Communication, Cultural and Media Studies: the Key Concepts*, 3rd edn (London, 2002; first published 1994).

Hicks, Dan, and Mary Beaudry, eds., *The Oxford Handbook of Material Culture Studies* (Oxford, 2010).

Jones, Lois Swan, *Art Information and the Internet: How to Find it, How to Use it* (Chicago and London, 1999).

Kelly, Michael, *Encyclopedia of Aesthetics*, 4 vols. (New York and Oxford, 1998).

Laplanche, J., and J.-B. Pontalis, *The Language of Psychoanalysis* (London, 1973; first published 1967).

Lenman, Robin, ed., *The Oxford Companion to the Photograph* (Oxford, 2005).

Lentricchia, Frank, and Thomas McLaughlin, eds., *Critical Terms for Literary Study*, 2nd edn (Chicago and London, 1995; first published 1990).

Mitchell, W. T. J., and Mark Hanson, eds., *Critical Terms for Media Studies* (Chicago, 2010).

Murray, Peter and Linda, *The Oxford Dictionary of Christian Art* (Oxford, 2004; first published 1996).

Nelson, Robert, and Richard Shiff, eds., *Critical Terms for Art History*, 2nd edn (Chicago and London, 2003; first published 1996).

Oliver, Paul. *Encyclopedia of Vernacular Architecture of the World*, 3 vols. (Cambridge, 1997).

Osborne, Harold, ed., *The Oxford Companion to the Decorative Arts*, corrected edn (Oxford, 1985; first published 1975).

Rapport, Nigel, and Joanna Overing, *Social and Cultural Anthropology: the Key Concepts*, 2nd edn (London and New York, 2007; first published 2000).

Helene Roberts, ed., *Encyclopedia of Comparative Iconography: Themes depicted in Works of Art*, 2 vols. (Chicago and London, 1998).

Roosens, Laurent, and Luc Salu, *History of Photography: a Bibliography of Books* (London, 1989–).

Smith, Paul, and Carolyn Wilde, eds., *A Companion to Art Theory* (Oxford, 2002).

Tilley, Christopher *et al.*, eds., *Handbook of Material Culture* (London, 2006).

Townsend, Dabney, *Historical Dictionary of Aesthetics* (Lanham, MD, and Oxford, 2006).

Trench, Lucy, ed., *Materials & Techniques in the Decorative Arts: an Illustrated Dictionary* (London, 2000).

Turner, Jane, ed., *The Dictionary of Art*, 34 vols. (New York and Basingstoke, 1996).

Wallis, Helen, and Arthur Robinson, *Cartographical Innovations: an International Handbook of Mapping Terms to 1900* (n.p., 1987).

Ward, Gerald, ed., *The Grove Encyclopedia of Materials and Techniques in Art* (New York and Oxford, 2008).

Williams, Raymond, *Keywords: a Vocabulary of Culture and Society*, rev. edn (London, 1983; first published 1976).

ILLUSTRATION CREDITS

The author and publishers gratefully acknowledge the following people and institutions for granting permission to use their images. Where no credit is listed, the illustration is taken from the author's collection.

I, 1: Churchill Archives Centre © Churchill College, Cambridge

II, 15, 16, 31, 50: © National Portrait Gallery, London

III: National History Museum, Sofia

IV: Reproduced with permission of the Thomas Coram Foundation for Children (Coram) / London Metropolitan Archives

V, XIII, XXVI, XXXIII, 4, 7, 8, 14, 17, 21, 22, 29, 30, 34, 40, 42, 49, 51: Cambridge University Library

VIII, 12: Howard Nelson

IX, 13: By the permission of the Master and Fellows of Trinity College, Cambridge

X, XV, 23: Francesco Filangeri

XI: New York Historical Society

XII: Watts Gallery, Compton, Surrey

XIV, XXIII, 46: © Fitzwilliam Museum, Cambridge

XVI: York Museums Trust, York Castle Museum

XVII, XIX, XXIV, XXXIV, 18, 28: © Victoria and Albert Museum, London

XVIII, XXII, 3, 19, 24, 38, 41: © Trustees of the British Museum

XX, 35, 37: Reproduced courtesy of Museum of Modern Art, New York

XXI: Nigel Young, Foster + Partners

XXV: Courtesy of the Pennsylvania Academy of the Fine Arts, Philadelphia. Gift of Mrs Sarah Harrison (The Joseph Harrison, Jr. Collection).

INDEX